Jihadi Culture on the World Wide Web

NEW DIRECTIONS IN TERRORISM STUDIES

A series edited by

Max Taylor

Professor in International Relations (retired), University of St Andrews, Scotland where he was formerly Director of the Centre for the Study of Terrorism and Political Violence

P. M. Currie

Senior Visiting Fellow at the School of International Relations at the University of St Andrews, Scotland

John Horgan

Associate Professor of Science, Technology and Society and Director of the International Centre for the Study of Terrorism at Pennsylvania State University, USA

New Directions in Terrorism Studies aims to introduce new and innovative approaches to understanding terrorism and the terrorist. It does this by bringing forward innovative ideas and concepts to assist the practitioner, analyst and academic to better understand and respond to the threat of terrorism, challenging existing assumptions and moving the debate forward into new areas.

The approach is characterized by an emphasis on intellectual quality and rigour, interdisciplinary perspectives, and a drawing together of theory and practice. The key qualities of the series are contemporary relevance, accessibility and innovation.

Jihadi Culture on the World Wide Web

GILBERT RAMSAY

Bloomsbury Academic
An imprint of Bloomsbury Publishing Plc

B L O O M S B U R Y
NEW YORK • LONDON • NEW DELHI • SYDNEY

Bloomsbury Academic
An imprint of Bloomsbury Publishing Inc

1385 Broadway
New York
NY 10018
USA

50 Bedford Square
London
WC1B 3DP
UK

www.bloomsbury.com

BLOOMSBURY and the Diana logo are trademarks of Bloomsbury Publishing Plc

First published 2013
Paperback edition first published 2015

© Gilbert Ramsay, 2013

All rights reserved. No part of this publication may be reproduced or transmitted in any form or by any means, electronic or mechanical, including photocopying, recording, or any information storage or retrieval system, without prior permission in writing from the publishers.

No responsibility for loss caused to any individual or organization acting on or refraining from action as a result of the material in this publication can be accepted by Bloomsbury or the author.

Library of Congress Cataloging-in-Publication Data
Ramsay, Gilbert.
Jihadi Culture on the World Wide Web/Gilbert Ramsay. – 1
p. cm.
Includes bibliographical references and index.
ISBN 978-1-4411-7562-5 (hardback)
1. Terrorism–Religious aspects–Islam. 2. Jihad–Computer network resources.
3. Terrorism–Computer network resources. I. Title.
BP190.5.T47R36 2013
363.3250285'4678–dc23
2013018695

ISBN: HB: 978-1-4411-7562-5
PB: 978-1-5013-0767-6
ePDF: 978-1-4411-2439-5
ePUB: 978-1-4411-5812-3

Series: New Directions in Terrorism Studies

Typeset by Deanta Global Publishing Services, Chennai, India

For Dina, my sweetheart.

Contents

Acknowledgements viii

1 Terror on the internet? 1
2 Alternative media and its alternatives 25
3 Jihadi content on the World Wide Web 51
4 Jihadi forums in their own words 79
5 Disagreeable disagreements 105
6 Being a jihadi on the internet 131
7 Some other 'jihadi' consumption cultures: Crusaderism, war porn, shock 159
8 Jihadism between fantasy and virtuality, a tentative conclusion 181

Notes 207
Glossary of Arabic terms 231
Bibliography 237
Index 249

Acknowledgements

My journey to this book has been a long one, and there are numerous people to thank along the way. Clearly, without the support, encouragement and intellectual input of my tireless supervisors at St Andrews, first Alex Schmid and then Max Taylor, I would certainly never have finished the dissertation on which this book is based. But without Mark Currie's warm encouragement, that dissertation might still be languishing on the shelves of the University library. Of course, I must also mention the rest of my wonderful colleagues at the School of International Relations at the University of St Andrews, especially at my particular workplace, the Handa Centre for Terrorism Research. In addition to my time at St Andrews, my thinking was also shaped in important ways during the sabbatical year I took to write a report for the United Nations, working under the able direction of Richard Barrett. In addition to providing limitless support, my beloved wife Dina and my darling son Adam have had a lot to put up with and have done so with more good grace than I probably deserve. I have had a lot to learn as a first-time author, including a lot a probably should have known already, but my editors: first Marie Claire, at Continuum, and latterly Matthew Kopel at Bloomsbury have been enormously helpful.

1

Terror on the internet?

In the years after 9/11 – and especially following the invasion of Iraq – there was a proliferation of 'jihadi' websites, blogs, forums and other online media.[1] For some commentators, these amounted to nothing less than a 'terrorist' invasion of a new domain: cyberspace. The internet, so they insisted, was providing a new 'safe haven' for Al Qaeda in which it could plan, recruit, raise funds and generally replace the capabilities it lost with its bases in Afghanistan.[2] For others, for all their sound and fury, they signified a good deal less than this.

These claims have not gone away. But now that we are more than a decade from 9/11, now that occupying forces have left Iraq, now that we are the better part of a decade from the last major Al Qaeda attack on a Western country to have been successfully carried out, now that the battered NATO campaign in Afghanistan is winding down, now that epochal events such as the global financial crisis and the Arabic revolutions have provided new things for security analysts to fret about, now that American assassins have shot Osama Bin Laden in the head and dumped his corpse at the bottom of the Indian Ocean, now that hellfire missiles have accounted for much of the rest of the Al Qaeda leadership – and a good many innocent bystanders as well; now that, for good or ill, all these things have happened, we can perhaps at least get some distance on the subject. We can begin to ask, properly, what this online phenomenon really meant and what its continuing existence continues to mean.

That is what this book is about. It is an attempt to step back from the intensity, even hysteria of the discussion about 'jihadism' online and to try to view it as something of potential interest, not just as a possible security threat (though that should not be altogether discounted), or as a source of 'open source intelligence' but also, perhaps, as something of cultural interest in its own right – something which blurs the boundaries between political reality, myth, legend and, ultimately, fantasy.

In trying to do this, I make no claims to comprehensiveness. I have before me a huge empirical and theoretical terrain which I have no intention of mapping out completely – even to the extent of sketching the coastline of every continent. No doubt someone will one day produce a fascinating history of the emergence of the first online communities to describe themselves as 'jihadi', of the curious characters who dedicated themselves to tracking them with a fanaticism not much short of those who served as their online quarries, of the virtual war both sides thought they were fighting.

But this book neither provides, nor pretends to provide, such an overarching analysis. As argument requires, I shall touch on some of these themes, but no more than that. I am, in any case, wary of producing precisely the same too neat 'narrative' of online jihadi action as that which informs both jihadis and those most dedicated to studying them. Empirically, I shall be much more concerned with small – I hope – telling details than with exhaustive overviews. Often, my examples will be drawn from what is ordinary, mundane, routine or even seemingly peripheral about 'jihadi' content and activity online. I shall, for example, be as much interested in matters such as how internet 'jihadis' go about requesting a suitable online signature, or with the kinds of musing that get posted in the unglamorous 'general' sections of jihadi forums as with, for example, the acrimonious wars of words between Zarqawists and al-Maqdisists, or between partisans of Al Qaeda and the Islamic Army of Iraq which tore 'jihadist' communities apart, splitting whole forums down the middle.[3]

Still less shall I aim to provide a 'behind the scenes' exposé of the genuine connections that do of course exist between the media apparatuses of jihadist groups and their more 'kinetic' aspects. Again, this is an important subject, and the day will come when it will be possible to chronicle it adequately. But again this is not my subject – except in so far as some treatment of it is essential to my overall argument.

It might be imagined, then, that this book is intended to be a rarified academic exercise, remote from 'real world' concerns about security. It is true that this book is premised on the idea that the notion of online jihadism as a security threat in itself has been badly overrated. And yet, as I shall go on to argue, the thesis that one can talk, in some sense, about a distinctive 'jihadi culture' online, dependent, but not reducible to the real-world violence which it claims to be premised on, as well as being of interest in its own right, must also be an important part of any attempt to understand the practical issue of so-called 'violent radicalization' among self-styled supporters of Al Qaeda.

The real puzzle here is not so much trying to understand why a relatively few people, through a more or less comprehensible set of psycho-social processes, leave their ordinary lives to carry out acts of extraordinary violence; but rather the so-called 'problem of specificity': why relatively many others who possess apparently similar beliefs and commitments do nothing of the kind.[4] By better understanding how online jihadism actually works for those who engage in it– the pleasures, rewards and self-justifications that accompany membership in one of the subcultures which thrive on the consumption of digital jihadi content – one can, I suggest, begin to explain some of its puzzles; for example, why even apparently 'extremist' engagement online seems to seldom lead to actual violence. By turning the idea of a pathway through 'violent radicalism' into violence on its head and asking what *protects* people who seem to be ideologically committed to violent action from getting bodily involved, I would suggest that we are better placed to develop rational, measured approaches to deal with the threat of terrorism and to avoid excessive, illiberal and counterproductive attempts to further police and securitize the internet medium itself.[5]

At this point, a different sort of reader is perhaps equally concerned that I am so immediately back to talking about violence, security and 'radicalisation'.[6] Are we to believe that anything which is 'jihadi' is somehow automatically associated with terrorism? Don't I know (this reader may be wondering) that for many Muslims the 'true meaning' of jihad is the *jihad al-akbar* – an inner spiritual struggle to live morally? I don't want to get ahead of myself, as this issue will come up again later on, but a few words of clarification are probably needed at this point.

Jihād is the verbal noun of the form-three Arabic verb *jāhada*, which literally means (very helpfully) 'to do jihad'. Similarly, basic Arabic grammar tells us that a person who practices jihad is a *mujahid*. The triliteral root, *j-h-d*, is associated with the concept of 'striving', and the form-one verb from the same root unequivocally means 'to strive'. To give a corresponding example of why this is not necessarily a helpful indication of precise meaning, the form-one verb *sa'ada* means 'to be happy', whereas form-two verb *sā'ada* means 'to help'. Since, to the best of my knowledge, the words *jāhada* and *jihad* do not have ordinary language uses independent of their sacred ones, there is not much to go on in ascribing them meanings other than to look at how they are used in these contexts.

The verb *jāhada*, when specifically followed by the words *fi sabil Allah* ('in the path of God'), has generally been assumed to have the meaning of fighting holy war for the purpose of exalting God's word. Whether this implies a literal war against unbelievers or a figurative war against one's own internal unbelief and, if the former, when it is appropriate to fight this war has been a matter of profound contention throughout the history of Islam until the present day. While I shall occasionally make reference to this debate, I shall say as little about it as possible. There are Islamic scholars with lifetimes of training who can pronounce on this matter. There are ordinary Muslims with very strong personal convictions of their own. There are also many good and accessible books on the subject by non-Muslim experts. Michael Bonner's *Jihad in Islamic History: Doctrines and Practice* would be one good starting point.[7] Such books are useful as guides to understanding how the concept has been officially understood within Islamic theology. To get a sense of the range of ways in which Muslims (particularly those living in the West) actually understand the word, Gabriele Marranci's *Jihad Beyond Islam* is helpful.[8] For a bigger, statistical picture of Muslim attitudes, Esposito and Mogahed's *Who Speaks for Islam: What a Billion Muslims Really Think* provides a thorough assessment.[9]

This book, however, is not really about jihad at all. It is about digital content which has been described – usually by the person distributing it, and without pejorative implication – as 'jihadi'. More particularly, it is about a political/religious movement and, for our purposes, an online subculture of people who describe themselves (alongside other labels) as 'jihadis'. As we shall see in subsequent chapter, it so happens that when content is described as 'jihadi' it almost always has something to do with militancy, or at the very least contentious political striving against violent oppressors.

To say this is not by any means to say that such content is necessarily associated with or advocating 'terrorism', assuming that that word has any reliable meaning at all.[10] Much of the contemporary violence which occurs under the name of jihad would be more appropriately described as guerrilla warfare than terrorism. Moreover, just because a person supports a group which carries out acts of terrorism alongside other forms of violence does not automatically mean that that person supports terrorism as such. For example, there are those who would claim to admire Al Qaeda but who would also deny that it was responsible for 9/11 and other mass-civilian casualty attacks. Are these people to be seen as supporters of terrorism or not?

However, contemporary usage in Arabic and English (and, apparently, in Urdu as well)[11] also suggests that where people are referred to (and may indeed refer to themselves) as *jihadis* (except perhaps where the word refers colloquially to a member of Palestinian Islamic Jihad), that term refers in practice to a supporter of what has been called 'Salafi Jihadism' (or, better, 'Jihadi Salafism').[12] In practice, this entails, among other things, support for a range of groups more or less affiliated or aligned with Al Qaeda, including at least their major acts of terrorism as well.

For all its problems, then, the term 'jihadi' has two great advantages: first, it is the term used, emically, by the subjects themselves. Secondly, it is also widely used in ordinary speech by others as well. For example, when the mainstream Arabic media speaks of 'jihadis' or 'jihadi groups', there is really no ambiguity about what they mean. Nor do such usages presume that what these groups are actually doing is legitimately *jihad*. All other labels we might apply to the same set of phenomena have the disadvantage of being too broad, too narrow, too inaccurate, too pejorative or too celebratory. There is no need to elaborate on this, as the cultural, subcultural and cybercultural story of how we get from *jihad* to *jihadi* to *a jihadi*, and of the battle of names that this gives rise to is one of the main themes of the book.

For the purposes of this chapter, it is enough to note that 'jihadism' on the internet has, rightly or wrongly, been to a great extent the concern of literature arising from the field of terrorism and political violence, and it is with this literature that we are now concerned.

When nineteen terrorists took over four airliners and flew them into two of America's most iconic and important buildings, killing nearly three thousand people, they both vindicated and confounded a decade of thinking about what the new threats to the world's aspiring hegemon were likely to be. On the one hand, here was a substate group, operating with a flattened hierarchy, motivated by religious fanaticism and unafraid of causing casualties unprecedented in the history of similar operations. On the other hand, the attack had been carried out not by means of a nuclear weapon supplied by a rogue Russian scientist or a devastating cyberattack or a genetically engineered doomsday virus, but rather by the clever hacking of a number of social, organizational and cultural rules: the relative ease with which a foreigner could enrol for higher education in the United States, the lack of security on internal flights and the assumption, good since the 1970s, that the best thing to do in the event of a hijacking was to sit still and let the hijackers get on with it. So deeply engrained were these assumptions that, so it seems, even Al Qaeda took a long time to realize that its own combination of access to operatives ready to do suicide missions and lack of scruples about deliberately causing mass civilian casualties had fundamentally changed the possibilities of aviation terrorism. We can see this from the fact that, only a few years earlier, brilliant minds like that of Ramzi Youssef were still devoting themselves (as indeed they are again now), to the creation of ever smaller and more concealable explosives to sneak onto airliners, rather than considering (at this point) the fact that an aircraft is itself a flying bomb of terrible destructive potential.[13]

The blindness of the world's security experts to this possibility is neatly summed up by Alan Stephens and Nicola Baker in their book *Making Sense of War*.

> Many of the Western strategic analysts orphaned by the Cold War were so impressed by the conventional technological capabilities of the United States that they attributed a similar or even more advanced level of prowess

to potential adversaries. This type of threat inflation was driven in part by the realisation that anyone wishing to fight the United States would have to resort to asymmetric warfare. . . . This kind of mindset was also influenced by the common strategic tendency to "mirror image." Having concluded that adversarial forces would seek to use non-conventional tactics and weapons, analysts focused their attention on the kinds of threats that actors in a high-technology environment like their own might generate. Thus, a whole literature sprang up on cyber warfare. . . . These kinds of preoccupations led many to ignore the possibility that less conventionally capable actors might opt instead for a low-technology approach, sneaking under the radar rather than trying to attack it. . . . Al Qaida fighters in Afghanistan did not hide in multi-storey, air-conditioned bunker networks as envisaged, but in caves scarcely big enough to shelter a goat. And they were just as likely to contact each other by human messenger, by post or even by pigeon as they were to hide encoded instructions on the Internet.[14]

But Stephens and Baker's critique goes too far. In some ways, Al Qaeda were very much the sort of opponent envisaged by strategic thinking in the previous decade. As Zanini and Richards had noted in a chapter of a RAND Corporation publication just a few months before the attacks:

In contrast, the newer and less hierarchical groups (such as Hamas; the Palestinian Islamic Jihad; Hizbollah; Algeria's Armed Islamic Group; the Egyptian Islamic Group; and Osama bin Laden's terrorist network, al-Qaeda) have become the most active organizations (Office of the Coordinator for Counterterrorism 2000). In these loosely organized groups with religious or ideological motives, operatives are part of a network that relies less on bureaucratic fiat and more on shared values and horizontal coordination mechanisms to accomplish its goals.[15]

These authors go on to argue in the same chapter that an important factor in enabling these 'lateral coordination mechanisms' was the advance of information technology, making communications quicker and cheaper for everyone. As they noted, eyewitness accounts reported that Bin Laden even then had access to computers, the internet and satellite phones from his base in Afghanistan, however, limited its facilities might have been in other senses.

Perhaps the real problem with this sensible observation was the way in which, it having been grasped that global changes in technology may have create certain new opportunities for (from the Western security standpoint) foes as well as friends, the insight was then reified into a notion of abstract threat remote from everyday life, and somehow uniquely related to the specific technology of the internet.

Thus, for example, Gabriel Weimann opens his 2006 book *Terror on the Internet: The New Arena, The New Challenges* with the following words:

> In the wake of September 11, 2001, terrorist attacks, a single question seemed to arise from all quarters: how could U.S authorities and intelligence agencies have failed to completely to detect the plot? Despite many unknowns, a common thread runs through most of their explanations, the FBI reports, and numerous analyses: the Internet played a key role in the terrorists' attack . . . the hard evidence is overwhelming[16]:

The 'hard evidence' that Weimann actually cites is an article in a law journal, based in turn on newspaper stories,[17] which claims that two of the 9/11 hijackers would not check into a hotel in Florida unless they had 'around the clock Internet access in their room . . . the terrorists also used the Internet to purchase "at least nine of their [airline] tickets" . . . and used the Web to steal social security number and obtain fake drivers' licenses'.

If we base our assessment on the information provided by the 9/11 Commission Report, it becomes clear that while the 9/11 hijackers did use the internet, and considered it important enough to teach the relatively poorly educated 'muscle hijackers' recruited from Saudi Arabia how to use it as one of the skills they would need to blend in in America,[18] it was hardly a *sine qua non* of the plot. The plotters seem to have relied more on security through obscurity than anything else, and they seem to have used unencrypted email more or less interchangeably with telephone calls as a means of communication. As the report notes, for the most secure communications, the network relied on human couriers. Indeed if we consider the number of long-distance flights that were made in laying the groundwork for the plan, one might argue that, even as a communications medium (i.e. laying aside the importance of the airliners as the main weapon for the attacks), the availability of relatively affordable civilian air travel would seem to have been at least as crucial to the viability of the Al Qaeda network as it was in 2001 as was the internet (or, for that matter, satellite phones, which are another technology again).[19]

The paradox of the literature on the relationship between Al Qaeda and the internet as it emerged in the decade following 9/11, perhaps particularly in its middle years, is that on the one hand it tends to be premised heavily on bringing the debate down to earth by debunking excessive concerns about 'cyberterrorism'. And yet, at the very same time, it seeks to replace this with the notion of, as the title of one notable *Foreign Affairs* article puts it, a 'real online terrorist threat'.[20] It is fully recognized by researchers working in this area that the types of internet use from which this threat is supposed to emerge are by and large 'its more prosaic properties' from a technical point of view; that the terrorists using the internet are ordinary people who use the internet 'like the rest of us', and that the dangers arising from their use of it are heterogeneous. And yet there seems to be an irresistible urge, nonetheless, to constitute 'terrorist use of the Internet' as a single research field in which terrorism comes to be talked about, even if only as a conceptual short hand, as a sort of unified essence which somehow inhabits cyberspace and, further, as if the internet represented a unique sphere for terrorist action, rather than one of many modern technologies all of which make it easier to do certain things.

A good example of this is a much-cited paper published in the military journal *Parameters* in 2003 called 'Al Qaeda and the Internet: The Danger of Cyberplanning'[21] by Lt Col. Timothy Thomas. Noting that 'cyberplanning may be a more important terrorist tool than the much touted and feared cyberterrorism option', the author goes on to offer no fewer than sixteen distinct things which the internet can be used by terrorists to do. The issue is not necessarily with the validity of any of the author's claims (though, as I shall go on to argue, for the really important tasks needed to maintain a terrorist organization, there is now good evidence that the internet is not nearly as useful as it has been said to be), but rather the too-neat word 'cyberplanning' with which he thinks he can encapsulate all of them. It is almost as if we were to come up with a single word to bring together all the various ways in which a terrorist group might make use of the railway network or the postal service.

Nor are such attempts restricted to the military-strategic literature. Numerous efforts at typologizing that various ways in which the internet is or might be used by terrorists are to be found in academic work from a variety of disciplines, much of it following the same basic intellectual trajectory. So, for example, to take two of the most important University academics working in the area, both Gabriel Weimann and Maura Conway published papers in the early to mid 2000s debunking fears about cyberterrorism,[22] while both also, around the same time, produced papers typologizing the broader phenomenon of 'terrorist use of the Internet'.[23] For both, it is accepted that these lists of various uses of the internet by terrorists are conceptually rough around the edges, and that uses are often overlapping. But neither seems to question the basic idea that 'terrorist use of the Internet' represents a single area of research waiting to be subdivided out by the researcher. As a case in point, consider the typologies below, set out by Weimann in 2004 and 2006 respectively.

A cursory examination of this list should satisfy the reader that the set of uses enumerated here don't just overlap, but seem to belong to quite different levels of analysis. 'Sharing information' is a fundamental function of the internet. 'Networking' is a matter of organizational structure which might

2004	2006
Psychological warfare	*Communicative uses* (black and white propaganda)
Publicity and propaganda	*Instrumental uses*
Data mining	Data mining
Fundraising	Fundraising
Recruitment and mobilization	Recruitment and mobilization
Networking	Networking
Sharing information	Training
Planning and coordination	Attacking other terrorists

FIGURE 1 *Weimann's typologies of terrorist use of the internet from a 2004 report and his 2006 book. Other typologies are to be found in Conway (2006), who also reviews typologies by Furnell and Warren, Cohen, Thomas and Weimann; in Reid (2008) and in Chen et al. (2007).*

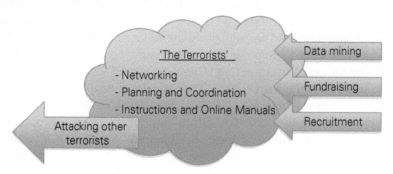

FIGURE 2 *The apparent interrelationship of Weimann's (2006) typology of terrorist uses of the internet. Some internet uses relate to 'inputs' into a notional terroristic actor, some into internal activities within that actor and one (verbal attacks on other terrorist groups) to an output from the actor.*

be accomplished by means of sharing information. Recruitment and training are (in principle) quite specific organizational activities which the internet could support in a variety of ways. But what is more problematic is the question of who, exactly, the terrorists are who lie behind all this, and how, exactly, the uses observed contribute to terrorism actually happening. If we are talking about a 'network' rather than a clear-cut organization, then on what basis do we judge whether a person who is carrying out a particular online activity is meaningfully a part of this loose-knit 'terrorist' entity or not? And if we are talking about outputs such as (Weimann means verbally) 'attacking other terrorists' which do not entail actual violence, then where, exactly, does the terrorism reside?

As a concrete illustration of this, consider the case of Tarek Mehanna. On the 12th April, 2012, this man was sentenced to seventeen years in jail by a Massachusetts court for the crime of providing material support to a terrorist organization.[24] What Mehanna had in fact been doing was translating and distributing online content on behalf of the Islamic State of Iraq – a branch of Al Qaeda. It is worth noting that in the United Kingdom, almost precisely the same case – that of Tsouli, Daour and Mughal, which we shall have reason to encounter again shortly – was tried with ultimately much the same outcome.[25] The defendants, who had been helping to distribute propaganda for the exact same organization, were found guilty of 'conspiracy to incite murder', and Tsouli, who was judged to have been the most active, was ultimately sent to jail for sixteen years. The major difference between the two cases, however, is that in the United States, where the first amendment of the US constitution provides powerful protections for freedom of speech, Mehanna was doing nothing illegal in distributing the content he was distributing.[26] Hence the charge of 'material' support. The ambiguity should be obvious here. Had Mehanna been a paid employee of Al Qaeda, he would clearly have been committing a crime, in so far as Al Qaeda is, in the United States, an illegal terrorist organization. Had he been doing the exact same things he was doing without any personal involvement with the organization, according to the US constitution he would just have clearly been innocent. The case then really had nothing to do with the harmfulness or otherwise of anything Mehanna did, but rather with the technicality of what it means to assist an organization.

A similar conceptual problem afflicts the other major preoccupation of early research on 'terrorist use of the Internet': the various attempts to 'map' or enumerate the terrorist 'presence' online. The following claim, by Weimann, for example, has now been cited so often (notwithstanding the fact that, whatever its validity at the time it is now plainly out of date) in the grey literature that it has taken on something of a life of its own.

> In 1998, fewer than half of the thirty organizations designated as foreign terrorist organizations by the U.S Department of State maintained Web sites; by the end of 1999, nearly all thirty terrorist groups had established their presence on the Net. Today there are more than forty active terrorist groups, each with an established presence on the Internet. A thorough and extensive scan of the Internet in 2003-5 revealed more than 4,300 Web sites serving terrorists and their supporters.[27]

Weimann insisted of this claim when he first published it: 'Our findings reveal a proliferation of radical Islamic websites. This is not a methodological bias, but rather a significant trend highlighted by our study'.[28] Indeed, how many of the sites he was talking about must have been 'radical Islamic websites' is indicated in the fact that, by 2008, he was asserting that Al Qaida alone now maintained more than 5,300 websites.[29]

This alarming sounding claim was, if anything, rather conservative. In 2008, the Anti-Defamation League kept an official tally of 8,000 'terrorist' websites,[30] whereas the Dark Web Portal project of the University of Arizona claims that, as of 2007, there were as many as 50,000 'terrorist' websites online.[31] This figure compares interestingly with Dubowitz's unsourced claim that 'In 1998, there were only 12 jihadist websites. By 2007, that number had increased to 50,000.' Yet again, so it seems, 'terrorist' is essentially a synonym for 'jihadist' or 'radical Islamic'.[32]

The problem, of course, with these tallies is again the question of what it means for a content item, encountered on the internet to be considered 'terrorist'. Weimann asserts in his book that he was 'Using the US State Department's list of terrorist organisations' to arrive at his total. But the problem is not as such one of defining terrorism or terrorist organizations, but rather of defining what it means for a website to be 'serving terrorists and their supporters'. After all, many *counter* terrorist websites offer access to material produced by 'terrorists' – indeed, in the jihadi magazine *Inspire*, readers are specifically advised not to visit jihadi websites, but instead to obtain ideological material from those agencies such as MEMRI which set out to monitor it.[33]

Moreover, as Weimann himself observed in 2002, the actual official websites maintained by terrorist organizations often kept well away from mentioning their own violent activities.[34] Do we count as a 'terrorist website' a website by a person who calls for violence against a particular group of people, even if its authors have no actual affiliation with terrorist activities whatsoever? Or do we count as a terrorist website a site which we happen to know, for one reason or another, to be affiliated to a 'terrorist organisation', even if it speaks only of a set of perfectly understandable political grievances, and says nothing about the idea of using violence to attain them? Or do we consider both to be instances of the same overall category? What if I have a site which supports Al Qaeda, but insists that Al Qaeda only ever kills on-duty soldiers in uniform as part of a just insurgency, and that all attempts to claim otherwise are malicious propaganda put about by a world Zionist conspiracy? What if I have a site which, for ostensibly 'descriptive' reasons, sketches out a strategy for a supposedly purely hypothetical campaign of terrorism against Muslim minorities in the West? What if I have a site which speculates philosophically that terrorism might under some circumstances be justified?[35]

Overall, there would seem to be two major problems with the 'terrorism on the Internet' literature, as it emerged in the years after 9/11. (It should be pointed out, in the interests of fairness, that Weimann and Conway, the two researchers I have singled out here as emblematic of the trend, would both appear themselves to have moved on significantly in their research output, in such a way that these limitations are not necessarily still characteristic of their more recent work.)

The first problem is that it is questionable how far 'terrorism on the Internet', or even 'terrorist use of the Internet', as such, is really a coherent object for research. Formulating the problem this way seems to confuse between at least two distinct issues: on the one hand, the question of how far the availability of the internet and specific ways in which it has been used has *caused acts of terrorist violence to happen* and, on the other hand, the question of how far certain movements, organizations or sets of ideas which, for some reason or other, have attracted the label 'terrorist' represent themselves online. Of course, these two areas may well be interconnected, but their connections cannot simply be taken for granted.

Ultimately then, the notion of 'terrorist use of the Internet' would seem to come unstuck on the vagueness inherent in the notion of 'terrorism' itself. The problem is not with the old cliché about the impossibility of defining terrorism, however. Rather, it is with the tendency for the meaning of the word, which surely ought to refer to certain specific sorts of violent action, to be applied to movements and ideologies which, however dangerous they seem, are not equivalent to actual violence happening in the world. As such, there is a tendency to lose sight of the real question that is surely at stake: does the

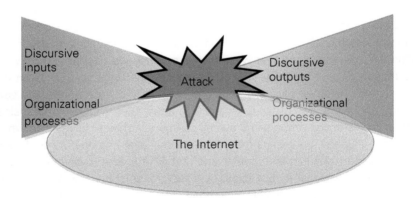

FIGURE 3 *A possible alternative model for thinking about the possible role of the internet in causing terrorism. Here the actual occurrence of violence is placed at the centre. Certain inputs are necessary for violence to occur and, in order for it to be meaningfully readable as 'terrorism', certain discursive and organizational outputs as well. The internet may (or may not) be used in carrying out any stage of this process.*

internet, in the final reckoning, actually cause acts of terrorism to take place that would not have taken place otherwise, or does it not? Without putting the concrete issue of acts of actual terrorist violence at the centre of the analysis, it is uncertain how any enquiry into 'terrorist use of the Internet', as such, can make sense.

Indeed, assuming that terrorism (meaning violence of certain kinds actually happening in the world) and 'terrorism on the Internet' are the same phenomenon seems to lead automatically to the assumption that the latter is inevitably threatening in just the same way as the former obviously is. As US senator Joseph Lieberman once said: 'we cannot afford to cede cyberspace to the Islamist terrorists, for if we do, they will successfully carry out attacks against us in our normal environment'.[36] This statement – albeit rhetorical – seems to assume simultaneously (1) that information networks constitute a 'space' which, like physical space, can be 'ceded' to another mutually exclusive occupant (2), that this space can be occupied by 'terrorists' (and presumably by extension by heating engineers, pigeon fanciers and US senators), (3) that the internet is not our 'normal environment', but rather some strange alternate reality parallel to the activities that make up ordinary life and finally (4) that there is a straightforward transition from one environment to the other, such that occupying cyberspace automatically makes it possible to threaten 'real' space.

We may note that even in advance of any consideration of the evidence, it is plain that these claims *cannot* be strictly accurate. Rather, (1) information networks are 'space' only in a metaphorical sense, and their 'occupation' by one set of data does not preclude their occupation by another any more than having books on one subject prevents a library from having books on another. (2) Terrorists cannot occupy cyberspace. They can use the internet. Ideas in support of terrorism can, however, occupy cyberspace in a metaphorical sense. (3) In the strict and specific sense used by an internet theorist such as Lawrence Lessig, 'cyberspace', meaning, paradigmatically at least, online environments such as *Second Life*, *World of Warcraft* or the various text-based MUDs and MOOs that preceded them can be understood as having a certain intentional alienness to ordinary life.[37] And indeed, while some uses of the internet by the 'terrorists' Lieberman is talking about may be relatable to notions of cyberspace, the actual media in these cases – websites, social media, email, etc. are now an integral part of many people's everyday routine – not some parallel dimension. (4) While it might be plausible to suppose that calling for people to do things may sometimes result in their doing them, there is no automatic relationship between a particular set of ideas being disseminated online and their actually being realized physically.

However – and here we now turn to the second problem with early writing on terrorist use of the internet – it also turns out that as more evidence has emerged in the literature on the subject from about 2008 onwards, and as terrorist violence itself has evolved, it has become increasingly clear that the relationship between the internet and the emergence of terrorist violence is, empirically speaking, a good deal more complex than has been supposed. Specifically, it seems that the internet is particularly unhelpful at offering a platform for those 'instrumental' uses of the internet which are most directly likely to be valuable in actually bringing acts of terrorism about (as opposed e.g. to making it easier to distribute propaganda after the event). Notably, the evidence that the internet is really useful as a tool for fund-raising, for training, for recruitment or for planning seems to be either thin or to point in the contrary direction.

With regard to fund-raising, the first question to ask is what really counts as internet fund-raising in the first place. Many of the more humdrum ways in which the internet might have a role in terrorist fund-raising seem to be fairly incidental and better treated under the rubric of the much-discussed topic of terrorism finance as a whole. For example, in 2009, the founders of an Islamic charity in the United States were given life sentences for, so it was claimed, channelling funds to Hamas, which the United States considers to be a terrorist organization. The Holy Land Foundation, like many charities, had a website which was used to solicit donations.[38] But it does seem that there are rather larger issues here than the fact that charities often have websites.

We would have on our hands a more remarkable example of the internet being used for terrorist fund-raising if terrorist groups were using the internet to solicit donations *directly*. It would seem that such things have occurred from time to time. For example, a group called the 'Islamic Army in Iraq' used to maintain a website called *nussra* which specifically allowed users to enter their credit card details and, ostensibly at least, to donate to the group.[39] But while examples like this make nice illustrations for PowerPoint presentations on the subject of terrorist finance on the internet, it seems highly unlikely that such short-lived, marginal and risky endeavours are important sources or revenue for such groups. Ask yourself the question – even if you supported an outlawed terrorist organization, would you really be prepared to put your name, address and credit card number onto a website claiming to belong to them?

A more plausible scenario would be one in which some form or other of cybercrime were used to raise money for terrorist purposes. In general, there is nothing abnormal about the idea of terrorists raising money by engaging in some more conventional crime and, in practice, it would seem that something along these lines may actually have happened – once. At the 2006 trial of Tsouli, Daour and Mughal, it was claimed that two of these men, it seems, had in addition to their propaganda activities also been involved in raising a very considerable amount of money – the figure sometimes given is $3.5 million – through online credit card fraud.⁴⁰

Assessing the significance of this incident is difficult, however, because the details surrounding it remain somewhat murky. Extraordinarily, the media at the time focused almost all its attention on Tsouli's online propaganda activities, treating the credit card story as a side issue. However, from what has been reported then and since, it seems that the men concerned, Tariq al-Daour and Younes Tsouli had bought credit card numbers from criminal forums such as Carderplanet and Shadowcrew and then laundered the money by using them to buy prepaid credit cards, egold and to play against each other on online gambling sites.⁴¹ It has to be said that this account, as it presently stands, seems unlikely to be the full story. Actually realizing money from stolen credit card numbers is generally recognized as much the most difficult part of this form of crime. This, after all, is the reason why the hackers who steal the numbers in the first place put them up for sale for a relative pittance rather than trying to withdraw cash from them themselves. And the amount of money which al-Daour and Tsouli are claimed to have raised is enormous. There is also the question of where the seed capital came from for obtaining the tens of thousands of credit card numbers they needed in the first place.

But even if we accept the story of al-Daour and Tsouli's credit card fraud at face value, it remains that this is an isolated incident which seems not to have been replicated (it would be harder to replicate it today anyway, since at least some of the loopholes used to extract money from the cards have been closed). Nonetheless, it is clearly of some concern.

One reason for this is precisely that online credit card fraud is an activity which can be more or less completed online without having to interface with the physical, embodied activities which actually doing terrorism implies. And it is precisely at this point that the real difficulties for using the internet as a tool for terrorism seem to emerge. The clearest example of this is with the idea of the internet as a 'virtual training camp'. This notion arose from the belief that the online availability of various jihadi weapons manuals, as well as recipes for bombs and poisons would facilitate a radical advancement in the ability of civilian amateurs to create and use deadly weapons. As work by Anne Stenersen has convincingly shown, the presence of these manuals was no proof of the existence of more structured forms of online training.⁴² Moreover, most of the actual bomb-making recipes being circulated were of dubious quality. But arguably, even the threat from good-quality bomb-making recipes on the internet is ultimately limited given the distinction between what Michael Kenney has influentially called *metis* and *techne*.⁴³ What this basically means is that there are some skills which cannot be taught simply through written instructions, but which must also be learnt through hands-on experience.

And bomb making, it turns out, is one of them. Numerous attempts have been made at constructing home-made bombs by jihadi and other sorts of terrorists. Few have been successful, and those that have been very successful have either used ready-made commercially available explosive (as in the Madrid bombings),[44] have had access to more formalized training elsewhere (as with the London bombings)[45] or have had extensive opportunity for hands-on practice (as with Anders Breivik).[46]

Something similar goes for attempts to use the internet in order to hatch plots for terrorist attacks or to gain new recruits. The problem here is that, as long as one is using the internet to talk to people that one doesn't already know and trust (and without this possibility, the value added by the internet in these areas seems rather limited), one simply doesn't know whom one is talking to. There will be more detail on how jihadis see this issue themselves later on, but the point has been well made by, among others, Raphael Pantucci, that the actual evidence from conspiracies such as that uncovered by the United Kingdom's police operation *Praline* suggests that the internet does a better job of compromising the plans of would-be terrorists than advancing them.[47]

The overall lesson from all of this is that while the internet may well offer a good means for terrorist groups to disseminate propaganda and cultivate supporters online, it is a much less useful way of supporting the material practices of actual terrorism. In consequence, the focus on the supposed terrorist threat from the internet has tended to shift in recent years away from Weimann's category of 'instrumental' uses and towards the idea of internet content as playing a role in more individualized 'grass roots' or 'self-starter' forms of 'violent radicalization'.

The idea that the internet offers a new kind of conduit for decentralized, media-based terrorist campaigns, in which dangerous 'memes' roam the ether, looking for 'vulnerable' bodies to colonize and bend to their sinister bidding is one that finds support in a number of high-profile incidents. Much was made of the fact, for example, that Major Nidal Malik Hassan, the American army psychologist who shot dead thirteen fellow soldiers at Fort Hood base in Texas, had been in email contact with the late Anwar al-'Awlaqi, a radical American-Yemeni cleric and, subsequently, an important member of Al Qaeda in the Arabian Peninsula. The same cleric was implicated when Roshonara Choudhry, a British psychology student, attempted to stab a member of parliament to death in his constituency office. She claimed shortly after to have resolved on this act after becoming fixated on his online sermons.

But the idea of the internet as a unique conduit for the viral spread of a new form of terrorist threat is one that, on closer examination, seems rather problematic. First, if one puts aside the idea of a supposedly uniquely virulent jihadist death cult and focuses on the material aspects, the handful of shootings, stabbings, arsons, amateur bomb attacks and one attempt to run over a crowd with a truck that characterize the universe of genuinely 'grass-roots' jihadist incidents in Western countries, it would seem that these melt rather easily into the overall background of idiosyncratically motivated mass shootings, stabbings, arsons and amateur bomb attacks that come part-and-parcel with the material culture of modern life. Nor is the supposed virulence of jihadist ideology as spread through the media so very surprising. While rigorous, statistical evidence might be equivocal (as it would have to be with regard to the slender evidence base for 'grass roots' jihadism), the anecdotal evidence for the existence of a 'media contagion' effect with regard to terrorism is substantial. For example, in *Insurgent Terrorism and the Western News Media*, Alex Schmid and Janny de Graaf have chronicled numerous cases where, a few weeks after the reporting of an act of terrorism in the media, a very similar act has seemingly spontaneously occurred somewhere else. Nor do such cases seem to be restricted to what we would easily call terrorism. For instance, there is some suggestion that the Port Arthur massacre, in which 35 people were shot dead, may have been triggered by media coverage of the similar massacre of primary school children which occurred at Dunblane six weeks previously. This is not to say that there is no such thing as 'self-starter' jihadist terrorism or that the internet has no role in at least some of the cases in which it has occurred. (Given the predominance of the internet as a platform for the consumption of media generally, and jihadist discourses in particular, it is actually difficult to imagine that it could be otherwise.) But once it is placed in this wider context, the threat this proposition presents and the novelty of this threat surely come into question.

Indeed, based on rigorous assessments of the best evidence available, even the limited proposition that the internet plays a significant role in cases of individual jihadist 'violent radicalisation' seems to be perhaps surprisingly questionable. While the consumption of extremist content is accepted as an indicative factor by the extremely empirically limited tools developed for the purpose of psychological risk assessment for involvement in acts of domestic political violence (which implies only correlation, not causation),[48] there is very little solid evidence that, across the aggregate of cases, it is a major cause of engagement in this sort of violence – such, at least, is the conclusion of the criminologists Wikström and Bouhana, having been charged in 2011 with producing a systematic 'rapid evidence assessment' of the available literature on 'Al Qaeda influenced radicalisation'.[49]

The fact that in Western societies, in which jihadists (many of whom, it is worth pointing out, are radicalized converts), represent a minute fringe of a fringe, do not have a problem with home-grown jihadist violence on anything like the scale that media attention to the phenomenon might suggest is, perhaps, not so very remarkable all things considered. But there is another dimension to this issue which has barely been explored. This is the apparent scarcity of cases of similar, individualized 'grass roots' violence even in Muslim-majority countries in which there would seem to be relatively well-established 'jihadi' subcultures. It is certainly true that jihadist militias of one sort or another have been rapidly able to spring to life within the context of violent insurgencies such as those in Libya and Syria. And it goes without saying that forms of jihadist violence have also struck in a variety of otherwise peaceful Muslim states. But it is easy to forget, in all the fixation with the threat of jihadist terrorism from Muslim-minority populations in Western countries that calls for 'individual jihad' by Al Qaeda ideologues are not purely (perhaps not even primarily) addressed to such minorities, but rather to individual Muslims in Muslim-majority states. Abu Mus'ab al-Suri's *The Global Islamic Resistance Call* – often seen as the definitive work on what the author calls 'individual terrorism' – was written in Arabic, for an Arabic speaking audience, and the majority of the targets he mentions within it are specifically located within the Muslim world.[50] The same goes for 'Abd al 'Aziz al-Muqrin's article 'The Targets within Cities'.[51] Or again, in the following forum post, an example of the sort of thing being posted quite commonly on Arabic forums around 2006, it would seem that the context in which the act is supposed to occur is not a Western country, but rather a Muslim-majority state.

> Go to the supermarket where he shops (the American pig) observe him well and keep close to his trolley in the supermarket. Let the poison be in a syringe. And if this pig puts in his trolley some fruits and vegetables which are not covered with a bag, spread it on the food without him knowing. It is preferable to put it on things like rocket, lettuce and the like. If not, you can stick the injection into any of the fruits – oranges, apples, whatever he has – even a fizzy drink like cola, and so on. With the permission of the only God, "who begat not, nor was begotten, nor ever had unto him his like" (q) he will die a horrible death. Imagine him dying and his soul leaving his body as he chokes.[52]

Given that Al Qaeda ideologues have been quite clear about the desirability of a campaign of individualized violence in the Muslim world, the very limited amount of violence of this sort which has actually occurred would seem to be quite revealing about the extent to which online exhortations – in the absence of material or organizational factors – are actually capable of producing action. As an illustration of this, let us take one particularly striking case – that of Saudi Arabia. Traffic data,[53] and the evidence of arrests,[54] as well as other factors[55] would suggest that this country is home to a relatively plentiful number of internet jihadists. And yet, since 2001, there have been, at the most generous estimate, less than two dozen acts of actual violence which might reasonably be ascribed to 'individual jihad', accounting all told for fifteen casualties (dead and wounded), and fire damage to one branch of MacDonald's.[56] Moreover, the fact that even these individualized attacks seem to cluster around 2004 (when the organized campaign of Al Qaeda in the Arabian Peninsula was at its height), and not in the later years (when the online jihadist media achieved its full development), would seem to further weaken the idea that online activism played a significant role in urging people to such acts of violence.

In other words, the case that the internet plays a major role in facilitating terrorism *directly* (whether by helping terrorists to organize it, or by radicalizing people into terrorism) seems to be far from proven. But perhaps this is rather too narrow a way of looking at things. After all, it may be that the internet facilitates terrorism and political violence in a more complex manner. For instance, it has been a commonplace of terrorism research that terrorism thrives on the so-called 'oxygen of publicity' – that terrorists deliberately create violence in order to cynically exploit the mass media to gain publicity for their cause, and that were such coverage not available, their violence would lose its purpose and therefore cease.[57] As a result, governments have at times gone to some lengths to limit the coverage of terrorism by mainstream news. Since the internet enables terrorists and militants to bypass this 'media blockade' and essentially report on themselves, it might be argued that this effectively removes a potential constraint on terrorism and therefore increases its attractiveness as a tactic. The relevance of this incentive has some empirical basis. In 2008, Asal and Harwood published a paper in *Studies and Conflict and Terrorism* in which they demonstrate a correlation between the number of casualties a terrorist group produces and the amount of hits it produces in a Google search.[58] Thus, it does not seem inherently implausible that publicity-seeking groups would deliberately attempt acts of mass-casualty terrorism for this purpose in the internet age.

Notwithstanding any correlation between the lethality of a terrorist group and the attention it gets, the hypothesis that this actually causes terrorism runs up against a rather serious problem: there is no unequivocal basis for saying that the amount of terrorism, or its lethality, has actually increased. The most authoritative database of terrorism incidents currently available, the Global Terrorism Database of the University of Maryland's START project records that terrorism – by number of incidents – reached a historical peak in 1992 before sharply declining to an all-time low at the end of the 1990s. Only in 2004 does the number of terrorist attacks begin to grow again, reaching a second peak in 2007 before declining once more.[59] But this apparent increase in terrorist attacks – notwithstanding claims made on the basis of older databases – is almost entirely the result of massive increases in terrorism in just two countries: Iraq and, after Iraq, Afghanistan. And when these two countries are removed from the reckoning, the dramatic increase after 2004 all but disappears. If Pakistan (another country which saw a dramatic rise in terrorist attacks after 2003) is also excluded, this accounts for what is left of the increase.

Even if we take as our yardstick the *lethality* of terrorist attacks, the picture is equivocal. Orla Lynch and Christopher Ryder have used GTD data to examine the casualty rates from all recorded terrorist attacks across the period it covers and found that there is no consistent upwards pattern. The lethality of terrorism has peaked three times – in 1983, 1998 and 2005, of which 1983 was the worst. After each peak, casualty figures have rapidly declined, with no reliable upwards trend.[60] If we take 1998 as our starting point (a year which marks a possibly significant change in the GTD's data sources), it is true that, even excluding Iraq and Afghanistan (and removing the major outlier represented by 9/11, which accounts for nearly half of the terrorism deaths in 2001), the trend line does give us, at best, a fairly shallow increase in the aggregate number of people killed by terrorism each year, taking us from around 3215 deaths worldwide to 4325 over a 12-year period – an increase of 34.5 per cent over the entire period – and one which the historical data suggests is by no means bound to be a long-term trend.

In short, there has been no overwhelming global surge in terrorist violence, whether measured by number of attacks, numbers killed or average lethality of attacks for which the internet needs to be held accountable. Terrorism remains as it has been – an episodic and localized phenomenon, and in so far as there have been dramatic spikes in the occurrence of terrorism, most of this has been caused – ironically – by the wars initiated supposedly in order to fight it. Moreover, there would seem to be some ground for saying that even here, what we are really looking at is not an increase in violence as such, but rather an increase in the use of specifically 'terrorist' tactics (use of roadside improvised explosive devices, suicide bombings and so on) in the overall context of wars which, though tragically bloody, have actually been rather less bloody than the best available historical comparisons. For the case of the war in Afghanistan, this is undoubtedly true. The United States has now been fighting here for roughly the same time it fought in Vietnam, in which time less than a twentieth as many American soldiers have died as did in that conflict.[61] Reliable figures for Afghan casualties are harder to obtain for the whole period of 'Operation Enduring Freedom'. But what figures are available would seem to suggest that Afghan deaths in Afghanistan have, during the period of NATO occupation been an order of magnitude, likely two orders of magnitude lower than deaths of Vietnamese during the period of American involvement in Vietnam.[62] With respect to Iraq, more and better studies present a picture of greater ambiguity. Death tolls for the Iraqi population range from around 100,000 to over a million.[63] However, it now would appear that, while still outrageous, the real figure is likely to be towards the lower end of this range, perhaps somewhere around the 200,000 mark.[64] If we interpret the Iraq conflict during its worst years as being as much a sectarian civil war as a war between US-coalition and Iraqi forces, then it might be reasonable (albeit the analogy is less precise) to compare this with the death toll of the Lebanese civil war, which seems to have produced in the region of 100,000 deaths in a population not much more than a tenth the size – up to 7 per cent of the entire population.[65]

Viewed in this wide-angle perspective, the 'terror wars' of Iraq and Afghanistan would seem to be exactly that: wars in which the use of spectacular, terrifying 'shock and awe' tactics by both sides has served to mask what is historically (even if it is unlikely to be very obvious to participants), if anything, a *decrease* in the overall bloodiness and savagery of conflict. Of course, much of this is due to restraint on the side of the attackers, who have used advanced techniques to aim their weapons and protect their own soldiers. But the fact remains that, even if the Taliban or the Islamic State of Iraq aspire to be much more lethal than they are, they have not succeeded. In the case of the former, one might argue that they have not needed to be, since they may very well come out winners of the conflict notwithstanding their relatively minuscule kill rate.

What does this have to say about the subject of jihadism on the internet? If it is far from clear that the internet causes terrorism in any easily discernible sense, and nor does it correlate with any otherwise unaccountable increase in terrorism or in political violence more generally, then it seems that we must find new questions to ask about the meaning and significance of the phenomenon. To some degree, the question 'how does the Internet fail to cause terrorism?' is an easy one to answer. At the instrumental and organizational level, as we have seen, it apparently fails to cause terrorism because, while it is a good way of facilitating the exchange of ideas, images and even emotions, it is rather less effective as a way of transferring the material capabilities that are necessary to translate these things to action.

With regard to the 'radicalized' individual who expresses a desire to get involved in the violence but does not, it is easy, in a general sense, to recognize that talking big and acting big will always be different things. And yet, while this gap may be easy to acknowledge from the bird's eye perspective, that is not the same as really understanding it. How, we might wonder, does it *work* to be a so-called 'violent radical' without actually being violent? And what might such a paradoxical situation – raised to the level of a collective phenomenon, placed before us by the accessibility of the online community, have to tell us about the meaning and future not just of terrorism, but perhaps of other things as well?

In the remainder of this book, I shall attempt to shed some light on these questions through an examination of the online culture of jihadism, with the emphasis on it as an *online* phenomenon premised first and foremost on a set of consumption behaviours, and forms of online sociality created around these. In the following chapter, I shall begin this task by considering in more depth the available theoretical approaches. I shall argue that attempts to understand online jihadism in terms of straightforwardly religious or political categories are inadequate and propose instead that we focus on more generalized notions of subculture, consumption practice and the nature of digital media as a way to look at the phenomenon afresh.

In Chapter 3, I move on to consider the difficulties of defining the phenomenon of 'jihadism', including so-called 'jihadi-salafism'. As an alternative to existing strategies at typologizing these phenomena, I shall attempt to reconstruct various senses of jihadism from the starting point of the general mass of 'jihadiyyat' on the Web. In doing so, I shall argue that, in addition to the specific armed groups and official ideological positions that help to give rise to variations in this content, it is possible to offer an alternative account of the emergence of distinct jihadi idioms within the interaction of the fundamental affordances of new media and the Web combined with a culturally determined vocabulary of 'jihadi' elements.

The following chapter moves on to the specific issue of jihadi Web forums. Drawing primarily on jihadi writings on the subject of the forums themselves, I attempt to tease out the odd contradictions that seem to beset this form, and the possible implications of these for understanding what online jihadi culture is actually about.

In Chapter 5, I move from the core of online jihadi culture towards its frontiers by examining arguments between self-styled jihadis and their dedicated opponents in an 'Islamic' Web forum. Through a close reading of these arguments, I try to further develop an understanding of the meanings and subculturally mediated values which internet jihadis cultivate through online activity and their imagined relationship with the mujahidin.

Chapter 6 develops and draws together the conclusions of the two preceding chapters by attempting to present an overall theory of how jihadism 'works' online, arguing that its contradictions and paradoxes, rather than undermining it, may in fact be crucial to its functioning.

Chapter 7 extends the approach of the book to the other side of the fence by considering the various ways in which jihadi content has been engaged with by 'counter-jihadi' or radical 'cultural conservative' actors, as well as by those interested in consuming jihadist content for the purpose of what looks initially like a non-ideological interesting in 'shock' material.

In the conclusion, I attempt to develop a more systematic conceptualization of the material of the book by positing that the 'online violent radical milieu', rather than being seen as connected in some necessary way to violence as such may instead represent a new phenomenon with distinctive characteristics of its own, sketching out what some of these might be.

2

Alternative media and its alternatives

If online jihadism is not to be understood simply in terms of a terrorist threat emanating from the internet medium, how, then, are we to understand it? Over the past decade, there has grown up a research field which is sometimes called 'jihadism studies'.[1] In contrast to the generalized terrorism specialists of the past, these are researchers who typically have a Middle Eastern studies background, including expertize in relevant languages. While many of them also have some association with military colleges and research establishments, there is little doubt that this new generation of researchers who began to rise to prominence in the second half of the past decade are dramatically better informed about their subject matter than all but a handful of the academic experts specializing in the area at the turn of the millennium.

In contrast to the 'terror on the Internet' perspective, researchers in this area tend to see the internet more as a resource than as a threat. They trawl jihadi forums and websites, drawing together highly detailed accounts of the nuances of ideological and tactical debates in Al Qaeda and similar movements. Often, they use the Web as the first outlet for their own work as well, through sites like *Jihadica*.

And yet, for all the great depth of knowledge, expertize and scholarly care exhibited by – to name just a handful, Thomas Hegghammer, Will McCants, Brynjar Lia and Nelly Lahoud – as a project, the loose, overlapping research area that is jihadism studies does, perhaps, have certain liabilities. It is, I would suggest, at its strongest when it comes closest to one of the two disciplinary poles with which it is associated: mainstream political science and mainstream Islamic studies. For example, Thomas Hegghammer's study of Al Qaeda in the Arabian Peninsula, already something of a classic, is as strong as it is because it is essentially a straightforward historical-political enquiry into a particular organization, enriched by the author's great command of a wide range of source material.[2] On the other hand, Nelly Lahoud's *The Jihadis' Path to Self Destruction* succeeds by being primarily a book about ideas – whether drawn from contemporary jihadi debates or from the historical comparison with Kharijism which the author sustains.[3] Here, it might be argued, is an attempt to produce something roughly comparable to conventional scholars of Islam such as David Cook, who study contemporary jihadist thought more or less as a continuation of an interest in the intellectual history of Islam with regard to subjects such as jihad, martyrdom and apocalypse.

Where 'jihadism studies' becomes more problematic is when it comes to be assumed that documents have a concrete real-world significance for no other reason than that they say they do. Emblematic of this is the project of, as the notable researcher Jarret Brachman puts it, 'stealing Al Qaeda's playbook'.[4] The basic idea here is that, by reading the 'strategic' documents and discussions which jihadis have online, it is possible to say something meaningful about what Al Qaeda and the 'global salafi jihad', as a single strategic actor, is likely to do. While plainly it does make sense for those charged with 'defeating' Al Qaeda to give attention to what 'the enemy' says about itself, taking this endeavour too literally seems to produce precisely the problem of 'mirroring' warned against by Stevens and Baker above. The danger is if it is assumed that, just because certain documents describe themselves as 'strategic', that it follows that they serve a similar function to strategic documents in relation to a structured, hierarchical, well-resourced and unitary organization like the US or (once upon a time) the Soviet militaries.

A good example of this is the claim which was often made after the Madrid bombings that the attack was inspired by an online document called 'Jihadi Iraq: hopes and dangers',[5] which analysed the various perceived weaknesses of the states involved in the occupying coalition and concluded that Spain was the weak link: a blow to Spain, so it insisted, would produce a domino effect which would unravel the coalition and leave the United States exposed and alone.

As it later turned out, plans for the attack had been set in motion long before this document appeared online.[6] Moreover, the attackers – who, after all, did not die in the blast – apparently intended to carry out further attacks, which would make little sense if they had achieved their object when Spain's incoming government did, in fact, choose to withdraw. Furthermore, the plausibility of the idea that attacking Spain would force it to withdraw is heavily dependent on the wisdom of hindsight, given that that is what actually happened. In reality, the reason the incumbent government lost the election, thereby ensuring that Spanish forces would be withdrawn, probably had more to do with the fact that the government lied about them, trying to portray them as the work of ETA, rather than with the attacks themselves.

Nonetheless, jihadi strategists were certainly eager to trumpet the effectiveness of the attacks *after the event*. Thus, Abu Mus'ab al-Suri makes this point in *The Global Islamic Resistance Call*,[7] as does another 'strategist' 'Abdul 'Aziz al-Muqrin in an article he published on targeting in the electronic magazine *The Training Camp of the Sabre (Mu'askir al-Battar)*.[8] Intriguingly, though, al-Muqrin, despite hailing the coercive success of the attacks on Spain, still lists Spain as one of his highest priorities for attack – something which would seem to undermine the whole point about coercive violence, whereby the coerced party has to know that it can end the violence by behaving as the coercer wishes.

What this episode serves to illustrate is partly that because global jihadism is not a unified, homogeneous phenomenon, it cannot be expected necessarily to implement any single strategy consistently. It also helps to show that, to the extent that jihadist organizations do act strategically, their strategy cannot necessarily be read off from documents that are freely available online. However, there may actually be something a little deeper at work here as well. Consider, for example, the following quotation from Osama bin Laden from a speech he gave in 2009.

> You are facing a universal crusade against all of you. This is Somalia on the southwestern extremity, and the crusaders have invaded it from land, air and sea. From the direction of the West, there is another crusader march – this one against the Sudan and advancing from Darfur. And only about 300 kilometres separate the coast of Sudan from the inviolable mosque in Mecca the venerable: i.e, within striking distance of Scud missiles.[9]

The idea that the United States intends to launch a full-on military assault on Saudi Arabia and that civil strife in Muslim countries such as insurgencies in Darfur or South Sudan are part of an overall plot to divide and rule the Muslim Ummah are familiar elements of Al Qaeda propaganda – or, for that matter, the wider tradition of Middle Eastern conspiracy theory. But in this particular speech, the title of which roughly translates as 'to battle, champions of Somalia' the absurdity of the logic is especially stark. Whether or not the United States sees it as in its interests to weaken Sudan, to maintain a sphere of influence in Somalia, or to retain its hegemony over Saudi Arabia, if it had the long-term goal of destroying Mecca, it would surely have done it by now. Or, if there is something holding it back from doing so, it is certainly not the need to get within 'striking distance of Scud missiles'.

The point is that while Bin Laden's language here is clearly 'strategic' in appearance (he is using the language of geopolitics, of troop formations, of marches and battlefronts), he may as well be talking about a game of *Risk* as about any actual events in the world. The purpose of his words, of course, may have an underlying strategy to it: he is trying to link the struggle of Al-Shabab Al-Mujahidin in Somalia to the worldwide struggle to which Al Qaeda is committed. But if so, the real meaning of Bin Laden's words lies not in the words themselves, but in his use of a strategic genre of ideological speech to achieve a particular social outcome.

If the 'jihadi strategic studies' literature is best understood not as actual strategy, but rather as a sort of rhetoric with a purpose potentially quite other than the explicit arguments it makes, then studying it in terms of the sorts of strategic framework with which military staff colleges are familiar is likely to be a waste of time. Indeed, one of the more entertaining ironies of the way in which jihadi strategic thought, in particular, is studied, is the way in which earnest attention is given to the thoughts of jihadi writers (who may be largely unknown except on account of these writings) who, in turn, are earnestly digesting the most fashionable American strategic doctrines of previous years: notions such as 'fourth' and 'fifth' generation warfare, 'full spectrum war', 'information war' and so on.[10]

Thus, if an older trend in scholarship on terrorism and political violence has at times fallen into the error of reifying the internet medium as a threat, its more cutting-edge representatives have, arguably, tended to fall into an opposite extreme: they have allowed the medium to disappear, and become, at times, overly fixated on content of the message as something of automatic relevance in and of itself.

But if 'jihadism studies' is somewhat limited in its ability to help us understand jihadism as an online phenomenon, it would seem that more mainstream scholarship on the subject of Islam and the internet has similar limitations with regard to its ability to accommodate the subject of jihadism. This is despite the fact that discussion of 'digital' Islam tends to proceed from an intellectual framework which – at first glance – seems well able to address the phenomenon. For instance, a major theme in pioneering work in the subject such as that of Jon Anderson and Dale Eickelman positions the emergence of online expression of Islam within a wider overall trend mass literacy and consequent 'scripturalism' analogous to the Reformation in Europe.[11]

Herein, however, we can perhaps also find a clue as to why Islamic studies has found internet jihadism such a generally difficult topic to broach. Drawing analogies about modernization from the European experience of it is, after all, as unsettling as it is normalizing. In pointing out as, for example Kai Hafez has quite recently done, that there is nothing so very alien about the turbulence of contemporary Islamic politics, since Europe went through much the same, it is difficult to gloss over the fact that this trajectory involved, for Europe, the Thirty Years' War, the First World War and the Holocaust.[12] Moreover, if one is to characterize the kind of Islam that Al Qaeda and the 'jihadi-salafi' movement stand for as 'scripturalist', that would seem potentially to imply that these things are, so to speak, built into the Islamic 'script'.

Another reason is, perhaps, the obverse of the problem encountered by those with a security and terrorism focus – namely, the concern that focusing on jihad on the internet comes uncomfortably close to the terrain of counterterrorism. Hence, for instance, in *Islam and the West*, Jocelyn Cesari complains that the study of Islam on the internet 'has primarily concerned itself with Islamic oriented activism'. This means that, in her view, the tendency has been to study 'Islam on the Internet', rather than 'Islam of the Internet'. And yet, when she comes to speak of 'cyberjihad' she describes it as 'a web waged war of ideas consisting primarily of increasing instances of agitation and propaganda in order to manipulate the thinking of the community'.[13] If focusing exclusively on online 'jihad' is perhaps considered a bit soft in terrorism and security circles, it may equally be a bit 'hard' for researchers focused on culture – particularly those who, understandably, do not wish to reinforce stereotypes about Islam as an inherently violent and warlike religion.

A rare exception to such tendencies is to be found in the work of Gary Bunt. Bunt is unusual in that, although a good deal of his work on online Islamic phenomena addresses jihadi aspects of this, he does this from a religious studies perspective which is a long way from the security focus typical of jihadism studies. As such, his work offers a refreshing alternative to approaches which would see such content solely in terms of a potential threat. Instead, Bunt approaches jihadi material on the internet as one aspect among many of a heterogeneous patchwork of 'cyber Islamic environments' – a term which, for Bunt, '[a]cknowledges diversity among and within different zones in cyberspace that represent varied Muslim worldviews within the House of Islam, all of which present a reference point of identity'.[14]

For Bunt, virtuality is absolutely at the heart of his approach – to the extent that his use of spatial metaphors can even seem a bit laboured as, for example, when he compares his adventures in cyberspace to the residency of Edward Lane in Cairo, or the travels of Ibn Battuta.[15] But he is sensitive to the difficulties of drawing too rigid a line between what happens online and what happens in 'real life'. As he observes at the beginning of his first book, *Virtually Islamic*:

> To an extent, the Cyber Islamic Environments I visit are simulations too, representations of the real and also representations of the ideal. Some contain depictions of physical objects: mosques, sacred texts, and images of Muslims. They also contain hard information and data, pure text without physical mass. The Qu'ran in cyberspace does not physically resemble the

Qur'an on my desk. The difference between Cyber Islamic environments and *Flight Simulator* is that the "fragmentation" can impact on the real lives of individuals, at significant and mundane levels.[16]

The questions raised by online religion are among the most interesting in internet studies. Indeed the very nature of religion – which surely pushes the philosophical notion of 'doing things with words' to its ultimate extreme – makes it a wonderful tool for exploring boundaries between 'virtual' and 'real'. Was the 'Church of the Holy Walnut' – set up on one of the early text-based online role playing games by a real-life Orthodox priest as a solution to the online community's problem of virtual gun proliferation a 'real' or 'imaginary' religion?[17] Is a digital Gohonzon a real Gohonzon?[18] Is it a sin to delete a digital Qur'an? Does the use of the internet by Orthodox Jews or Amish 'culture' the technology? Or in these cases is it really technology that is ultimately going to end up doing the culturing?[19]

However, notwithstanding Bunt's liberal use of spatial tropes in his writing about online Islam, there is a descriptive tendency to his work which, as Karim observed in a review of Bunt's second book, *Islam in the Digital Age*, is sometimes frustratingly lacking in theoretical substance.[20] At times, he seems unable to fully make up his mind as to whether he is writing about a distinct Islam 'of the Internet' or with more familiar, rather more 'down to earth' preoccupations in the study of contemporary Islamic culture, such as the dissipation of traditional authority.

In his most developed statement on the subject, the book *iMuslims*, he positions his work as offering a riposte to the claims of Electronic Colonialism Theory – a media studies perspective which sees electronic media as an extension of hegemony by core countries within the 'world system' over countries peripheral to it.[21] But he develops no detailed critical argument as to exactly why this is so. Indeed, rather uncomfortably, his work often seems at time to be premised on the idea that the juxtaposition of Islam and the internet is so incongruous as to be interesting in its own right.

This criticism is perhaps particularly true of Bunt's treatment of jihadi content on the internet. Bunt is at pains to point out that the mere existence of jihadi content online is not proof that it is linked to terrorism or poses some kind of threat. But it is still uncertain as to what *is* important about it. At one point he queries as to whether jihadi space must be regarded as sacred space – but there is no serious discussion of what it would mean for there to be 'sacred space' online, and what would follow from this with regard to jihadi material.[22]

Perhaps the underlying problem with Bunt's work – the thing which seems to inhibit him from developing any deeper theoretical account over the course of three books – is precisely the fact that he is ultimately trying to say something about 'Islam'. Because he offers no real frame of reference outside this subject, he finds himself caught in the dilemma which Frederic Volpi has perceptively observed when he asks: 'how one can move away from essentialist accounts of Islam without simply saying "there are different Islams"'.[23] The price that Bunt has to pay for candidly admitting the militant 'jihadi' parts of contemporary Islamic discourse into his overall picture of Islamic diversity and heterogeneity is that it makes possible only a rather thin overall account of contemporary Islam.

Thus, while it would of course be absurd to say that jihadism on the internet has nothing to do with religion (indeed, such claims often seem to lead in the direction of arbitrary distinctions between religion and ideology which ultimately do little more than feed into Western and, particularly American attempts to separate out quiescent and stabilizing 'religion' from contentious and rebellious 'ideology'),[24] it does seem that trying to understand jihadism within the wider context of an Islamic whole is inherently problematic. But if neither political violence nor religious studies offer useful vantage points on online jihadism, what then is left?

Perhaps the next most obvious approach would be to analyse online jihadi content as a media form, specifically as a form of 'alternative' media. According to Bailey, Cammaerts and Carpentier, there are four main approaches by which we can understand and define this concept.[25] Alternative media can be understood as media which serves, being produced and consumed within, a particular community; as media which is 'alternative' to some notion of the mainstream; as the product of 'civil society' and, finally, as a 'rhizomatic' phenomenon as outlined in the thinking of Deleuze and Guattari – defined by its amorphous nature, contingency and continuing subversion of established categories.

While the empirical reasons for thinking so will have to wait until the chapters to follow, it can be said with confidence that online jihadi content fits easily into the first two of these categories. It is certainly 'alternative' in the sense that it aims – quite explicitly – to offer a substitute for the mainstream corporate or, from a jihadi point of view, 'Ziono-Crusader' news. Moreover, it is constitutive of, and in turn constituted by particular communities (in the cases with which we are concerned, online communities), who both produce and consume it. How far it fits into the other two categories is less certain. Jihadi discourses in a general are, as we shall see, a genuine part of online 'Islamic' discussion and of discussion in specific contexts (such as Palestinian contexts) where armed resistance, whether it is framed as 'jihadi' or not, is a live issue in ordinary life. Thus, 'jihadi' content may, in certain times and contexts, have a part to play in certain public spheres. But to the extent that an actor's relationship with power is conceived as inevitably violent, civil society as such, meaning by definition a 'civil' sphere for public action mediating between rulers and ruled, seems something of a contradiction in terms. Moreover, while jihadi media is certainly more fluid in nature than reified notions of terror on the internet would suggest, the rhizomatic metaphor seems to invite analysing the phenomenon in terms of a general notion of social discourses relating to jihad rather than the more specific, bounded and generic forms which jihadi content in fact takes.

And yet, even when understood specifically in terms of its relationship to community, and its alterity to the mainstream, jihadi content would seem to pose some quite serious problems for existing theoretical perspectives in this area.

An interesting illustration of what these problems might be can be provided if we turn to one of the few existing examples of a specific attempt to analyse the phenomenon along these lines: Chase Knowles' exploratory use of Frankfurt School-influenced genre theory to the case of what she suggests we call 'Islamist Neorealism' (although it is specifically jihadi content which she actually addresses in her paper on this subject).[26] First, as Knowles notes in this paper, theories of political communication of the kind she is working with are generally poorly equipped to deal with content which mixes both political and religious themes while, on the other hand, theories of communication which attempt to incorporate specifically Islamic phenomena such as that proposed by Mowlana tend towards unhelpful 'reverse orientalist' essentialism.[27]

Moreover, as Knowles argues, 'Islamist neorealism' contains not only religious elements but also motifs which seem, in Western contexts, to have more to do with fictional genres than factual ones. There is, as she sees it, 'a major theoretical puzzle . . . in short: why are a range of non-fiction and fiction formats being hybridized into one collective visual, virtual paradigm?' Knowles seeks answers to this question through comparison between the Islamist 'web genre' and that of 'socialist realism', through the dependence of the material, as she sees it, on the 'fictional epic' and lastly through a 'dualism between text and spirit' which she calls 'infospirituality'.

The problem with these interesting ideas is that Knowles seems to be able to find no satisfactory way of integrating them. In the end, so it seems, politics is still politics and religion is still religion, and 'Islamist neo-Realism' is still just a hybrid bundle of the two. As she concludes, the two main rhetorical purposes of the genre she attempts to identify are the communication of a message of resistance through strategic narrative (the crafting of narratives for specific strategic aims) and the production of 'infospiritualism'. But how these two ends are connected or, if not, why they persistently coincide with one another in the same content 'genre' remains unexplained.

But perhaps the real underlying difficulty Knowles faces is the same as the one which, so I suggest, is encountered also by Bunt. This is, in essence, whether one takes jihadi material seriously and at face value (which implies engaging seriously with the vision of Islam it sets forth); or refuses to take the material at face value and claims instead that it has some underlying symbolic meaning accessible to the researcher but not the subjects, which puts the researcher in the seemingly patronizing (and hegemonic) position of claiming to better understand the true meaning of the subjects' claims than they do themselves.

Of course, this choice is not so stark where the researcher is dealing with militant content embedded in a wider social context. Significant amounts of attention can and have been devoted to the art and literature of martyrdom and militancy in, for example, Palestinian resistance[28] or the conflict in Northern Ireland.[29] There is also a (very small) empirical literature on the consumption of jihadi content by 'ordinary' Muslims and on the wider consumption of security discourses by publics in general.[30] In the former examples, however, the researcher is typically concerned with these as one cultural feature incorporated within and shedding light on a larger political struggle. In studying say, murals in Belfast or martyr posters in Gaza, it is relatively easy for the scholar to avoid having to position herself explicitly for or against the narrative of the content, and to treat the content instead as fairly straightforwardly expressive and performative, precisely because there are other narratives accessible to her within the bounds of the resistant community as a whole. In the latter, the breadth of the audience examined and its (unsurprising) lack of connection with 'radical' material and discourses means raises few really difficult interpretative problems for the researcher.

The problem is that the internet doesn't work that way. Or at least, it doesn't work that way for a case like that of specifically jihadi media. Here, the researcher is wilfully encountering not broad, territorially delimited societies and complete lived realities, but rather part-time subcultures explicitly premised on engagement with the mediated expression of particular (and in this case particularly 'radical') positions. This in turn makes it more difficult to assess their political meaning and potential in terms that do not avoid the researcher falling into uncomfortable value judgements. In short, it is relatively easy and comfortable to do a study in which one concludes the obvious point that 'not all Muslims are terrorists'. Or 'Muslims overwhelmingly reject violent extremism' or 'extremism has a particular social context in society x' or even 'the violent extremism in society x is simply a reflection of another sort of violent extremism in society y'. It is more difficult to say things that are not automatically securitizing and condemnatory about 'violent extremism' itself. Which leaves the question as to what one *does* say about it.

Indeed, oddly, there is a case for saying that as research into alternative political culture has become more nuanced and more open to difference, heterogeneity and plural understandings of resistance and power, including religious forms of alternative media, so has it actually become less able to resolve this dilemma.

In the past, when certain forms of cultural studies (particularly in their British and, specifically, Birmingham School variant) were at the height of their influence, there was a tendency – now often lampooned and stereotyped – to view almost any unconventional act, from violent crime to slightly idiosyncratic television watching habits as an example of resistance to the prevailing hegemonic order. For example, Dick Hebdige, in a classic analysis of youth subcultures of the 1960s and 1970s made the famous argument that these could be understood in terms of 'resistance through rituals', whereby working-class children were responding to the destruction of the old certainties of British industrial culture by creating deliberately extreme mélanges of proletarian style.[31] Some of the subcultures Hebdige was writing about did have quite clearly enunciated political ideologies, although, as revisionist critics like Muggleton have since argued, it tended to be the middle-class art-school members of these movements that played the key roles in this, while the actual working-class members of the movements often had much more idiosyncratic understandings of what they meant.[32] But the point was (and it is specifically this that forms the core of Muggleton's critique) that Hebdige did not apparently feel that it particularly mattered what the members of the subcultures actually said about themselves. He felt himself free to read into their style whatever ideological subtext he believed he could perceive in it.

Researchers like Hebdige believed they could do this because they subscribed, or have been interpreted as having subscribed, to a black-and-white view whereby all hegemony was essentially bad and all resistance to it essentially good. But while things have moved on since then in the sense that scholars have become more cautious about seeing all resistance as positive and more willing to reject 'unidimensional' interpretations of the potential of popular culture,[33] it can be argued that the essential underlying binary remains at work in much of the research that followed, in so far as the ultimate universal goal of liberation seems to remain. Thus, for example, John Downing, in his seminal *Radical Media*, setting out a more complex and multidimensional approach to his subject, notes that, unfortunately, American suffragists did not always support civil rights, American civil rights activists did not always support women's suffrage and the American labour movement didn't always support either.[34] But in all these cases, we can observe, liberation is clearly to be seen as an unalloyed good, even if these three different struggles did not always recognize it for the case of the other.

One price of this more down-to-earth approach is potentially that it seems to risk going to the opposite extreme, committing the researcher to a rather literal focus on discourse over the structural features of the worlds within which social phenomena occur. Indeed, it is telling that forms of analysis which look not so very different from the 'resistance through rituals' model for British youth subcultures of the 1970s still remain very much relevant in a work on Islamic phenomena such as Saba Mahmood's *Politics of Piety* in 2005, which seeks to explain women's activism within the socially conservative Muslim Brothers by presenting her subjects' actions as having a performative significance which goes beyond the explicit content of the party's formal principles.[35] Or again, with specific regard to the problem at hand, Siapera, writing about the political potential of internet use by Muslims has critiqued the rather rigid, Habermasian model of multiculturalism, in which politics and religion are kept firmly separate, and each group must unreservedly commit itself to a common, secularized political process. She argues instead for a more performative, dynamic understanding of the medium's dialogical potential.[36]

Another problem with alternative media approaches which have moved away from structuralist readings of resistance is, paradoxically, that they seem to place the researcher in a position which is in a sense no less judgemental than it was before. Whereas, in the previous case, the scholar's job might (*in extremis*) have been to show why any anti-establishment act amounted to an act of resistance – even over the self-understanding of the subject – in the latter it becomes (to simplify a good deal) the scholar's job to pick through a variety of 'alternative' and resistant practices and decide which bits are progressive and good and which are regressive and bad. In other words, while selection may be a more nuanced business, the fundamental underlying binary remains.

The source of this binary at work in approaches to alternative media such as Downing's seems ultimately to be a belief in liberation as a sort of transcendent good, a single true north to which all political struggle, at every level, ought ultimately to aspire. But this underlying idea seems to suffer from two fundamental problems. First, liberty and therefore 'liberation' is not an absolute, but is itself socially constructed; and indeed the meaningful enjoyment of liberty actually requires (according to all manner of philosophical positions) that the individual be determined in all sorts of ways: bound into structures of shared cultural meaning and value, bound into shared institutions of collective governance, charged with unshirkable duties over one's stake on the common good and so on and so on.[37] Without these things, one is not 'liberated', but abject, at the mercy of whatever managerial power is closest at hand. Lila Abu Lughod has, for example, observed something along these lines in noting that acts of seeming resistance may be better understood as diagnostics of power, showing us how people are moving smoothly from one form of domination to another than actual processes of liberation.[38]

What such an understanding may suggest is that, in assessing the potential, meaning and indeed value of a given subculture, there are other things we may wish to be concerned about than how closely it relates to a progressive political ideal. But what might these be? As the cultural theorist Lawrence Grossberg is once said to have said, 'if studying popular culture is not political, then what good is it?'[39]

One possible answer to this question is that if 'alternative', more participatory cultural forms do not necessarily fulfil the promise of bringing about revolutionary change, they may at least help individuals to cope with some of what Giddens calls the 'consequences of modernity'. For Giddens, the vast, structural changes in the organization of human societies which result from 'late' or 'high' modernity have profound consequences at the micro-level of individual psychology, particularly in the ways they threaten what he calls 'ontological security'.[40]

Ontological security, for Giddens, refers broadly speaking to the basic human need to feel that things make sense, that one's life means something, that one occupies a clear identity, that one's life history tells a coherent story. For Giddens, the concept can be related to existentialism, to the radical doubt of Wittgenstein and the Kierkegaardian notion of a dread which can be overcome only by taking a 'leap of faith' into choosing a moral life even when it cannot be fully justified by reason.[41] But of course there is nothing inherently modern about existential angst as such. For example, the great eleventh-century Islamic theologian, Al-Ghazali, coming to the shocking conclusion that it was not possible to prove the existence of God through logic alone, seems to have a profound personal breakdown which led him to abandon his career and family and seek refuge for a time in mysticism and seclusion.[42] The anti-rationalist conclusions he reached were of enormous later importance for Islamic thought. Or we can go further back still, to one of the earliest literary works in existence, the Babylonian *Dialogue of Pessimism*, in which a master, in dialogue with his clever slave, exhibits agonizing indecision over the point of various possible personal and social activities before contemplating suicide.[43]

For Giddens, what is particularly significant, however, about the 'late modern' age is its inherently 'reflexive' nature.[44] Late modern institutions are 'post-traditional'; they are technocratic; they are founded on open-endedness, on lack of finality, on doubt. For Beck, they replace the traditional past with the 'onrushing future'.[45] For Alasdair Macintyre, they replace the values enshrined in a shared moral tradition with the myth of the scientific manager as the enlightened leader of human institutions to whichever goal they happen to be directed.[46]

As a result, the traditions and forms of solidarity in which people find meaning and around which people orient their lives are continually coming into question. The sorts of anxieties which were once peripheral to the everyday struggles for existence of most humans become an increasingly normal and common part of everyday life. Social concerns of every kind find themselves called to account, forced to explain the rationale for relations and collective practices which were once simply taken for granted. At the same time, cultural forms are 'disembedded' – lifted from one context, in which they made one sort of sense – and transposed to another, in which, as with a musical phrase or a clause in a sentence, they may in this new context end up meaning something else altogether.[47]

The specific value of such visions of late/high/postmodernity is that they seem to create a new problematic for research beyond dynamics of liberation and oppression. By viewing the erosion of traditional orders as producing specific crises of individual meaning, it becomes appropriate to ask of particular subcultures not just whether they are conducive to resistance or passivity, or whether they support liberation or oppression (which is not to say that these are no longer appropriate questions to ask), but also whether they help to overcome, for their members, some of the traumatic and socially disruptive consequences of transitions to modernity.

At its broadest, the concept of new subcultural forms specifically relating to postmodern challenges to traditional and even modernist institutions of mass authority is one which has already been applied to a very broad range of cases. Indeed, it relates very closely to Olivier Roy's enormously influential thinking on 'neofundamentalism' and its role in the establishment of new, though apparently ultra-traditional forms of globalized Islam.[48] Indeed, in more recent work, Roy has argued for the particular case of Al Qaeda support in Western countries, that it is best understood not in conventional political terms, but as what he calls a 'youth movement'.

And yet while ideas of this nature may have little difficulty getting traction elsewhere, the notion of subculture as something essentially inward looking, premised more on the creation of a sense of belonging and ontological security among its members would seem to remain under-explored in the still politically focused literature on alternative media.

This may be to a significant degree because such conclusions are, understandably, profoundly disturbing to the aspirations of alternative media itself, as well as the hopes of those who study it. But it is also because work on alternative media has typically focused on how it is produced, and for what explicit purpose, rather than on how it is consumed, and how the subcultures of consumption it supports relate structurally to the overall society in which they are located.

While a relatively slim literature does exist premised on examining alternative media and, more generally, new social movements and politicized subcultures along roughly these lines, the general purpose of this literature seems to be to critique its potential rather than to offer a new set of standards by which to assess it. Thus, for example, in one rather acerbic analysis of labour relations at the *Honolulu Weekly*, an 'alternative' newspaper in Hawaii, it is observed that despite the progressive views put forward by this paper, its treatment of employees was actually markedly worse than that at a 'mainstream' competitor.[49] A more extensive statement of the argument that seems to be implicit here is to be found in Heath and Potter's *The Rebel Sell*. Here, it is proposed that Western countercultural groups which claim to resist capitalism, through their very determination to challenge the basic social codes of mass society, end up undermining the possibilities for collective solidarity that are needed to create meaningful alternatives to extreme, free market capitalism.[50] Ironies (self-conscious of course) such as the creation of branded trainers by an anti-consumer group like Adbusters are, for these authors, actually an automatic outcome of the structural implications of a society fragmented along subcultural lines. Freedom of choice about what set of social mores one subscribes to and freedom of choice about what sort of stereo one buys go hand in hand.

Possibly more useful than such critiques, however, are accounts of the subcultural functions of alternative media which go beyond merely attacking its lack of obvious mainstream success and instead focus more explicitly on the extent to which it fulfils the purpose of building alternative communities as a good in itself. Where this relates to the larger suggested project of the 'alternative public sphere', we are basically looking at a postponement of the same binary vision discussed above.[51] Nonetheless, such analyses can help to provide insight into how alternative media works as a means of building community and shared value. A potentially more fundamental, but so far under-explored shift is, however, hinted at by exploratory work such as that of Jennifer Rauch, looking at ways in which the consumption of alternative media is ritualized and related to issues such as personal identity in ways which seem more reminiscent of the relations consumers have to art and fiction than to content with the ostensibly instrumental goals to which left-progressive alternative media typically aspires.[52]

How could we go about understanding alternative media if it were to turn out that it had less to do with its explicit political goals than both its participants and its analysts might like to believe? The obvious point of comparison would seem to be with those subcultures concerned not explicitly with producing and consuming political media, but rather with entertainment proper, in other words, with fandom.

Indeed, as it happens, there have been various, albeit problematic suggestions (over and above that of Roy) that engagement in online jihadism may indeed be usefully compared to forms of popular entertainment consumption. The most obvious of these is the coinage of the term 'jihobbyist' by Jarret Brachman, an independent researcher and consultant on global jihadism who has in the past worked on various reports for Westpoint Military Academy. In his 2009 book *Global Jihadism: Theory and Practice*, Brachman defines the term as meaning:

> ... an enthusiast of the global Jihadist movement, someone who enjoys thinking about and watching the activities of the groups from the first and second tiers, but generally they have no connection to al-Qaida or any other formal Jihadist groups. And it is unlikely they will ever actually do anything that directly supports the movement.
>
> So Jihobbyists may do it from the comfort of their home computer or their local coffee shop, but they are still actively seeking to move forward the Jihadist agenda. By hosting Jihadist websites, designing propaganda posters, editing al-Qaida videos, recording soundtracks (nashids) for those videos, compiling speeches from famous Jihadist shaikhs and packaging them into easily downloadable files or writing training manuals, these individuals help to form the base that keeps the movement afloat. Some become obsessed with the brutal beheading, sniper or explosives videos. Others would rather spend their time reading thousand-page books about the history of the movement.[53]

Contained within this definition are many of the deep ambiguities which seem to characterize Brachman's relationship with this term. On the one hand, he presents the 'jihobbyist' as rather a comical, inept figure. Indeed, in some of his less formal online writing he had spoken of 'jihobbyists' as 'orcs' or as 'utter dolts in their Mommy's basement'.[54] And yet elsewhere he has offered rather more nuanced and considered opinions about those individuals he deems to fall into the category, as when he insisted:

> 1. There are thousands of individuals from all walks of life and corners of the Earth who are actively using the Internet to consume and promote al-Qaeda and the global movement that it purports to spearhead. This, in fact, is the new al-Qaeda.
>
> 2. Many of these individuals are not full-time al-Qaeda propagandists. Far from it. They probably have never nor will never meet anyone officially associated with the actual al-Qaeda group. They just believe in the mission, the goal, the methodology or the allure. It is their version of fantasy football.

3. These individuals are also not one-dimensional. They have close friendships, good families, enjoy past-times and seem to have high self-esteem. They might also work out and take tough-guy pictures of themselves.

4. The Internet activity of these individuals tends to reflect the fact that supporting al-Qaeda fits into just one piece of the pie that is their lives.[55]

Another major difficulty Brachman seems to have is with determining whether he considers his 'jihobbyists' to represent a security threat or not. While the very notion of the jihobbyist seems to imply a person whose interest in Al Qaeda is largely recreational, as opposed to representing a genuine commitment, Brachman also seems intent on insisting that jihobbyists do, after all, 'keep the jihad afloat', and that they may even be dangerous themselves. Indeed, his attempts at finding a more robust conceptual framework for understanding jihadism from the perspective of cultural consumption and leisure seem to be essentially directed towards the ultimate goal of salvaging some notion of such forms of engagement as representing a security concern. This, at any rate, seems to be the main point raised in a *Foreign Affairs* article he published with Alix Levine, in which he insists that jihadi online milieus exhibit deliberate elements of 'gamification', aimed at radicalizing new members through competitive processes of acquiring reputation points and similar rewards.[56]

The limitations of Brachman's approach should be fairly apparent and will in any case be discussed later on. However, it is worth noting that Brachman is not altogether alone in comparing online jihadi engagement to less self-consciously ideological and political practices. Consider, for instance, the following example.

> Indeed, most of them are good people from among those who promote support for the mujahidin – on the forums – but they play their part to the fullest extent – to the benefit of RAND Corporation naturally. For all the cursing and insulting that takes place towards the Islamic Army in particular, and others in general, and the declarations that basically the sole true jihad is the jihad of Al Qaeda, none else, and that the rest are fighting for the benefit of nationalism and tribalism and we do not know what; but essentially it hurts that which is hurt by the Jews and the Christians by means of splitting Al Qaeda – or the Islamic State of Iraq – from the rest. (The rest of the factions particularly and the rest of the Muslims in general by the broadcast of schisms and difference between the sons of a single *manhaj* and a single religion and a single jihad).
>
> And this "work" is dear to them, whether intentional or unintentional, and it is [in effect] their implementation of the schemes of the enemies

by proxy, and if they were calling for support of the mujahidin (and there is no room for naivety), and God knows the hands that lie behind these things, realistically the net is 90% ignorant people . . . and what is more likely than that a scheming Jew or a treacherous heretic should broadcast words bubbling with enthusiasm calling for the support of those. And what is broadcast thus except poisons of a certain type: Al Qaeda is the hope of the Muslims, none other, and the State is the foundation for the coming caliphate – words of unification before monotheism (as if the rest were polytheists or people of innovation) – the attributes of the manhaj and so on from the ringing declarations which steal the minds of the "fans," 90% of whom have no religious knowledge whatsoever, and which captivate them like teenagers. *Indeed the majority of them in the recent yesterday were football fans, and think that this business is the same with the names changed.*[57]

The example (emphasis in the original) comes from a post on the forum Muslm.net dating from 2007 – the year of the 'surge' in Iraq and the Al-Anbar Awakening, which split Iraq's Sunni resistance, with Al Qaeda-affiliated groups continuing their fight against those they perceived to be on the side of the occupying forces, while some non-Al Qaeda-affiliated groups chose instead to turn their weapons on Al Qaeda, perceiving them now to be a greater immediate evil than the occupation itself.[58]

The pressure this put on the insurgency as a whole led to angry exchanges between supporters of Al Qaeda and those of non-Al Qaeda-affiliated groups (even if they had not, at least at the time, abandoned the insurgency). Supporters of the insurgency in Iraq began to realize that this factionalism was a problem in itself, and many saw the hand of the United States in the online as well as the offline strife gripping the movement. They insisted that a covert programme by RAND Corporation was being used to sow dissent between partisans of Al Qaeda and of the other groups. It is this view which the post above is trying to address. For this forum member, it is not necessary to invoke the malign influence of US power to explain the dissent. Rather, the problem is to be found in the irresponsible action of those online activists he calls 'fans'.

Less specifically, it is of some interest to consider how acquitted suspects in cases revolving around the use of the internet in relation to alleged support for Al Qaeda have themselves used language with the purpose of publicly trivializing their own actions. For example, Mohammed Atif Siddique, a Scottish Muslim who was sentenced to jail under the British Terrorism Act 2006 for but subsequently acquitted for allegedly 'collecting terrorist-related information, setting up websites . . . and circulating inflammatory terrorist publications', said of himself on acquittal 'I'm hardly a terrorist, I'm more of a numpty'.[59] Another similarly controversial case, Samina Malik, who was also convicted before having her charges overturned on appeal, later described the militant poems she had written on the backs of receipts at the shop she worked in as 'meaningless', and said that she had given herself the online nickname of 'Lyrical Terrorist' simply because it 'sounded cool'.[60]

In such examples, we see an implied binary distinction between serious online support for Al Qaeda and frivolous engagement which is more concerned with 'cool' and attitude than with any considered intention to contribute to violent action. Compared to the public statements of Siddique and Malik, the first quotation does, however, seem somewhat more nuanced, attributing to the online 'fan' of Al Qaeda not so much a lukewarm commitment, as an excessive partisan enthusiasm which is lacking in appropriate circumspection and restraint.

Interestingly, the views of fandom presented in both Brachman's account and that of the Muslm.net member seem closely relatable to the popular images of fandom which early scholarship on the phenomenon set out specifically to critique.

For instance in *Textual Poachers*, one of the earliest major works of cultural scholarship on fandom, Henry Jenkins observed for the case of television fans that they were typically stigmatized as:

- Brainless consumers who will buy anything associated with the show and its cast
- Who devote their lives to the cultivation of worthless knowledge
- Are feminized and/or desexualised
- Are infantile, emotionally and intellectually immature
- Are unable to separate fantasy from reality[61]

The problem this seems to raise for any serious attempt to consider jihadism through the prism of theories of fandom and similar forms of subculturally mediated popular entertainment consumption is that the notion of jihadism as fandom – whether used to imply foolishness or threat or both would seem to recall precisely the types of stigma which fan scholars reject for actual fans. Indeed, even beyond Jenkins' portrayal of the public perception of the fan as a rather laughable figure we have what Joli Jensen, at around the same time, called the 'pathological stereotype' of fandom: the notion of fans as a crazed mob, or as dangerous loners prone to celebrity stalking, or even murder (as e.g. with the assassination of John Lennon).[62] Camille Bacon Smith, another important early writer on fandom, opens her book with a humorous anecdote in which a group of female science fiction fans are made to feel so uncomfortable by the reaction of a man in the hotel lobby where they are assembling for a convention, that they quip about themselves being a 'terrorist society'.[63]

To arrive at any useful comparison, then, between the ways in which fans consume and produce texts and the ways in which online jihadis do, it is plainly necessary to eschew, from the outset, any notion that jihadis are literally a kind of fan and, instead, to try to show how insights from the fandom literature may serve to inform an understanding of how online jihadi practices might work. What the study of fandom would appear to have to offer here might be understood as a kind of natural experiment. Fan communities, in principle, would seem to look like online religious or political communities in reverse. While the latter are in principle premised on a shared and non-negotiable ideology, but may in reality be bound together more by subcultural practices of collective consumption and production, mutual aesthetics and raw sociality (what the theorist Michel Maffesoli refers to as the 'glischomorphic tendency' of humans),[64] so the former are in principle premised on shared consumption and production practices, and mutual aesthetics but may, out of these produce things which look rather like ideology or even quasi-religious ritual.

As a theoretical device, then, the fan community can be taken to serve as a sort of postmodern equivalent of the 'savage tribe' or early anthropology. In looking at how ideology and community grow, in the case of fandom, out of affect, we are, in a sense, doing something similar to what Durkheim was doing in asking about what the 'elementary forms of the religious life' could tell him about the elaborate, institutional mass religion of his own day.[65]

Indeed, for Lawrence Grossberg, in a highly influential essay, it is 'affective sensibility' which lies at the heart of fandom as a phenomenon.[66] He argues that media consumption in the saturated landscape of the present day (and the present day, for Grossberg, is 1992) involves the creation of 'mattering maps' by individuals, linking one 'affective investment' to another in an overall 'portfolio'. Lawrence's concept, which introduces the rather counterintuitive idea of an underlying structure governing emotional response, seems, for one thing, to offer a neat complement to sociological and, specifically, social movement theory ideas about 'framing'. It also suggests the idea that these affective investments in texts provide individuals with a certain amount of control over their emotional states. This in turn creates a paradox, interestingly explored by Matt Hills in his work on horror fandom, whereby certain kinds of material are deliberately and knowingly consumed which, so it would appear, are specifically associated with negative mental states.[67] For Hills, this is to be understood in terms of a sense of insider superiority and mental strength, but the notion also seems to raise interesting questions about the consumption of content in order deliberately to arouse one's own feelings of, for example, outrage.

The question of how texts engage readers emotionally is, of course, ultimately enormous, encompassing the whole discipline of rhetoric, literary criticism and beyond. But in cultural studies generally, and perhaps particularly in fandom, the emotional engagement of reader with text has typically been understood as relying particularly on the active and creative participation of the reader. The most obvious example is of course the work of Barthes who, in *The Pleasure of the Text*, stresses again and again how enjoyment in reading derives from its haphazardness – the author's uncertainty about the reader, the reader's inconsistency in that actual practice of reading, the 'play of language', the way the author's ultimate meaning always slightly recedes from the reader's grasp.[68] This is of course especially true of the indescribable 'bliss' which Barthes famously contrasts with mere mundane *plaisir*. But the idea that the subversive potential of reading and consumption is somehow a joyous activity is also very much present in other much referred to theorists such as Michel de Certeau[69] and Mikhail Bakhtin.[70]

Thus, work on fandom has tended to inherit a cultural studies perspective in which there is an intimate and dynamic relationship between the emotional resources 'invested' in texts, and the active and productive participation of the reader in consuming them. A particularly influential example of how such 'resistant reading' works in practice is Janice Radway's now classic study *Reading the Romance*.[71] Here, the author examines the consumption practices of a group of ordinary American housewives in the small town of Smithton in relation to light romance novels. The point at issue is that these novels are typically seen as escapist 'trash' fiction, premised on highly stereotyped and regressive ideas about gender relations. However, by examining how the novels are actually read and understood by the particular group concerned, Radway claims that a very different picture of their potential emerges. First, the embodied practices of reading – which involve the expenditure of household income, and the taking of personal time away from traditional household chores and responsibilities amounted, for the women of Smithton, to a minor but significant rebellion and assertion of independence. Second, the novels sustained a sense of community among the local women which further helped to provide alternatives to the domestic sphere. Third, the selective criteria which the women applied to the novels emphasized not the traditional values they enshrined, as represented by the marriage that served as the culmination of almost every story, but rather the flouting of convention and rebellious 'feistiness' of the heroines prior to their eventual domestication. Paradoxically, the inevitable romance of the novels was in a sense rather incidental to what the readers enjoyed about them.

A crucial point about Radway's focus on the role of readers and their communities in filling out the seemingly limited and stereotyped texts they were consuming comes into focus if we consider the difference between the kind of 'genre' literature represented by the romance novel, and the novel as such, according to Mikhail Bakhtin. For Bakhtin, the defining feature of the novel proper is precisely its defiance of genre – its 'heteroglossia'. What Bakhtin seems to mean by this is that the 'real', 'serious' novel, paradoxically, can be known by the fact that it incorporates some of the subversion originally reserved for the specific genres of parody such that, for example, Don Quixote, a great and enduring novel, is actually a parody of a genre of romance fiction which Don Quixote itself has outlasted. For Bakhtin, it is a crucial point about genre fiction – at least as represented in the history of Western literature, though he also passingly notes its existence in Ottoman culture as well – that serious, tragic genres always had parodic, comic counterparts.[72] Thus, for Bakhtin the process which Radway captures in her observation of readers in a small American town would seem to be a more or less universal law of the reception of serious genre works – that the audience is expected to respond to them 'dialogically', filling them out by bringing them down to earth, subjecting them to sacred defilement, incorporating them into their quotidian lives and so on. Thus, the novel as such (perhaps one could also add the symphony?) represents a remarkable index of the coming of modernity in so far as it represents not a particular speech act within a more or less known social context, but rather the attempt by the author to put down on paper a representation of an entire 'virtual community', with all its dialogical complexity and lack of finality.

The idea of texts – perhaps especially generic texts – as only fully existing through their dialogical extension into a receptive community implies that the 'portfolio of affective investments' assembled by a reader is potentially a fungible currency. This leads naturally to another crucial concept in fan studies – Bourdieu's notion of 'cultural capital'. In Bourdieu's thought, human social life is lived out in a series of bounded 'fields', within which various forms of more or less exchangeable 'capital' are available.[73] By investing in cultural capital (such as taste in the 'right' sorts of music, art, architecture and so on), a person can help to ensure their membership of a particular social context – a fact which helps to explain some limitations to social mobility.[74] For popular cultural audience theorists such as John Fiske, subcultural groupings such as fan communities also produce their own distinctive versions of cultural capital, the accumulation of which is governed by its own rules.[75]

Thus fandom, as scholarship has typically understood it, consists of a set of complex and interrelated processes. In one sense, it is an individual process by which meaning is actively discovered in texts and texts are in turn charged with meaning. And yet even as an apparently solitary activity, this process is inherently dialogical and therefore social. It is dialogical in the sense that the fan is in active dialogue with the text and with the authorial minds which encoded it. But, particularly for the case of television fandom (arguably the most written about form of the phenomenon), it is also dialogical the text itself presents a vision of a particular imagined human society into which the viewer/reader can imaginatively insert herself.

Because of the dialogical nature of fandom even at the seemingly individual level, however, fandom is inherently supportive of forms of collective consumption and community. Moreover, under such circumstances, the combination of the fan's individual dialogical relationship with the text and the association of other fans in a fan community seems to have a multiplier effect, such as to produce a sense of intense sociality which is greater than the sum of its parts. Thus, for Jenkins and Bacon Smith, the poignancy of the fan communities they observed lay in the fact that while the community amounted only to a 'weekend world', lived out in hotel lobby conventions and, between times through virtual communities sustained initially by handmade fanzines and later by the internet, nonetheless this 'weekend world' seemed to the fan to have much more social substance and reality than the ordinary world of 'mundania' outside.[76] This intense experience of belonging was reinforced by the way in which fans actively produced and performed their fandom, creating what Jenkins calls an 'art world' of fan folk-music, fan art and fan literature, as well as dances, costumed performances and the like acted out at conventions.[77] The overall effect seems to be understandable in terms of the notion of 'synecdoche', the rhetorical principle whereby the part stands for the whole: the actual human contact of fans does not amount to a full community in the traditional sense; the imagined world of the texts which the fans engage offers a much fuller and more rounded out vision of a complete life, but it is, of course, a fiction. By acting out the former against the backdrop of the latter, it is possible for each to fill in the other's deficiencies, creating a stable sense of belonging.

It is no coincidence that the television fan communities explored by Jenkins and Bacon Smith in the early 1990s closely resembled the 'virtual communities' which would soon after become a key concept in writing about cultural phenomena on the internet. As Howard Rheingold observes in his book *The Virtual Community: Homesteading on the Electronic Frontier*, the people who initially brought to life the specific bulletin board-based system with which has was concerned were Deadheads (Grateful Dead fans) who 'came online and seemed to know instinctively how to use the system to create a community around themselves'.[78] As with other fans who were early adopters of the internet, it wasn't instinctive. It was because they had already learnt by long experience how to sustain a fragmented community around a shared pop-cultural interest.

There is, then, an important relationship between the consumer/producer communities epitomized by fans and the communities sustained by media production/consumption (or, as it is now often called, 'prosumption') on the internet. Indeed, for Robert Kozinets, an 'ethnographic' marketing research scholar heavily influenced by work on fandom, online communities can, as a point of methodology, all be understood and analysed first and foremost in terms of online media consumption practices.[79]

If this is so, however, it raises an interesting question – of particular significance for our purposes – about how far the 'cyberculture' of the internet is in fact just a particular and contingent 'culturing' of technology by what may be a predominantly Western social form. Were this to be the case, it would seriously challenge the applicability of notions of fandom to jihadism on the internet a general phenomenon.

A plausible clue to the resolution of this dilemma can actually be found in Rheingold's example itself. For the case with which he was concerned, we can note that while the Grateful Dead fans seemed to have an uncannily natural understanding of how the technology could be used to support an online community, the role they played was not to monopolize the medium, but rather to catalyse the wider community that would form around 'The Well'. In other words, what they did was not to invent the social possibilities of the medium, so much as to discover them.

A useful way of understanding what was going on can be found in a concept widespread in ecological psychology and the sociology of engineering: the notion of affordance. Essentially, an affordance is a latent possibility, built into the structure of an object or an environment with which a person interacts; but one which has to be perceived. The keys on my keyboard afford typing, not just because it is physically possible for me to press down on them and produce characters on a screen, but also because of my perception that this is a thing I can do. For Gibson, the psychologist who first developed a theoretical account of the idea, affordances are all about explaining how humans process visual data in the first place.[80] Gibson thought that we always, immediately and automatically perceive objects visually in terms of the affordances we see in them. For Norman, a psychologist of design who picked up on Gibson's ideas and modified them, it is the other way round: affordance is about designing objects so that their correct use is immediately apparent and obvious.[81] Later work has become more concerned with how people come to be able to perceive new affordances of objects.

Specifically in relation to the sociology of technology, however, the concept of affordance has represented a useful middle ground between the technologically determinist view that human life is wholly shaped by the possibilities offered by technology, and the view that the possibilities of technology are wholly culturally determined.[82] What affordance seems to say is that there are certain specific possibilities built into technological artefacts, but that whether they are perceived or deployed is a matter for human culture.

It would seem that this is what happened in Rheingold's example. The electronic bulletin board had a set of fundamental 'action possibilities' associated with it, which could be used to create a certain sort of deterritorialized, topically focused, elective community. But the change fact that Grateful Dead fans had already been trying to create a similar sort of community in the absence of this particular technological prosthesis meant that they were in a better position to perceive these possibilities than others were. However, once others had perceived them as well, the community they developed necessarily functioned along similar lines, as dictated by what the technology allowed.

What are the core affordances of the internet? This is obviously a vast question which humanity has only begun to answer, and there is a correspondingly enormous and hardly unanimous literature on the topic. For the purposes of this book, a useful theoretical approach is offered by the work of Lev Manovich. For Manovich, there is a fundamental distinction to be drawn first of all between 'cyberculture' – that is, the cultural and social forms which new media supports, and new media itself. Though he does not use the term himself, Manovich's understanding of the latter can usefully be viewed in terms of affordances.[83] On the one hand, Manovich is keen to avoid understanding new media simply in terms of computers and digital technology. As he argues, it is perfectly possible of old media forms such as books or radio to happen to be digitized. On the other hand, he perceives certain characteristics particularly distinctive of new media as preceding computers and electronic data. At the same time, it is clear that digitization of data and its algorithmic manipulation by software has an enormous impact in terms of making new media forms ubiquitous.

For Manovich, the fundamental formal characteristic underpinning new media is the montage – as opposed to the narrative. All new media items are, so he argues, essentially surface representations of an underlying database in which information is stored numerically. In consequence, new media artefacts differ from other media types in the fact that there is never, in principle, a final version. The new media artefact can always exist in variants and is always subject to manipulation by automated processes. In Manovich's thought, these properties have consequences. New media, which is manipulated visibly by a particular vocabulary drawn from cinema (panning, zooming, etc.) and which is manipulated invisibly by specific computer languages written by particular people, represents a contingent language which has to be learnt. But there is something all-enveloping about this language which transcends the particularities of content to become, so it seems, a universal human mode of expression.

Since Manovich is a theorist of new media, rather than of cyberculture, it is useful to supplement his vision with a more particularly 'cybercultural' one. A particularly useful one within the paradigm of fan studies is offered by the work of Pierre Levy, whose theories play much the same role in the later writings of Henry Jenkins as do those of Michel de Certeau in his earlier ones.[84] Levy is in a sense the extreme example of a 'techno-optimist' within the grand debate between optimists, pessimists and 'realists' which has dominated discussions of the cultural potential of the internet. In what is perhaps his most read book, *Collective Intelligence*, he famously speaks of what he calls an 'achievable utopia'.[85] But the real roots of Levy's thinking can actually be located in his work on the concept of virtuality.[86] Just as, new media, for Manovich, is facilitated but not reducible to the properties of digital information technology, so for Levy, virtuality is not simply a consequence of computer simulation, but is something much older and deeper which this technology helps, to use a Heideggerian term, to 'bring forth'.[87] Virtuality is not opposed to reality, for Levy, but rather to actuality. It is a real state in which things are becoming, as opposed to being concretely present in the here and now. It is this insight that is essential to Levy's basically optimistic vision, for it is this which enables him to escape thinking that a culture dominated by internet technology must be one in which people are trapped in an illusion, and to replace this idea with the notion that they are inhabiting a state of continuous and creative becoming. The idea may sound mystical, but in some ways it is obviously not at all. Every time one pays with a bank note which 'promises to pay the bearer on demand' an identically meaningless piece of paper, or one enters into a contract backed up by a threat of violent coercion which it is extremely unlikely will ever be visited, one is entering the world of the virtual.

How does this all relate to fandom? And, more to the point, how does this all relate to understanding jihadi culture on the internet. What fandom gives us, so I have tried to argue, is a way of thinking about how, in a world dominated by acts of media consumption – which, after all, is ultimately what the internet is – people are able to produce value and meaning. Indeed, these processes are all the more important where people are faced with the universal language of new media and the bewildering, proliferating promises of virtuality. For it is only by consumptive practices capable of producing meaning, value and particularity that a world of universality and potentiality can be lived in the here and now. How this relates to the particular case of internet jihadism is a question for the rest of the book.

3

Jihadi content on the World Wide Web

A good deal of writing now exists on the question of how best to define and typologize 'jihadism'. As I touched on at the outset of the book, the term has the advantage that it is used self-descriptively. There are people who call themselves 'jihadis' and who speak of a 'jihadi movement' or 'jihadi current' to which they belong. Nor are these claims completely synonymous with the classical words *jihad* and *mujahid*. They are deliberately used as technical terms specific to contemporary situations. At the same time, they do carry with them the implication of an association with *jihad*, so that those who are specifically concerned with delegitimizing jihadis are more likely to speak (in Arabic) of 'terrorism' (*irhab*), 'extremism' (*tatarruf*) and so on.

Jihadism tends to be viewed in one of two ways: either as a behaviour or tactic synonymous with the use of political violence by Islamist groups in general, or as a particular ideology, theology and world view. In the former case, it tends to be typologized based on the notion of a hierarchy of enemies. Thus, influentially, Gerges has classified jihadisms as irredentist, revolutionary, classical and global.[1] Irredentist jihad(ism), such as that of Palestinian groups, seeks to attack a specific enemy across a political boundary. Revolutionary jihad seeks to overthrow a state government. Classical jihad seeks to defend a Muslim people against an outside aggressor. Global jihad (of which Al Qaeda is the main, if not sole example) commits itself to a geographically unlimited battle.

In the latter case, jihadism is typically associated closely with Salafism, as for example in widely used terms such as the 'Global Salafi Jihad'.[2] Salafism, strictly speaking, is belief in a form of Islam which claims to be premised on a strict return to the path of the 'pious predecessors' (*al-salaf al-salih*), entailing a highly literalistic focus on the original sources of the religion (the Qur'an and Sunna), while rejecting any formal adherence (*taqlid*) to the classical law schools established over centuries in Sunni Islam.[3] Contemporary Salafism – as has been stated in numerous previous accounts – developed in two main strands – or, perhaps, as two completely different phenomena deploying the same term.[4] First, there is a modernist and politicized strand originating with thinkers like Jamal al-Din al-Afghani and Muhammad Abduh, which diagnosed excessive adherence to tradition as the reason for the relative decline of the Muslim world, and hoped to revitalize the religion and the society of its adherents by cutting away these accretions and returning to the source. Second, (the form which is usually meant when people speak of Salafism today) there is a more puritanical and typically less worldly form which developed largely out of Saudi Wahhabism (originally an eighteenth-century revival movement which had become the official version of Islam of the Saudi state). This already highly scripturalist and literalist version of Islam was further developed by the work of the hadith scholar Nasir al-Din al-Albani whose daring re-examination of the authenticity of these classical narrations helped to undercut the automatic authority of the law schools dominant in the interpretation of Sunni Islam.[5]

Contemporary global jihadism – as ideology or theology – is generally held to represent the meeting point of these two strands, taking its main intellectual inspiration from the literalism of the latter, but introducing into it the political concerns of the former. In another very influential typology, Quintan Wiktorowicz has argued that contemporary Salafism can be divided into 'purist', 'politico' and 'jihadi' forms: the first aiming to purify society by correcting their own behaviour and gradually recruiting others, the second aiming to achieve political influence over government and the last rejecting the possibility of participating in the political process and seeking instead a total war against both regimes at home and their unbelieving masters abroad.[6]

Theologically, jihadi-salafists are characterized broadly speaking by their insistence that the governments of Muslim countries, because they wilfully refuse to implement the Islamic shari'a, are therefore apostates and must be overthrown. They may also argue that this leads to a situation analogous to the occupation of the entire Muslim world by enemy forces. In such a situation, an unlimited defensive jihad is called for. This jihad is an individual obligation to all Muslim men of suitable age and bodily fitness.[7]

And yet, as Thomas Hegghammer has incisively observed, the term 'jihadi' or 'jihadi-salafist' is one which, measured against the actual phenomena to which the term is applied, may not be as neat and helpful as it seems.[8] Even from the highly simplified account just presented, the ambiguities and fracture points should be obvious. 'Salafist', to begin with, potentially refers, as we have just seen, to at least two quite different groupings of religious and social phenomena. This is particularly confusing when it is considered that the term 'Salafist' is often used today, roughly synonymously with Roy's notion of 'neofundamentalism',[9] in contradistinction to the 'Islamism' (or, ikhwanism) of the Muslim Brothers, even though the foundational thinkers of the Muslim brothers such as Sayyid Qutb were once seen as very much a part of the *salafiyya* tradition of Al-Afghani and Abduh.[10] It is further confused by the fact that quintessentially 'jihadi' thinkers such as Abdullah Azzam were not Salafists (at any rate, not in the Wahhabi sense). Indeed, Azzam recommended that those Arabs who traveled to practice, as they saw it, jihad in Afghanistan, should try to blend into the local culture by submitting to the practices of the traditional *Hanafi* law school to which Sunni Afghans almost universally subscribe: an idea which runs directly contrary to fundamentalist Salafism's rejection of the *taqlid* of schools of law.[11]

On the other hand, the notion that 'jihadism' is a distinct system of thought (as opposed to a political strategy) only when viewed as a subcategory of Salafism is necessarily misleading. After all, any political group which has decided to undertake 'jihad' must necessarily have a political (and therefore ideological) account of what it is doing. This suggests that there must be a distinct 'jihadism' of supposedly non-'Salafist' groups such as Hamas. Moreover, even with regard to what is called 'jihadi-salafism' there are obvious complexities. Hegghammer observes how Abu Muhammad al-Maqdisi, one of the central scholars of self-declared jihadi-salafism, tried to prevent people from traveling to do jihad in Bosnia, which he saw as a distraction from revolutionary jihad at home.[12] Another supposedly core 'jihadi' scholar, Abu Basir al-Tartusi, specifically condemned the London bombings and has argued on the basis of the idea of a 'contract of security' between Muslims living in non-Muslim countries and their 'hosts' that similar acts of terrorism are illegitimate.[13] Thus it follows that 'jihadi salafism' is not necessarily 'global jihadism'. On the other hand, it is not necessarily clear that 'global jihadism' is automatically equivalent to 'salafi' jihadism, as evidenced by the relative lack of interest of strategic theorists of global jihad such as Abu Mus'ab al-Suri in the strictures of 'salafism'.

In one respect at least, scholars of politics often resemble the objects of their study: both are intimately concerned with drawing up ever more precise and accurate accounts of the ideological minutiae that distinguish various groups. This is, potentially, a problematic fact. Treated with insufficient reflexivity, it may seem that these historical distinctions – rather than the contemporary discursive processes by which they are wielded – have importance in and of themselves. Faisal Devji, for example, has criticized what he sees as an excessive concern with 'genealogy' in Islamist movements, whereby, for example, it is assumed that the 'roots' of contemporary radical movements are inherently vital to understanding their essences, while other possible connections (Devji thinks that he sees interesting parallels between global jihadism and its traditional nemesis, Twelver Shi'ism) are thereby overlooked.[14]

In this chapter, I tentatively propose to trace an alternative account of 'jihadism' – specifically as we find it online – by taking as my starting point not 'jihadism' per se, but rather through developing and problematizing, and then broadly exploring, a notion of 'the jihadi'. What do I mean by 'the jihadi'? As a starting point, 'the jihadi' is simply anything which someone (particularly if that someone would probably identify as a Muslim) has labeled as such. Of course, this starting point is a simplification. Practically speaking, Arabic Web users (of course, not all Muslims are Arabic speakers, but most Arabic speakers are Muslims) do not necessarily draw any consistent distinction between, say, a 'jihadi-video' and a 'jihad-video'. 'The jihadi' in the sense I wish to use it is therefore another heuristic, like 'jihadism', rather than an incontestable empirical reality. Nonetheless, it is one which has some basis in usage, and which, extended, seems to yield a worthwhile conceptual distinction.

Indeed, the notion of a thing being 'jihadi' is interesting almost precisely because it seems so banal. The form 'jihadi', in contemporary Arabic, basically means – or at least, appears to mean – nothing more controversial than 'pertaining to jihad'. The final suffix, that single 'i' (the letter) *ya* in Arabic, marks out the word as an Arabic construction called a *nisba*, a 'gentilic' form which indicates membership of a class. As the grammarians Badawi, Carter and Gully note, the *nisba* in contemporary Arabic has become exceptionally productive. Perhaps imitating the similar productivity of endings like 'ish' and 'ic' in European languages, one can now speak, say, of a thing being '*dimuqrati*' (democratic), '*saddami*' (Saddamist), '*radikali*' (radical), '*iliktruni*' (electronic) and so on.

And yet, in the very contemporary productivity of the *nisba*, the way in which it is often casually used to create new coinages, would seem to lie the conundrum. On the one hand, the ordinariness of the usage means that there is nothing *inherently* ideological about the term. To say that a video, for example, is 'jihadi' is not inevitably to bracket it off as having to do with 'jihad' in inverted commas, rather than the true, authentic jihad of the true, authentic Islam. And yet, at the same time, it carries with it a certain insinuation that this could be the case. This is, in part, because it sometimes is the case – as the examples above suggest, the *nisba* is often used for political and similarly abstract terms; and in part it is because the contemporary openness of the *nisba* class contrasts sharply with usage in the classical Arabic from which the authentic 'jihad' arises, in which it was tightly restricted to words relating to places and tribes. The prophet Muhammad was *Qurayshi* (from the tribe of Quraysh) and *Makkawi* (from the city of Mecca). But he certainly was not, nor were any of his works, in contemporary usage, 'jihadi'. The term, therefore, serves as an emblem of a present-day reality in which cultural universals have been replaced with a new master-ideology of choice. Indeed, even somewhat earlier usages of the term 'jihadi' seem to reinforce this notion. In an Arabic dictionary from the late 1920s, for example, the word 'jihadi' is offered as meaning simply 'military', a synonym for the word *harbi*, from *harb*, meaning 'war'. The notion that *jihad* and, therefore, anything that was *jihadi* represented some special category, distinct from the ordinary workings of politics and society, seems to be absent.

As such, the notion of 'the jihadi' serves to mark out a special kind of terrain lying constantly between 'jihad' as the authentic and rightful property of 'true' Islam, and 'jihadism' as something which, by virtue of being a particular ideology subscribed to by some, but certainly not all Muslims, is clearly in some sense problematic. 'The jihadi' also seems to mark out and draw attention to another key point: whereas the terms 'jihad' and 'jihadism' seem to hold out the promise of essential realities lying offstage, which can be grasped, however partially, through examination of their manifestations, consideration of 'the jihadi' invites us to think from the outset in constructivist terms, treating specific 'jihadi' items as logically prior, rather than posterior, to such abstractions. And yet this, too, seems to challenge the very nature of these categories, in so far as it invites us to ask whether the cultural productions of 'jihadism' (its videos, songs, websites and so on) arise from its intellectual beliefs or whether, conceivably, it could be the other way around. 'The jihadi' as a concept also seems to help remind us of the gulf that may exist between representations of a thing and accepted notions of what that thing is. For example, consider the difference between what the inhabitants of English-speaking countries would typically consider to be 'Christmassy' and what they might say about what Christmas is. Even the fire breathing evangelical given to lamenting the progressive loss of the 'true meaning of Christmas' would be likely, at least in an off-guard moment, to perceive images of Yule logs, Christmas trees, robin redbreasts, etc. etc. as 'Christmassy', that is indexical of a cultural construction called 'Christmas'.

'The jihadi', then, can be taken as standing for the sphere of cultural representations of jihad. To say that something is 'jihadi' does not inherently commit a Muslim to saying that it is holy and right, nor to saying that it is not. The sum total of all that is 'jihadi' does not add up to jihad, but rather to its man-made allegory.

What, in practice, is 'the jihadi', and where, on the Web, is it to be found? As a very broad starting point, *Google Trends* data from 2004 to the present suggests that by far the most common search queries to be associated with the term 'jihadi' are 'nashid', followed by 'Salafi', 'forum' (including the names of

jihadi	al-jihadi	jihadiyya	al-jihadiyya	al-jihad
jihadi nashid	jihadi forum	jihadi nashids	jihadi salafism	Islamic jihad
jihadi poetry	salafi	jihadi websites	salafism	websites of jihad
jihadi website	direct (news)	jihadi nashids mp3	jihadi forums	Voice of Jihad
nashids		nashids	jihadi nashids	jihad movement
		nashids mp3	nashids	jihad photographs
		Islamic jihadi nashids	jihadi websites	jihad network
		jihadi website	jihadi firdaws	jihad in Iraq
		jihadi forums	al-firdaws	nashids of jihad
		films	jihadi al-fallujah	jihad and tawhid
		jihadi nashid download	al-fallujah	the base of jihad (Qa'idat al-Jihad)

FIGURE 4 *Google trends results illustrating most popular searches for 'jihadi' content in Arabic.*

certain specific 'jihadi' forums, 'website', 'poetry' and 'films') – results which very much accord with the less scientific impression likely to be formed by anyone who has experience of searching the Web for jihadi content. It is perhaps also interesting to note that many of the most commonly related search queries to 'al-jihad' also seem to relate to searches for types of media content: 'websites', the 'voice of jihad', 'pictures of jihad', 'network of jihad' and so on.

These results serve to provide a vivid illustration of the existence of various sorts of *jihadiyyat* (particularly, of course, the jihadi 'hymn', or *nashid*, which we will come back to), being uploaded and consumed across various online locations. What sort of locations? Given the way in which jihadi content has been securitized, the picture with regard to its general distribution and availability online has been a somewhat paradoxical one of, on the one hand, marginality and, on the other, ubiquity. Jihadi websites tend (though not always) to have a rather short lifespan. Jihadi video, audio and text files, made available often through remote file-hosting sites, typically rely on a strategy of redundancy. Forum posts offering such material are inevitably followed by dozens of links – most of them, equally inevitably, defunct. At the same time, however, content advertising itself as 'jihadi' remains easily accessible on mainstream sites. Posts appear quite openly on large Arabic Web forums such as Al Jazeera Chat, Al-Sahat, Swalifsoft which offer downloads of jihadi files, and 'jihadi' material is easily locatable on social media sites such as YouTube, Facebook or Twitter.

The combined effect of the increasing dominance of 'Web 2.0' sites such as YouTube and Facebook over previously popular Web forums, together with the difficulty (to be explored further in the subsequent chapter) of establishing clearly jihadi Web space, has seemingly had the effect to some extent of fracturing and – as one analyst puts it 'atomising' jihadi content online.[15] And yet in spite of this, it is still more or less possible to speak of a 'jihadiness' which extends outwards in what are roughly concentric circles. In the inner circle are sites which claim themselves to be 'jihadi'. Beyond this are certain sites dedicated to 'Islamic' material which may offer 'jihadi' content as one category among others.

Finally, jihadi content appears in various ways on mainstream sites. Sometimes, this is the result of dedicated and potentially self-styled 'jihadis' who appear to devote significant effort to distributing files as widely as possible. In other contexts (e.g. political discussion forums such as Al-Saha or Al Jazeera Talk), there may be more active participation by jihadi members. Under some circumstances, 'jihadi' items may also be posted by forum members who do not present themselves, in other respects, as typically 'jihadi' at all, for example, members whose profile pictures are of actors or music stars.

The significance of this essentially unsurprising arrangement is perhaps more readily explained if this order is reversed. The idea that 'mainstream' Arabic sites might have a certain amount of engagement with 'jihadi' content of one sort or another is, of course, hardly shocking, when we consider that public support for groups with a 'jihadi' element such as Hamas, or resistant groups in Iraq has long been substantial in the Middle East, and that even support for Al Qaeda has not been negligible in certain places and times.[16] Nor again is the idea that certain 'Islamic' sites might sometimes incorporate 'jihadi' elements.

What is, however, of potential interest is the way in which the linked structure of the Web seems to draw out and foreground from this cultural backdrop a logic of selection and consumption which is, one might suppose, ultimately as subversive as enabling. 'The Islamic', viewed from the standpoint of a general interest Arabic forum such as *Al-Saha* or *Al Jazeera Talk* is, necessarily, one subfield among various others (on Al-Saha, motor-maintenance would be another). A large, mainstream forum such as Al-Saha's users, being Arabs (or at any rate proficient Arabic users), are by and large likely also to be Muslims. Al-Saha is, therefore, a more or less 'Muslim' online environment. By contrast, being 'Islamic' within this space is simply one choice among others. Contrary to the general tone of much writing on 'digital Islam', what is problematic about the Web would seem, then, to be precisely not that it is somehow resistant to being 'cultured', but that it lends itself too readily to different 'cultural' choices – thus unmasking the glibly elective nature of the culturing process.

The same, then, goes for the 'jihadi' field as sometimes offered within particular 'Islamic' sites. The fact that space online is zoned topically means that the availability of jihadi content necessarily holds out at least the possibility of the availability, also, of jihadi space. And yet the Web is not, in contrast to the hard drive, organized as the hierarchical branching structure beloved of a new media theorist such as Manovich, but precisely as a Web, in which the subordination of one topic to another is only a contingent artefact of human perception.[17] From the point of view of the hyperlink, 'Islamic' and generically Arabic space may equally well be viewed as subfields of the jihadi. Worked-out ideology and the seemingly banal logic of Web browsing are thus, potentially, two sides of the same coin. Or, as we shall see, being ideologically 'jihadist' and being, so to speak 'into jihad' – are rather hard to distinguish as online phenomena.

To illustrate this point, let us now consider an illustration from the opposite direction. Rather than starting out with the general distribution of (Arabic language) 'jihadi' content on the Web as a whole, we shall begin this time with a clear-cut example of a 'jihadi' website and consider from there how it maintains a sense of 'jihadiness' through its selection and ordering of data. The site in question shall be Tawhed.ws, 'The Pulpit of *Tawhid* and *Jihad*', a site often taken to be the online epicentre of self-styled 'jihadi-salafism'. The website, which advertises affiliation with a number of 'jihadi-salafi' scholars, including Abu Basir al-Tartusi and Abu Qatada al-Falastini, is however particularly the project of perhaps the most important jihadi shaykh of all, Abu Muhammad al-Maqdisi. This association is unquestionably accurate with regard to that section of the site entitled 'the library of Shaykh al-Maqdisi'.

The library is subcategorized initially into three main sections: *The Manhaj of the Sunna* (which is devoted to prose texts), *The Voice of Tawhid* (to multimedia content) and a section called *'Ayun al-Kalm*, the meaning of which is not wholly clear and is conceivably supposed to be ambiguous. *'Ayun'* is the plural of *'ayn*, meaning an eye or a wellspring. It also conveys a sense of something being choice, or excellent. *Kalm*, on the other hand, has two distinct meanings: in the first it means language or speech, in the second, an open wound. Whatever the name of the section is supposed to convey, its content is poetry, organized in turn under five headings. Two of these are dedicated to a selected 'best of' and to miscellaneous material. The other three are topical, consisting of poems on 'jihad and martyrdom', 'ethics and sentiments' and 'the contemporary situation'. Broadly, the first is devoted to poems celebrating combat, the second to more personal and intimate themes, the third to poems bewailing the oppression of Muslims.

We may observe that all of these texts are located on what is clearly and self-declaredly a jihadi site both in the sense that Abu Muhammad al-Maqdisi openly positions himself as 'jihadi-salafi' and writes of his followers as the 'people of jihad', but also in that the website itself is a 'pulpit of tawhid and jihad'. However, within the overall context of a 'jihadi' site, there is, of course, material that is more and less directly relevant to 'jihad'. Within the library of Abu Muhammad al-Maqdisi, content of the former sort is mainly located within a subsection entitled (after a famous book by 'Abd al-Salam Faraj), 'the neglected obligation', a section which is in turn subdivided as follows:

What is striking about being brought face to face with an online collection such as this would seem to be the way in which it illustrates Manovich's point regarding the inherent supremacy of database over narrative in new media forms or, to use the terminology of the cognitive psychologist Jerome Bruner, of paradigmatic over narrative ways of thinking.[18] Even though *tawhed.ws* would seem to be a website profoundly concerned with presenting a unified and coherent ideological message, the very nature of the 'library' (as opposed to the linear form of the individual texts in contains) seems such as to invite a certain heterogeneity and plurality. 'The jihadi' as presented here broken down into its constituent parts, becomes – as, of course, it must – a heterogeneous mix of dispassionate strategic thinking, practical knowhow, shari'atic reasoning, collective sentiment and highly personal concerns with living a virtuous life – not only on the battlefield, but in the private and domestic spheres as well.

A library, however (or at any rate a cataloguing system), is probably not the ideal place to grasp the essence of a new media idiom. Manovich insists that the roots of the 'language of new media' are ineluctably visual, lying in the first 'screens' used to display bourgeois art, the programmable patterns of the Jacquard loom, and finally the cinema.[19] Therefore, it is perhaps not to texts, but rather to images that we ought first to turn in order to produce any overarching analysis of the core elements of 'the jihadi'.

In interesting starting point for such an analysis would seem to be offered by a particular type of the popular *jihadiyya* which circulate the Web: the jihadi *bitaqa* or 'card'. *Bitaqat* are stand-alone graphic designs, suitable for use, for example, as forum signatures. Often, they seem to have the purpose of conveying a value or a sentimental message, and in addition to their purely visual components, they typically include a short text – a popular saying, for example, or slogan of some kind.

'Islamic' *bitaqat* represent one category of which, conforming to the pattern sketched out above, there are in turn various subcategories, the jihadi

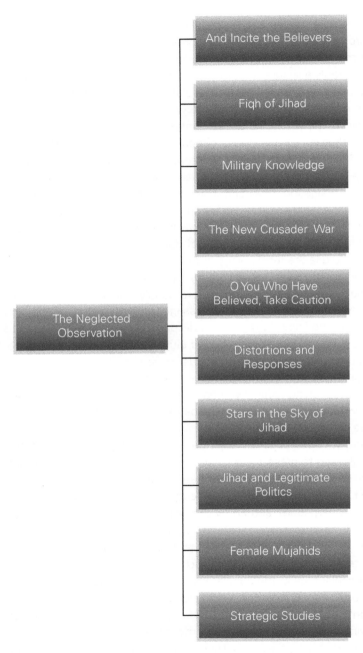

FIGURE 5 *Text categories in the 'neglected obligation' section of Al-Maqdisi's online library.*

bitaqa being one of these. On one website which appears to be particularly popular for this content, *Luqman al-Hakim*,[20] *bitaqat* are organized under three headings: *da'wi* (aimed at promoting Islam), *'ibadi* (aimed at celebrating or, perhaps, reminding people of the acts of Islamic acts of worship) and jihadi *bitaqat*. One may also encounter, for example, *bitaqat* devoted to *raqa'iq* – the Islamic virtue of soft-heartedness.

We might therefore reasonably expect jihadi *bitaqat* to offer a deliberate microcosm of how 'the jihadi' is represented. And so, indeed, would seem to be the case. One yardstick for demonstrating this is provided by a research project published by Westpoint military academy aimed at identifying and classifying the main 'visual motifs in jihadi propaganda'.[21] In just thirty-three jihadi *bitaqat* available on *Luqman al-Hakim*, for example, images corresponding to nineteen of Westpoint's twenty categories of image are present, with 40 per cent of the specific motifs it identified represented as well. On the other hand, the *bitaqat* included just one specific motif – the clenched fist – which seems to be specifically absent from the list identified by Westpoint.

The generally close fit between the images displayed on jihadi *bitaqat* and those identified by Westpoint's study of 'jihadi propaganda' in general appears to suggest the existence of a more or less common repertoire of jihadi images. This supposition would also seem to be supported by repeated Google image searches which I conducted between 2010 and 2012, looking simply for images that had been classified in Arabic (by anyone and for any reason at all), as 'jihadi'. Here again, the categories into which the images seemed to fall, irrespective of the variety of sources and contexts from which they came, seemed to be essentially the same as those previously identified by Westpoint.

There is, it should be noted, one important – even rather glaring – exception to this. Both with regard to the specific case of online collections of jihadi *bitaqat* and the general one of images which have been labeled by someone, somewhere, writing in Arabic, as 'jihadi', there is one very commonly recurring set of images which, for one reason or another, Westpoint makes no specific reference to, other than through a general category of 'modern weapons' (which in its report are always in the hands of Muslims): this is, imagery associated with violence *against* Muslims. The iconic images of the tank, helicopter, jet fighter or conventionally equipped Western soldier are all present on the *bitaqat* on *Luqman al-Hakim* (and even more so in some other online collections; and were equally prominent in 'jihadi' images returned by Web searches.

Nonetheless, this fact – while surely significant – does not detract from the overall point that 'the jihadi', in all its diversity, seems to be represented through a more or less closed, and more or less common set of motifs.

Nature Images	Sun
	Moon
	Water
	Flora
	Landscapes
	Animals
	Weather
Geography, Political Symbols and States	Globe/World
	States/Flags
	Holy Places
	Significant Events
People	Political Leaders
	Martyrs
	Women
	Children
Weapons, Warfare and the Afterlife	The Afterlife
	Weapons
	Blood
	Colours
	Hands

FIGURE 6 *Westpoint's Categories of Image in 'Jihadi Propaganda'.*

Thematically, eight main concerns – combat, oppression, solidarity, place, history, community, piety and cosmic order – seem sufficient to summarize what virtually all jihadi content would seem to be about. But what is more significant is the extent to which these broad themes seem, in turn, to be represented by a relatively narrow, stereotypical and constantly repeated repertoire of images which, at least at the level on which we find the *bitaqat*, seem to be the common property of 'the jihadi' as a whole.

Indeed, this would seem to be paradoxically attested to even by the degree to which identifiable differences between ideological varieties of jihadism seem to be represented in assemblages of jihadi content such as *bitaqat*. Thus, on *Luqman*, we see some *bitaqat* featuring the Palestinian flag or the military slacks, balaclava and bandana typical of the Qassam brigades, another showing the Iraqi flag, and yet others with the silhouetted cavalier figures, medieval weaponry and stylized landscapes particularly typical of Salafist jihadism; but all are offered up together, as if all partook of what is ultimately a single, unified stock of jihadi iconography, choices within which are no more than a matter of taste.

Something rather similar seems to go for that most popular of jihadi content, the jihadi nashid. It has already been noted that the consumption and distribution of jihadi nashids appears, at least at certain times, to be a relatively mainstream phenomenon. Moreover, jihadi nashids seem to cross what might appear to be ideological boundaries with relative ease. To offer a recent example, a list of well-known nashids including examples such as *jihadina* by the popular *munshid* Abu 'Ali which it is not uncommon to hear soundtrack the content of Al Qaeda affiliates is also to be found on a forum dedicated to the theoretically secular Free Syrian Army.[22] Or, again, a montage of operational footage from the Al Qaeda affiliate Islamic State of Iraq might be accompanied by the nashid *Blow Up the Cursed One O Daughter of Jihad* – which, given its subject matter – might perhaps be expected to be the property of Palestinian Islamic Jihad.[23] Indeed, as Behnam Said has observed in a very useful recent article on the subject, many of the most popular jihadi nashids today in fact originate from the late 1970s and 1980s, meaning that they predate many of the major organizational distinctions between jihadist groups (if not Islamic movements) in the present day.[24] Nonetheless, some nashids are clearly identified as specifically relating to a particular group, as in examples such as an advertised 'collection of 300 hamasi jihadi nashids'.[25]

Indeed, the popularity and attractiveness of the nashid form has not gone unnoticed by organized jihadist groups. In the late scholar and activist Anwar al-'Awlaqi's *44 Ways to Serve Jihad*, the production and dissemination of nashids is given an entry all to itself. In the English-language jihadi magazine *Jihad Recollections*, an article by 'Abdur Rahman' observes that:

> Anasheed is a phenomenon that has rippled throughout the Ummah of Muhammad, peace be upon him. There isn't a person who aspires to jihad today that doesn't know at least one catchy nasheed by heart. Be it a video of a raging battle, a Mujahid shooting mortars, the setting off of a IED or simply sitting amongst other Mujahideen, 9 times out of 10 you'll find these videos being accompanied by *Jihadi Anasheed*.[26]

The author of this article goes on to argue that, in the digital age, the nashid plays an analogous role to that of poetry in assisting the original rise of Islam.

A *nashid*, generally speaking, is an Islamic hymn. Indeed, the word is sometimes applied to all forms of music with Islamic religious import. Typically, however, nashids are, at least in the present day, à capella songs for one or more male voices. Instruments, which are often considered *haram* by strict Muslims[27] rarely, but do sometimes, appear in accompaniment. However, voices are often multi-layered and manipulated with studio effects. Nashids of one sort or another have seemingly always existed in Islam – including at least one which is a fundamental part of the religion – the *Talbiyah* – a nashid sung by pilgrims on *Hajj* and *'Umra*.[28] However, the contemporary, sometimes almost choral (though generally unison) vocal form of the Islamic nashid,[29] as represented by most 'jihadi' nashids may be a relatively modern introduction.[30] Certainly, the effects applied to the voices, which may approach the imitation of musical instruments, give the form a specifically contemporary quality.

There is no clear boundary line between the musical jihadi nashid and the jihadi poem (often described as a *qasida*, which is technically a particular classical form of poem).[31] Where the lyrics to jihadi *anashid* are offered alone, they may be described as 'jihadi poetry', or nashid lyrics and poems may be offered together undifferentiated. Conversely, of course, a jihadi poem may be set to music. Since we are primarily concerned with text in the analysis that follows, the two forms can be treated as identical to all intents and purposes.

Said convincingly proposes that jihadi nashids can usually be categorized into four main types: 'battle hymns', songs about martyrs, mourning songs and praise songs.[32] But these categories do not, on their own, convey any very strong flavour of the actual tone and emotive content of these works, and world views they seem, for all their stylization, to convey.

For instance, there seems to be an interesting distinction that can be drawn between those works which seem to be deeply concerned with the sacred relationship between an idealized vision of the Islamic hero, and the community on whose behalf they fight, and those in which, by contrast, the poet's voice seems to be more reflective, and even more isolated. For instance, in a 'martyrdom' nashid, like *Khudhu Qalban (Take a Heart)*, the poet graphically – almost cannibalistically – connects the bodily sacrifice of the martyr to the collective well-being of the community, saying:

> Take a heart, hardened like iron . . . take it and attack all the Jews
> Take my soul to shade you all . . . so that if it did not live, it flutters from afar
> Sons of my people, be patient, for the dawn has come . . . and the sun of victory has risen anew
> Take my eyes on the noblest of youth . . . tomorrow the blind will see anew
> Take from me my two hands, even if they were broken . . . my hand alone obstructs my redemption
> Take my skin, make from it a fuse . . . or a slingshot for a babe or child[33]

But a similar spirit also seems to infuse a nashid that might be classified as a 'battle hymn', such as *Labbayk, Islam al-Butula*.

> Here for you, heroic Islam, all of us will sacrifice in your defence
> Here for you, and make from our skulls for the integrity of your glory
> Here for you, if the standard should grow thirsty, the youth will pour out blood for it
>
> This host shall gather tomorrow in my country in its completeness
> And it will rise up to shatter falsehood in my territory
> And it will rise up on the horizons of the proud ones of my people
>
> Jerusalem, I have pledged you the value of my blood
> I have sworn that I will not permit and allow the despoiling of my honour
> Beit Hanoun and Haifa and Galilee groaned and my anger awoke

In such cases, the point is not just the notion of martyrdom (literal or figurative), but also the way in which the authorial voice typically seems to present itself as speaking for, and reaffirming commitment to, a whole people who are ultimately portrayed as all being party to the struggle. This social reality is put forward as an eternal, unshakeable fact, and the struggle of the narrator is contextualized within it. Indeed, there seems to be a strong theme of equivalence between the collectivity of the people, the physical body of the narrator (or the heroes whose praise is being sung) and the land itself. Oppression and martyrdom, for example, 'plant' a seed which will grow into 'thorns of vengeance' among the coming generation.[34] In *Blow Up The Cursed One O Daughter of Jihad*, this idea of sowing the dragon's teeth is expressed even more directly when it says 'pour out your blood, for if good blood falls upon the ground it will grow into soldiers in the time of need'.[35] Other references are still more graphic: 'Our skulls are offered so that your [Islam's] honour can remain whole', says one song.[36]

Indeed, so closed is the imaginative system – so fixated on the triangular relationship between martyr, community and the eternal (as much of the natural world as the divine) – that even violence against the enemy seems at times to disappear into abstraction. The hero dies fighting the enemy. But it is the gore of his own demise, his 'pledge . . . of blood' that is emphasized – not that of his opponents. Constantly present in the violence of the fighter is the equal and greater violence done to the fighter's people: 'a generation refusing injustice' is raised by the blows and injustices of the enemy.[37] But the main role of the heroes thereby produced is, in turn, to die heroically. The concern here is not, it seems, the actual physical destruction of the community, but its social death, its dissolution through loss of honour. Indeed, even the afterlife seems, in such works, to be of secondary importance to the life of the collectivity, a point seen above in the concern of the martyr for his soul to shade his fellows, or elsewhere in the popular motif of the martyr wishing his life back in order to sacrifice it again. Religion in these poems, as powerful as it is, seems to be invoked almost in a sense that Durkheim might have approved of, as 'a figurative expression of the society'.[38]

Other nashids, by contrast – while not using a fundamentally different imaginative vocabulary – seem to project a much less secure sense of belonging. Here, the community – or at least the narrator's membership of it – seems not necessarily to be a given. Feelings of commonality may be temporary, and the narrator may even appear to express notions of alienation and nostalgia. No longer does the author merely celebrate the outstanding dedication of a third person hero. Rather, he is at pains to declare his own loyalty. In the case of one example by a person who writes under the pen name of 'poet of Al Qaida', it is the very act of producing poetry itself which affirms the writer's commitment.

> Do not doubt my heart, O friend
> I am the pure one, and your outpouring that cries out
> My arm rhymes precious verses
> Over the concert of the swords, and the shields
> Proud, sweet rhymes
> Calls- "come to prayer, come to salvation" to the people of jihad.
> It paints its letters, it makes my hymn become
> As sharp as the spear of *Al-Samhariyyat*
> I have given my slaughter to the Islamic state
> I have sworn allegiance to it, and forfeited all return.
> I reach out to the Amir with an overflow of longing
> So reach out so that we can swear allegiance by hand[39]

Indeed, as can readily be noted, the possibility that the writer's sincerity might be doubted is offered at the very inception of the work. Elsewhere, the community and solidarity expressed in the first category is represented as a longing for a time which has now vanished.

> Where are our days? Where?.... Where have we spent them?
> They went in the blinking of an eye.... O my places, remember them
>
> O blessed Kandahar ... the Lord keep her
> .... by jihad.... The Guide build her
>
> Paradise of the merciful ... noble Kabul
> By God, we are not pleased ... with injustice anywhere[40]

Perhaps as a consequence of this, these poems seem simultaneously more concerned with violence against a specific enemy and less sure about the prospect of salvation. As one nashid asks: 'One day a whole Ummah will kneel... in healing gloom... To an important question... did you do your duty to the prophet?'.[41] No longer is the existence of an afterlife merely a matter for celebration. Now, it is a matter for concerned personal reflection, which presumably is compounded for some by feelings of distance and lack of agency, as for the author of *O World What is this Silence?* Who in conclusion to events in Chechnya can offer only that:

> The Russians will continue the fighting... and we shall continue to be pious while others sleep.[42]

In yet other nashids, the notion of an intimate link between fighter and people seems to become lost in an unrelenting focus on combat with the enemy. For instance, in a nashid such as *For Each Army We Have a Fallujah and For Each Bush a Zarqawi*, there is little attempt to conceal the theme behind metaphorical abstractions. Another popular Iraqi nashid, *Blow them Up*, is still more direct:

> ... kill them
> Shred them, scatter them, capture them... and slaughter them
> Burn them, drown them, round them up and reap them...
> ask the Lord for steadfastness and longanimity... and defeat them.[43]

At this point, it is useful to compare the well-developed Arabic-language tradition of jihadi nashid with its rather more limited English-language counterpart. Islamic music in English is of course much more limited generally than it is in Arabic, although with the globalization of Islam there are now major Anglophone Islamic artists such as Sami Yusuf or Yusuf Islam.[44]

Specifically 'jihadi' music and poetry in English is, however, for understandable reasons, probably a disproportionately slender resource even within this more limited context. Far fewer Muslims for whom English would be the first choice for self-expression have direct experience of the sorts of situation which is the theme of jihadi content. Moreover, even allowing for generally greater protections to freedom of expression in Anglophone countries, 'jihadism' is generally far more securitized against, as evidenced, for example, by the controversial conviction (later overturned on appeal) of the so-called lyrical terrorist Samina Malik, a shop clerk whose presence on jihadist sites, possession of various widespread weapons manuals and personal writings on subjects such as 'How to Behead' were initially judged to constitute 'records likely to be used for terrorism'.[45]

Some attempts to introduce poetry to English-language jihadi content have the appearance of self-conscious efforts to replicate the Arabic idiom. This would seem to be so, for example, for the case of *Inspire* magazine – a much-publicized attempt by Al Qaeda in the Arabian Peninsula, under the editorship of the American Samir Khan – to replicate in English the basic model of the Arabic-language jihadi propaganda magazine. There have also been attempts to imitate in English something of the unaccompanied musical style of the Arabic nashid. A more problematic category is so-called jihadi rap. Notwithstanding the huge amount of publicity which songs such as Soul Salah Crew's *Dirty Kuffar* attracted,[46] there are very few examples which can safely be said to belong to this genre. Some of the work of a group mainly active in the late 1990s called 'Soldiers of Allah' deals with jihad in ways which are recognizably similar to Arabic jihadi content,[47] as do a few other examples such as 'Muslim Bilal's' instrument-free rap song 'Like a Soldier'[48] or some of the work of the group B.I.A.S.[49] Since this content seems seldom to be described as 'jihadi' by those who make it, and since it exists on a clear thematic continuum with politically motivated rap music made by Muslims (and indeed by non-Muslims), it is generally difficult to discuss such examples comfortably under the 'jihadi' heading as a group.

Content items which are distributed as English-language 'jihadi nashids' tend to be significantly less sophisticated than their Arabic counterparts, and to make fairly simplistic, didactic and even stilted use of a limited range of topics and themes. Nonetheless, they do broadly resemble the latter category of more globally oriented nashid outlined above in their individualistic focus, their foregrounding of specifically theological matters (such as the heavenly reward that awaits the martyr) and their specific interest in identifying the *kafir* enemy as an object of hostility. The nashid 'mother don't be sad',[50] for example, focuses on a stereotypical theme to be found even in medieval jihad literature – the need for the aspiring mujahid or *shahid* to justify the claims of jihad over those of family, while the nashid 'I love you my bro' emphasizes the alternative sense of brotherhood which is supposed to be found in the practice of jihad. Here again we have a theme which is well established in classical writing on violent jihad. However, within the much more constrained overall repertoire of the English jihadi nashid, this specific concern with issues of individuality, alienation, separation from family and rediscovery of new forms of metaphorical kinship seems particularly salient.

We can extend this discussion by considering a class of jihadiyyat which combine both the graphic designs considered above, nashid music and animated poetic text all at the same time: the jihadi flash animation. Like the *bitaqat* and the *anashid*, these *flashat* are generally offered as a subset of the wider category of *islamiyyat*. And, in much the same fashion, they seem to draw on a common vocabulary to express a variety of styles which, while not explicitly pertaining to different jihadist ideologies, are at least suggestive of them.

Indeed, an interesting feature which seems widespread in these items is the almost saturated feel that they create through layer upon layer of media. In addition to montages of images and simple animated graphics, these items make extensive use of quite lengthy poetic text which is often presented as if it were a visual element in its own right, with camera-style techniques of scrolling and panning used for emphasis.[51]

On top of this, there will generally be a nashid providing the soundtrack, and the words to the nashid (which are, of course another poem) may be different to the words which appear visually. There may even be some use of interactivity. For example in the animation *Prison is a Paradise or an Inferno*, the viewer starts the piece by unlocking a jail cell with a virtual key. In *Open Fire!* (The imperative is, intriguingly, directed at a female listener), the viewer's eye is drawn in through rapidly moving crosshairs.[52]

Overall then, there is in these forms a rather interesting contrast between the generally circumscribed range of messages and motifs which the jihadi idiom allows, and, on the other hand, the multiple *forms* and types of speech which are being thrown together. It is as if, in the excess of multiple media layers, the form wishes to compensate or even transgress the rather limited range of expression it allows. This is not to say, however, that the form is wholly limited to the endless remixing of identical elements. For instance, in a video entitled *The Arrow of Yesterday Continues*, a standard narrative about solidarity in the face of Zionist oppression is complicated by the fact that it is presented as happening inside a television, within a simple CG rendering of a prosperous, Western-style living room. But even here, the original form of presentation still encloses identical basic material.

One more – albeit tentative – observation may be pertinent here. For all the emotiveness of their content, the visual form of the jihadi animation seems to have the consequence of removing from the picture the sense of personal narrative which we have seen to be so important with regard to poetry and nashid. Whereas in these, the author's beliefs, intentions, resolutions and even self-doubts are a crucial part of the emotional effect, the jihadi animation, even as it incorporates nashids into the overall assemblage, seems inevitably to create a certain sense of distance: the creator is presenting us with an artefact designed – very clearly *designed* – to produce an emotional reaction, and in this sense, the creator's action, unlike the personal commitment expressed in the nashid, is complete. What is being offered is, so it seems, not a cry from the heart but, rather a product, a form of action.

Jihadiyyat and ideological partisanship

So far, I have emphasized the extent to which ideological boundaries between different movements and groups seem to become blurred at the level of the production and consumption of online jihadi content. Jihadi nashids, while sometimes specifically the work of a particular militant group, appear to cross boundaries between supporters of different forms of jihadism, and even between supporters of Islamist and non-Islamist forms of militancy. Collections of jihadi *bitaqat* offer a smorgasbord of different designs, some implying an interest in one group or tendency, some in another.

What I have not discussed so far, however, is how, out of this putatively shared stock of jihadi motifs, the individual idioms of different jihadist groups are constructed. Developing such a discussion is important to my argument, in so far as I aspire ultimately to show how distinctions which appear to be profoundly rooted in ideological differences can, potentially, also be located in the logic governing the range of images by which jihad is represented – in other words, that a jihadi idiom broadly identifiable with what might often be called (if sometimes misleadingly) 'salafi' jihadism is, viewed from the combinatorial possibilities available in the stock of jihadi motifs, more or less an inevitability.

A brief illustration of how this might work can be provided if we return, briefly, to the highly stereotypical and circumscribed set of images in the jihadi *bitaqat* discussed above. I have already proposed, loosely, that some examples here apparently aim to represent an Ikhwani vision of jihad, while others seem more consonant with what might be interpreted as a 'Salafi' one. To cite two obviously contrasting examples, in one, a silhouetted horseman stands holding the black war-banner, the *raya*. In another, a child stares through a jagged hole in the wall, defiantly holding a Palestinian flag as a fire burns in the background.

In this case, there seems to be no iconographic overlap at all, to the extent that – were the two designs not offered as part of the same collection, there would be no reason to consider them part of the same visual language. But is this more generally true? In this collection, for example, there are some images: the sword, in particular, which appears seven times, which seem never to appear alongside others, such as the national flag (Palestine and, in stylized fashion, Iraq), children or enemy weapons.

Indeed, it might be suggested that there are really three basic categories of jihadi image. One set relates to militancy and resistance in a general sense – we might equally expect to find them, *mutatis mutandis*, in relation to any armed struggle, jihadi or otherwise. A second relates to the way in which, generally, Islam (or, perhaps better the '*Islamic*') seems to be visually represented online. Images such as mosques, books, sunrises, moons and so on are equally to be found in *da'wi* or other categories of *islamiyyat*. Finally, there is a small set of images which seem to be *specifically* jihadi – the sword, banner, horse, etc.

Here, again, the *bitaqat* offer a succinct illustration of the point. Many of the cards feature a quotation from the Qur'an or hadith as the main text, and two of them include hadiths on the relative virtues of jihad compared to other activities. In two of these, the hadith quoted compares jihad to other possible commitments. In one, the text reads:

> The prophet was asked what is the best deed. He said: "faith in God and His prophet". It was said: "what then?" He said: "jihad in the path of God." It was said: "what then?" He said: "a blessed *hajj*."

The designer of this card has had to try to find a single image to represent each of these deeds. *Hajj* can easily be shown through the image of the Ka'ba – the shrine in Mecca which Muslim pilgrims circumambulate as the culmination of this ritual. Faith is portrayed by means of the index finger, extension of which accompanies the declaration of faith in Muslim prayer. The corresponding image for *jihad* is a silhouetted horseman bearing sword and banner. In the second of these, the narration of the prophet is as follows:

> The prophet said: there are three things which it is a duty unto God to assist: a wedding which wants honour, a library which wants alms, and jihad in the path of God.

Here, the image chosen is a more contemporary one: *jihad* is represented by a man with a long beard, dressed in turban and *shalwar qamis*, bearing a Kalashnikov rifle.

What is interesting – so it would seem – is that the idioms of certain ideological forms of jihadism (specifically, 'national' jihadisms such as that represented by Palestinian or, in past years at least, elements of the insurgency in Iraq) seem to specifically eschew images which are seemingly religious and militant at the same time, preferring instead to produce composites of images which are *either* religious *or* militant. By contrast, other forms of jihadism (those which seem, with respect to online material, to be most prototypically and generically 'jihadi') are most clearly defined by images of precisely this sort: that is, images which seem at once 'militant' and 'Islamic'.

Realizing 'the Jihadi'

To develop and explore this point further, let us now consider some specific examples of propaganda content clearly attributable to particular, ideologically distinct, organizations. Specifically, I now propose to examine videos produced by three groups: Hamas, a group ideologically affiliated with the Muslim Brothers, and moving between both militant 'jihad' and other, non-violent political strategies; the Islamic Army of Iraq, a specifically insurgent group which displayed both Salafist and nationalist elements, and the Al Qaeda affiliate Islamic Army of Iraq. The aim, in discussing the material, I should stress, is not in any way to produce a comprehensive assessment of the propaganda of any of these organizations. Nor is any claim made that the texts are strictly comparable in a general sense. Rather they are chosen to illustrate a set of ideal types of solution achieved in jihadi propaganda to the problem just outlined. The specific texts in question shall be the Qassam Brigades' *Convey the Voice of the Wrathful Hero*,[53] the Islamic Army of Iraq's *Baghdad Sniper 2*[54] and the Al-Qassam Brigades', and the first part of the Al Qaeda affiliate Islamic State of Iraq's series *Knights of Martyrdom*.[55]

Convey the Voice of the Wrathful Hero[56] is a song accompanied by a video montage celebrating the armed wing of Hamas. The music – in common with some other specifically *Hamasi* nashids – violates fundamentalist convention by including instrumental accompaniment including bass and keyboards, and indeed the song much more closely resembles secular Levantine music than Islamic nashids in general. The montage opens in the green wash of night vision with Qassami riflemen creeping forwards. The image of an explosion bursts through the scene, to reveal the logo of the Qassam Brigades: itself a composite image including the Dome of the Rock, a kalashnikov, and a green flag with the *shahada*. The video then cuts rapidly to footage of Qassamis on parade. Shot from below, the approaching group presents the impression of overrunning the viewer. Over the imagery are sung the words:

> Convey the voice of the wrathful hero
> To the world I write "Qassami"
> To tarry at the gates of glory
> And honour the Ummah with feverish blood

The bulk of the video is concerned with displaying the Qassamis as a formidable and courageous fighting force, drilling, firing rockets and machine guns and advancing in squadrons. A section around the middle of the video celebrates individual Qassamis, and towards the end we see progressively growing crowds of flag-waving supporters.

Two brief shots show also a Qassami in a quiet moment, reading a Qur'an, and one shows a collective *du'a* prayer – the Qassamis are good Muslims, and the song in the background makes it clear that they are 'Islam's army', fighting for the Islamic nation. The film also dwells repeatedly on photographs of Qassami martyrs against a rolling blue sky. Most of the video, however, is concerned with purely military and social affairs. Indeed, even the language of the song is essentially secular, its words in colloquial Arabic and even the name of the group being given the characteristically Gazan pronunciation of 'Gassami', while the thumping drums and bass of the accompaniment speak more of the idiom of popular song than of sacred chant.

Juba, the sniper of Baghdad, represents perhaps the most sophisticated trans-media project ever attempted by a militant group. Using montaged footage of individual sniper operations, the Islamic Army of Iraq apparently succeeded in producing an artificially constructed viral internet hero with his own website, anashid and numerous self-declared 'fans' (as can be seen in the use of 'Juba' as a nickname element).[57] In keeping with this, *Juba 2*, the second Baghdad Sniper is a sophisticated piece of work, which cleverly integrates the core 'jihadi' themes. After an initial sequence, portraying a man in a balaclava cocking a sniper rifle, over which the production is credited to the central media foundation of the Islamic Army in Iraq, and offering it as an Eid present to the "people of monotheism", the video opens with the sounding of the *adhan* (the Muslim call for prayer). A door opens and the same man in a balaclava enters into a sparsely furnished white room, still carrying his rifle. He sets this carefully down on a table, together with a side arm, a mobile phone, a radio and some bullets. He turns to a wall chart, on which are written the prophetical words 'do not associate with an unbeliever, and fight him into the everlasting fire'. He scores off another mark on a growing tally, and sits down to write a communique to the Muslim Ummah, referencing the blood of 'our Muslim grandfathers' and the shame of its desecration by the same Jews and Crusaders. 'What will we say' he asks, 'on Judgement Day?'

Knights of Martyrdom is a series of operation videos celebrating suicide bombings by the Islamic State of Iraq. The element of particular interest is not so much the operational footage itself, which more or less follows the conventions of such content, but rather the computer animation with which the series begins. This displays a green and well-tended garden, chirruping with birdsong – a typically Islamic vision of paradise which seems, perhaps, all the more effective for its virtuality. The (imaginary) camera pans over the scene to show us something shocking and incongruous. In the middle of the delicate garden is the hulking shape of a large lorry. The door of the lorry opens. Using the cinematic language of the 'first person' computer game, the camera zooms in, and we find ourselves looking at the dashboard, as if we are seated in the cab. The door closes, as if the viewer has closed it. The lorry drives off. Suddenly, it is not on grass anymore, but a dusty desert road. At the end of the road is a stylized military compound, dominated by a large, red cross. The truck drives into the compound. There is a cry of 'Allahu Akbar'. At this very moment, the computer animation switches to live footage of an explosion at the end of a desert road, just like the one represented in CG.

Let us consider in turn how each of these well-made and interesting examples of propaganda footage by a jihadi group expresses 'jihadiness'. The Qassami video, *Convey the Voice of the Wrathful Hero*, as noted, uses a mixture of purely military scenes, together with a few scenes of Qassamis in specifically and conventionally pious contexts. Scenes connected with martyrdom also have a religious context in so far as Islamic iconography is an integral part of Qassami practices in this regard. However, these occasional images of religious ritual are not really incorporated into the overall narrative. One could remove them or replace them with some alternative cultural gesture, and the video, being mostly concerned with the Qassamis' military discipline, courage and popular support, would still make sense. Essentially, this is militarism with some use of obvious religious motifs.

In *Juba 2*, religious motifs are not simply overlayed, but become an integral part of the narrative. First, while the Qassam brigades are said to be fighting for Islam in some unspecified sense (bound up with the inherent sacredness of Palestine), in *Juba 2*, politics (i.e. power relations between different actors) is expressed in terms of specifically religious issues. It is the desecration of mosques and the Qur'an, the shame of the Ummah and the failure to implement shari'a that are the main grievances voiced by the sniper. Religious ritual is also integrated into the narrative structure of the video. From the context, we *assume* that Juba has just finished praying. Or, if he hasn't, that he ought to be. So when he lays down his weapons and carefully checks off his latest kill, the care with which he does it brings to mind the same ritual care that would be brought to ritual ablutions. And yet, as integral as this is to setting up the scenes that follow, the actual violence, when it comes is, is still wholly temporal in content. Indeed, later on in the video, an interview with the 'commander of the sniper brigade in Baghdad' provides a wholly rationalistic and operational-sounding justification for the use of sniping which seems almost to defy the absolutist and deontological admonitions which have just preceded. If the Qassami video *overlays* select and rather general religious signs on its otherwise generically militant material, the Islamic Army of Iraq one works by *juxtaposing* distinct religious and militant narratives.

By contrast, almost everything in the *Knights of Martyrdom* animation seems designed to avoid this interpretation. Eternal reward in heaven is not a way of reconciling the viewer to the death of the hero – it is where the action starts. When the weapon appears, we are not witnessing the sacralization of a worldly object, but the opposite: the jarring introduction of the profane into the sacred. The use of graphics – including the large cross which both marks out and obscures that actual, real-life army base which the truck will blow up in – seems intended, like some sort of 'augmented reality' not to obscure, but rather to reveal the true essences which underlie the physical event which is about to occur. Wherever the mind might be tempted to offer an alternative interpretation, we are, it seems, continually forced back to the idea of suicide bombing as – to use Faisal Devji's terminology – an unmistakably 'ethical act'.[58] The jihadi, in this Al Qaeda video, is realized not by *overlay* or *juxtaposition* but rather by the *integration* of the 'militant' and the 'Islamic' into a single thing.

It is, of course, important to note that this integration is less successfully achieved in the actual film footage that follows in which, for obvious reasons, elements of the humdrum and the profane necessarily intrude. But what is striking is that even at their most idealized and stylized, neither the Hamas nor the Islamic Army of Iraq videos seem even to attempt something similar. Jihadiness in the Qassami footage never seems to mean more than to pray *and* fight (as two separate, but mutually supportive activities in the context of a wider community). In the Islamic Army of Iraq context, it means to pray *then* fight (as an index of the piety of a specific hero, an inseparable part of the overall narrative of his actions). In the Al Qaeda video, there is at least an attempt to find a visual idiom for showing fighting as a kind of prayer.[59]

Explaining 'synthetic' and 'integrated' Jihadism

What the above analysis seems to suggest is that the production of different ideological idioms within jihadi content is indeed effected not so much by the introduction of entirely distinct elements (although some elements, as we have seen, such as medieval weaponry, tend to be absent from the more nationalist forms of jihadism, whereas, obviously, specifically nationalist elements are absent from its more fundamentalist and globalized expressions). Rather, it is achieved by the extent to which the elements which make up jihadi content are integrated with one another. It is worth noting at this point that the need to 'integrate' may, as argued above, be as reflective of the nature of new media content as any larger process. Hamas content, so it would seem, assumes a certain pre-existing integration of its major themes within the mind of the consumer. Al Qaeda content, on the other hand, attempts as far as possible to integrate themes of militancy and spirituality within the content itself, even down to the specific elements selected.

The implication here would seem to be that Al Qaeda, relative to groups such as Hamas, is genuinely more 'purist' with regard to the extent to which it presents jihad as central to its meaning and purpose – hardly a surprising conclusion. But the real point being made here is that the various apparent 'levels' of 'jihadiness' seem to be more or less inherent in the way that mediated representations of jihad are structured. A 'jihadi' nashid, or a *bitaqa*, as we have seen, is as likely to be associated with Hamas as with Al Qaeda. On the other hand, a 'jihadi' *forum* – which is not to say, of course, that there are not Hamas-affiliated Web forums – almost certainly implies a forum which, broadly speaking, is likely to be not just generically 'jihadi', but roughly speaking what we would call 'jihadi-salafi' in orientation. The same is true, incidentally, of the 'jihadi book'.[60] Again, in contrast to the nashid, a Web search for 'jihadi books' is a fairly reliable way of bringing up the list of currently active 'jihadi' forums. Search for 'hamasi nashids', and one consistently returns around of 50,000 hits. Search for 'hamasi books' and the hit count is in the low digits, with results referring to standard Muslim Brothers texts like the work of Sayyid Qutb and Hassan Banna. By contrast, a search for 'jihadi books' returns, at the last count, 63,700 hits, of which the first five are specifically 'jihadi' (and pro-Al Qaeda) sites. A typical list of such 'jihadi books' (this one, in fact, from a non-jihadi forum) reads as follows:

- *The Future of the Peninsula and of Iraq* by the martyr (God willing), Yusuf al-'Uyayri.
- *The American Presence in the Peninsula: Its Truth and its Aims*, Yusuf al-'Uyayri (may God accept him)
- *Guidance for the Confused on the Permissibility of Killing Prisoners*, Yusuf al 'Uyayri
- *O Mujahidin, the Spirit, not the World*, Abdullah Al-Rashid
- *Thus we See the Jihad, and we Desire it*, Hazim al-Madani
- *The Creed of the Saved Sect*, Abdul Majid Muhammad Muni', may God accept him in the heights
- *The Whinnying of the Horses in Explanation of the Book of Jihad* Abd al-Rahim al-Shafi'i
- *The Late Warning Concerning the Most Important Important Matters Necessary* 'Izz al-Din al-Maqdisi

And so on. This particular list goes on to offer eleven books by Abdullah Azzam, as well as volumes by Abu Muhammad al-Maqdisi and Ayman al-Zawahiri. These are plainly not just Islamic books dealing with jihad. For example, there is virtually no chance of encountering Shaykh Yusuf al-Qaradawi's (2009) *Fiqh al-Jihad* listed as a 'jihadi book', even though it is perhaps the most significant book of Islamic jurisprudence on that subject published in recent years.[61]

What this seems to suggest is that jihadism, as we find it online, may in a sense be seen as a logical necessity of the way the Web arranges data: the availability of certain choices makes inherently possible the emergence of certain sorts of space. Topically organized space in turn implies ideology, where the topic in question is conducive to interpretation along those lines.

I do not mean by this to suggest that we must understand the emergence of jihadism deterministically. A combinatorial possibility does not inevitably mean that a combination will actually exist or be used. Nor, it follows, do I mean to suggest that the actual salience of jihadi content is unconnected to realities on the ground. Nor again am I suggesting that the elements that make up 'the jihadi' are themselves somehow eternally pre-set elements of an essentialized notion of Islam or Middle Eastern culture.

There is no need to deny that the specific jihadi forms we encounter on the Web are anything more than surface representations of more deeply rooted ideological tendencies. And yet I would like to suggest that what I have presented is not just a demonstration of the methodological possibility of (re)constructing the particular forms of jihadism already recognized in the literature on the sole basis of 'jihadi' Web content. I have also presented a possible alternative view of these phenomena, whereby the specific textual issues that define particular ideological boundaries (e.g. beliefs about the permissibility of elections, about the global nature of the obligation of defensive jihad, about the permissibility of the *taqlid* of traditional law schools)[62] can realistically be seen as subordinate, in the development of contemporary forms of jihadi engagement, to the processes of the production and consumption of more literary and artistic forms of jihadi content, to the material practices of engaging with them, and even to the way information is ordered and structured by the Web. If so, it is not implausible to see jihadism on the internet as a form of 'affective investment', beginning with processes of collection and distribution which, with deeper and more socialized commitment, acquires ideological clothing: an ideological clothing represented specifically by the inherent possibility of distinctively 'jihadi' forms not only of dynamic content, but also of virtual space.

4

Jihadi forums in their own words

In this chapter, and the one that follows, I shall examine the phenomenon of jihadism on Web forums in Arabic, whether on specifically 'jihadi' forums (the subject of this chapter) or in the form of self-styled 'jihadi' activists on forums with a wider sphere of interest. While recent years have seen the Web forum increasingly eclipsed by more or less equivalent applications built into social media, Web forums remain important for online communities seeking online spaces special to themselves and distinct from the mainstream. Moreover, the Web forum, as successor to the electronic bulletin board, has a venerable place in the history of online community, providing the site for numerous studies on the potential and meaning of internet media.

Web forums, viewed in terms of their general characteristics, have an interesting hybridity. They afford anonymous (or apparently anonymous) real time or nearly real time, many to many conversations. But they also permit asynchronous forms of exchange, because of the fact – also significant – that they automatically preserve dialogue history. They are (or can be made to be) universally viewable. At the same time, dialogue can be (or can be made to be) restricted to a limited circle of forum members. Taken together, these characteristics mean that Web forums, as a form, occupy an ambiguous territory between publicness and privacy, between anonymity and 'pseudonymity',[1] and between functioning as 'chat rooms' and as something closer to a multi-authored document. This is further complicated, for the case of the contemporary Web forum, by the ease with which it is possible to post images, embed video and provide links to other media.

Web forums and bulletin boards have been central to discussions of the internet as a platform for both virtual community and the development the internet as a space for dialogue and the possible development of public spheres, with significant differences of opinion as to their potential. As was touched on in Chapter 2, 'cyber-optimists' such as Howard Rheingold[2] have seen bulletin boards as capable of sustaining rich and vibrant online communities. Others have also argued (including for the specific case of the Muslim world) that the internet may present the opportunity to develop public spheres – spaces for rational dialogue, as theorized most notably by Jürgen Habermas[3] – which lie outside the power of state and commercial institutions, but allow citizens to participate informally in the formulation, critique and development of politics. Others have been more sceptical about such claims. Mark Aakhus, for example, argues that the very openness of Web forums limits their usefulness as vehicles for serious deliberation, since there is nothing compelling posters to finish arguments they have started.[4] Cass Sunstein worries, by contrast, that the fact that membership of forums is self-selecting risks a situation of group polarization, whereby, by a well-established mechanism of group psychology, those who socialize exclusively with those of similar opinions become more hardened in these opinions.[5]

Regardless of their wider potential and the particular uses to which they are put, the collaborative nature of Web forums, the typical use of nicknames by their users, and their tendency to attract a finite and regular membership mean that they have at least the potential to sustain immersive communities capable of generating a powerful sense of online place. Certainly, those Web forums which describe themselves as 'jihadi' would seem to remain the only parts of the Web that provide the sense of uniquely jihadi environment and therefore where uniquely, exclusively 'jihadi' communities coming to being. *Jihad* (in the jihadi understanding) may belong to the battlefield, but the forums are where *jihadism* happens. But what, exactly, does happen on jihadi forums? What does it mean to be a member of one? What does 'doing jihadism' (as opposed to jihad) involve?

First, what do we mean by a 'jihadi forum'? For reasons we have already established while, in principle, the term does not exclude forums dedicated to non-'salafi' jihadi groups, it turns out that forums that actually *call themselves* 'jihadi forums' do in fact tend to be synonymous with forums that support what is sometimes called 'jihadi salafism'. To sum up the argument of the previous chapter, 'jihadi salafism', understood as a more or less scripted ideology can also be viewed from a subcultural point of view in terms of an identity created through the selection of a particular combination of pre-existing elements: notably, an exclusive focus on 'the jihadi' as located within a stylized set of elements defined (appropriately or no) as 'the Islamic'. So-called 'Salafism' (a term which is often in fact applied to 'neofundamentalist' forms which are not strictly Salafist)[6] is perhaps better understood from the perspective of the internet simply as that topical space which is conceived of as exclusively 'Islamic' (and which therefore by logical necessity represents itself as disembedding 'Islam' from other areas of life). That portion of 'the jihadi' which is reached as a subtopic of 'the Islamic' is 'jihadi-salafism'. And 'jihadi forums' are what happens when this topical field is itself represented as a space of its own – or, more accurately, when 'the Islamic' and other topical fields are viewed as if exclusively from the standpoint of 'the jihadi'.

Over the years, these forums have developed a distinctive visual idiom such that it is usually possible to identify a new one at a glance. This is not just a matter of the combination of specific elements of the jihadi idiom, but is also matter of layout. Typically, the head of the page will feature an oblong banner of a single colour, enriched with effects such as fading or decorative patterns of shade. On the right-hand side of this will be the name of the forum written in elaborate, calligraphic script. To the left will be a generic set of familiar symbols: a Qur'an, a Kalashnikov, a horseman. Below this there will scrolling text, usually advertising the latest releases from the 'Islamic media foundations' of the various groups the forum supports (usually Al Qaeda affiliates) and below this a succession of colourful flash banners advertising further releases. Only after scrolling some way down do we come to the forum's various sub sections. The first section of a jihadi forum will invariably be devoted to publishing new communiqués from militant groups. There is more variation as to what other sections are included. There may be a section devoted to Islamic theology, a section devoted to wider news about the 'situation of the Islamic Ummah'. Quite commonly, there is also a 'general section'. A closed off section may exist exclusive to the management of the forum. More specialized sections may include, for example, sections for material in other languages; a section dealing with technical information relating to computers and security, or even a section for 'the Islamic hacker'; a section for 'questions and answers (usually on practical matters relating to design software or using the forum); a section on Arabic language and grammar or a section especially for women. Shumukh Al-Islam, and the time of writing, still maintains a 'training camp' devoted to providing information on bomb-making and military techniques. But this seems to be exceptional, and generally material of this sort would appear to be of less significance than it was in the past.

It is true that a few forums represent in-between cases from an ideological point of view. Al-Buraq forum (the surviving offshoot of a forum which split into two rivals each bearing the same name) has some of the same material that other jihadi forums have, but is dedicated to the non-Al Qaeda Salafist-Nationalist group of the Islamic Army of Iraq.[7] *Al-Aqsa Gate* wavers between looking more and less like a typical jihadi forum, but is focused on jihadi-salafi groups in Palestine, specifically Gaza. *Hanayn* disseminates Al Qaeda content, but is less exclusive, and during the Arab Spring it tried for a time to rebrand itself as a forum specifically dedicated to Arabic revolutions. However, these are exceptional enough, and sufficiently unusual compared to more typical examples (such as *Shumukh al-Islam, Ansar al-Mujahidin, Al-Jihad al-'Alami, Layuth al-Islam, Sanam al-Islam, 'Ushaq al-Hur* being some active example at the time of writing) as to make generalizations reasonably safe.

Another complicating factor in defining the 'jihadi forum' is that any given jihadi forum typically serves merely as the focal point for a wider 'Islamic network' making use of numerous different internet applications. As with most Web forums, their users will also be kept up to date with the latest releases and news by means of regular emails. A private messaging service is built into the forum – sometimes accessible only to the more senior members. For a long time, PalTalk, a real-time audio chat service was popular, with many 'Islamic networks' maintaining their own rooms. Today, jihadi forums have their own YouTube channels, Twitter accounts and may even venture into producing their own content – blurring the boundary between themselves and the 'Islamic media foundations' charged with actually creating the videos and communiqués disseminated by fighting groups and jihadist scholars – and example, perhaps, of the phenomenon of media 'convergence' increasingly noted by media scholars such as Henry Jenkins.[8]

As a more concrete illustration of what the term 'jihadi forum' entails, consider the following exchange which occurred on the forum 'Swalifsoft' in 2007. 'Castle of Palestine' is hoping to set up a new site and makes the following opening.

> Peace be upon you, dear brothers, I have vowed to disseminate these materials on the Internet, wherever I have membership, and especially on swalif-soft. The brothers of the mujahidin in Palestine want to establish a website for themselves, and they need the following:
>
> 1 News scripts for jihadi news
> 2 Scripts for articles with photos, where biographies of the souls of martyrs can be disseminated
> 3 Unique anashid scripts which could include albums and videoclips
> 4 Hosting on a Russian server, so that the Jews can't hit it.
> 5 Support for an email server
> 6 A flexible mail menu script – so that we can send the members the latest news

The response he gets is mixed. 'I hope', objects one member, 'that this website doesn't serve the takfiri ideology of the followers of Bin Laden'. To which 'Castle of Palestine' responds:

> Dear brother – I said that the website is "jihadi" so "the message can be known by its title." Whoever would like to help, they are welcome. If you don't like it, just say a word of goodness and pray for your brothers in Palestine.[9]

Even with regard to the very particular Palestinian context, the term 'jihadi website' is expected, so it seems, to be self-explanatory. So, too, are the basic functions the site is expected to fulfil: to serve as a platform for the content of 'the brothers of the mujahidin'. But what the real significance may be of the convergence of this ideological orientation, and this type of online activism is the question to which I turn in this chapter.

Until a few years ago, at least, a typical account of how jihadi forums originated might have gone something as follows: websites supporting jihadi groups have been in existence in one way or another since the 1990s, the obvious example being Azzam.com or sites related to the ongoing Chechen wars like Qoqaz.net. By the end of the 1990s, groups in Chechnya were filming operations, including beheadings, which sometimes ended up online. After 9/11, Al Qaeda in the Arabian Peninsula began producing its own material for online dissemination, including a website, Neda.com. After the invasion of Iraq and the consequent insurgency, however, footage of operations started to be produced on a scale never seen before. Getting this footage onto the Web was a challenge, particularly given the narrower bandwidth generally available at the time. Online activists such as 'Irhabi007' (Younes Tsouli) and 'Muhibb al-Shaykhayn al-Tunisi' helped to solve this problem,[10] receiving content from people like Abu Maysara al-Iraqi, press secretary for Abu Mus'ab al-Zarqawi's Al Qaeda in the Land of the Two Rivers, and doing the work of editing, preparing, reformatting and disseminating it. The initial online point of contact for this was Al-Ansar.com, which was in effect the world's first jihadi forum.

After Tsouli was arrested and Ansar.com went offline, a more regularized distribution system was created. This involved creating Al-Fajr media, a centralized agency for preparing and disseminating propaganda created by the media production arms of groups affiliated to Al Qaeda, and an online network centred around four main Web forums: Al-Hisba, Al-Ikhlas, Al-Buraq and Al-Firdaws, as well as various other lesser, and less official examples. This network survived until late 2008, when three of the four forums went permanently offline. The fourth and last, Al-Hisbah, followed them early in 2009.[11] Since then, a relatively stable situation seems to have emerged, whereby content is distributed on a variety of jihadi forums, with one taking an informal leading role (first a forum called *Al-Falluja* then, when it closed down, another called *Shumukh al-Islam*), and with some enjoying closer links to distributors than others, but without the semi-formalized arrangement that seems to have existed before.

Does this narrative still stand up? Certain facts have since emerged which, at least, are problematic for it. The discovery that one major jihadi forum (suspected to have been Al-Hisba) was in fact a joint-run Saudi-CIA intelligence front, until it was shut down by a cyberattack from the US Army (which was unaware of this fact), injects at least a note of uncertainty about what was really going on behind the scenes.[12] Another rather surprising little detail is that Al-Ansar, the first real jihadi forum, apparently closed down for the seemingly trivial reason that Younes Tsouli, its then administrator, simply failed to pay to renew its hosting.[13]

However, what is perhaps most problematic about this sort of account is that it is largely top down, focused on the perceived instrumental needs of Al Qaeda, and how concerns such as the jihadi forum helped to offer practical solutions for them. This is, of course, a very important part of the story. But what it ignores is the more 'bottom up', organic side to how the forums came into being. Consider, for example, the following account:

> Arabic forums started to appear approximately ten years ago, and the first one to appear was al-Sahat, as I recall. In 1999, "Ana Arabi" [I am an Arab] appeared, which the Saudi intelligence bought, and renamed "Ana al-Muslim." [I am the Muslim]. At the same time Al-Sahab website appeared, which was Islamic in the beginning. In 2000–2001, the website Islam Online appeared. The writers on the Internet at that time went in different directions. I moved on to the website "Jawab." There was a chatroom mainly for Egyptians. And the groups that were taking part in dialogue on the Net were generally limited. There was Ali al-Qurani, who debated against the Rafidi Shiites in al-Sahat, and against him there was a man called Al-Malak al-Tair [the flying angel], and with him speedbird, and a group of people who were supposed to be Sunnis. On the other hand there was audio chat in PalTalk. Most of this was Muslims against Christians. And the strange thing was that all these forums, except Islamway, remain online up till now. Others came and went and didn't leave much effect other than on a few people.
>
> In 2001 and after the two blessed battles of September, Islamway was gone. Islamway was an Egyptian forum in general. It was led by the low down, dirty traitor Baramuda al-Samadi. And this is how the forum started.

In 2001, when Islamway was gone, they replaced it with several forums. There was al-Tajdeed, al Qala'a, al-Islah wal Tawhid and Bab al Arab beside Ana Muslim. Then the Orthodox Carmathians took Al-Sahab and expelled all the Muslims from it. The only jihadi forum on the net was al-Tawhid, and it is said (but God knows) that the Sheikh Abu Qatada used to write in it and the Sheikh Abu Hamza al-Masri as well. On the other hand Al-Islah, Al-Tajdeed and Al-Qala'a were all political forums which included jihadis among their members and allowed them. Of course, we can't blame the respected Sheikhs, the owners of Islah and Tajdid, because they are known by name. They are pursued and threatened by the authorities, so they shouldn't be blamed for that . . .

At the end of 2003, Al-Ansar forum appeared, and was the first true jihadi forum at that time. Before, there was a website called jihad.net, and its owner was captured, and there was no way for anyone seeking to support to jihad to write on any forum at all.[14]

This extended quotation sketches a picture of a lively scene in which a distinctively 'jihadi' milieu evolves not just as a response to specific developments in the political sphere (although these are clearly very important), but also as a gradual process of diversification and specialization which seems to mirror the development and expansion of Arabic on the Web in general. Discussion moves from generalized sites such as Al-Saha to more specialized Islamic sites before the eventual emergence of specifically 'jihadi' sites.

This quotation comes from a lengthy post from 2009, the title of which roughly translates as 'Jihadi Forums: What they Have, What they Need', posted by the administrator of a forum active around 2010 called 'Madad al-Suyuf', an individual who called himself 'Abu Harith al-Mihdar'. It is useful at this point to introduce the document and its author a little more. The document under the title 'a history of jihadi forums' was translated in part by the analyst Ann Stenersen.[15] In that form, it has been criticized by Aaron Weisburd, a long-time observer of jihadi media, for what he claims are inaccuracies.[16] But to see the document simply as a factual record – or even as a 'history' per se is, I would suggest, to misunderstand its real purpose and value. What the post intends to be – as its title suggests – is not a history per se, but rather an evaluation of the meaning and potential of the jihadi forum, a kind of internal critique based on the subjective experience of a long-time internet jihadi.

Who is (was?) 'Abu Harith al-Mihdar?' According to the journalist Sayyid Zaid, writing on *Islam Online*, and another piece in *Al Arabiya*, Abu Harith al-Mihdar's real name is Walid al-Mihdar al-Shadhili. Zaid says he is an Egyptian Islamic scholar, who studied in Mecca and Pakistan before going into exile in London.

For a long time, the Whois lookup details of his site openly revealed it to be registered in the name of a certain Ahmed al-Sharkawi of the London borough of Camden. This Al-Sharkawi, incidentally, would appear to be the same communications engineer who, in 2007, got into the news when his daughter Salma, who had been removed by social workers and taken into foster care, died in a car accident while traveling with a council worker. According to the Quilliam foundation report, *Cheering for Osama*, Al-Sharkawi and Al-Mihdar are one and the same person, although a more plausible explanation would presumably be that Al-Sharkawi, as a communications professional, was managing the site on the shaykh's behalf.

Other claims have been made about Al-Mihdar's identity in online gossip on jihadi and Islamist forums. In one discussion on the Muslm.net, it was claimed that he had been thrown out of countless forums before for disagreeable behaviour, and or logging in with an Israeli IP address. Al-Buraq presents an elaborate biography, claiming that the whole identity of Al-Mihdar is a front for a Jewish imposter by the name of Nadhim al-Maghribi.[17]

These claims reveal something of the uncertainties in dealing with the world of the jihadi forum. They also give a flavour of the rather hostile, backbiting social environment it offers. The main reason for these claims is likely to be that Al-Mihdar was, during the time he was active, a very controversial figure in jihadi circles. The forum Madad al-Suyuf was distinctive for being the main representative of the 'neo-Zarqawist' faction of the jihadi movement. This division dates back to the acrimony that resulted when Abu Muhammad al-Maqdisi, a pre-eminent jihadi theologian and Abu Mus'ab al-Zarqawi's spiritual mentor, fell out with his protégé over the brutality of his actions in Iraq.[18] The mainstream of the jihadi movement broadly took the side of Al-Maqdisi. But for many jihadis (notably, for many internet jihadis), Al-Zarqawi was a great hero and icon. They insisted that, as a mujahid in the field, Al-Zarqawi was in a better position to judge what actions were necessary and that, basically, the theologian Al-Maqdisi should mind his own business. Al-Mihdar became a leading ideological figure in this movement, launching scathing online screeds against Al-Maqdisi as well as another cleric important to the jihadi movement, Hani Al-Siba'i.[19]

But in a sense, it is precisely the subjectivity of Al-Mihdar's account, delivered both as an insider and as an outsider, which makes it so interesting. On the one hand, he is unflinching in his criticism of what he sees as the shortcomings of the forums. But he locates his critique in practical and specific details about their running. In summary, what Al-Mihdar argues is that jihadi forums should not be put on a pedestal. They exist to disseminate ideology, and attempts to make them something more than this are simply ways of undermining this basic goal and sowing discord. And yet, if we analyse what he says in more detail, it becomes – as I shall argue – increasingly clear that the discord which Al-Mihdar and many others see as a particular liability of the enterprise is, looked at another way, its central feature.

A revealing specific in this regard is the question of openness. For Al-Mihdar, trying to protect a forum by restricting membership to invitation is a pointless misunderstanding of the fundamental nature of the medium. As he argues:

> This is a dubious strategy, which I have no doubt was originally suggested by intelligence. Besides which, it has a problem. Why? Here's why. Why do you close a forum? If you think that it is to prevent intelligence from entering, I say: how do you know that there aren't intelligence already among the members? If you say that you know them all individually, I say: then why do some of them subsequently get ejected? Anyway, Al-Hisba used to use this method, with open membership for the media agency. In the end, all these secrets are available to any foreigner in a foreign country, as long as he has an email address with a foreign or Arabic newspaper or television channel he will be able to get into the forum.

The point that Al-Mihdar is making is a very common one to make in jihadi writing online and is, in itself, hardly controversial. Here, for example is the guidance which the official website of Al Qaeda in the Islamic Maghreb gave to users of jihadi forums:

> It is no longer unknown to anyone how important are chat rooms on the Internet, and the effect achieved in international communications, so that it has come to pass that by means of them major newspapers and satellite channels seek out and publish the jihadi news (they contain). And the mujahidin have benefited from the Internet, and in particular from this application, a benefit praised in particular for the ending of the . . . and the breaking of the Zionist/Crusader stranglehold over the media which has constrained the mujahidin for long years.
>
> Intelligence apparatuses in all their varieties have become sensible of this danger [i.e. the propagation of jihadi news via Internet forums], as if they saw in these chat rooms an irreplaceable chance to trap whomever they may of the "terrorists," or whoever is opposed to this or that institution. And they have made great efforts to break into the chat rooms, inserting their members to trip up whomever they can thereby, or by putting pressure on the owners of those chat rooms to cooperate with them in such things, and indeed the CIA announced lately on the channel CNN that it was planning to set up Arabic language chat rooms to trap "jihadis."

The document goes on to give ten rules for would-be participants in jihadi forums to keep themselves secure, of which the first and last are worth quoting specifically:

- Remember that people you meet on the Internet may not be who they say they are
- If you just want to chat and make friends, jihadi forums aren't for you![20]

Indeed, in Al-Mihdar's opinion, closing a forum is not just an obstacle to its fulfilment of its mission, it is also bad for the forum community itself.

> When they closed the membership in Al-Ansar there was a total disaster, as I mentioned before, because membership was limited to a certain type of people. And thus they opened the door to factionalism and splitting inside the forum. Not only that, but people were even afraid of writing frankly. And the situation continued like this for a period. Then the website was closed and removed forever.

What is interesting in both of these examples – one from a 'central' Al Qaeda source and another from an outsider – is that both condemn not only the use of jihadi forums as places to develop offline connections, but also as places for sociality in general. Indeed, as Al-Mihdar argues:

> Forums are either about disseminating ideology, like al-Madad (and this is what it was meant to be from the beginning), or forums for dialogue, in which there are replies and proofs and questions, and there are only a few of these. Examples of forums which spread ideology include the forum of Sheikh Nasir al-Fahd, God have mercy on him. He used to put theological research on it, and didn't discuss anything. And now there is al-Athari, which aims to expose the disgrace of Madkhalism. There is also the forum of the Egyptian Jama'a al-Islamiyya. These do their work successfully and achieve their aims, though we have our differences with them. The dialogue forums are very few and rare. They include, for example, al-Sahat al-Hurra, and to establish a forum like this requires experienced moderators, who delete whatever is unnecessary from the point of view of whoever is behind the forum. So if somebody adds to a forum a post which consists of nothing but swearing it is deleted, and if somebody makes a post which presents a good argument they leave it, even if it is against the opinions of the moderators.

We may note that the only example of a 'discussion forum' which Al-Mihdar mentions is not a jihadi forum at all. And indeed Al-Mihdar is as scathing about the potential of jihadi forums as platforms for meaningful dialogue.

I prepared a study of the forum Al-Hisba with the help of a team from Al-Madad. They gave me the number of members registered online daily. Then we calculated the number of members who genuinely contributed posts to the forum. Then we calculated the number of members who participated by making a comment. Then we calculated the number of members who say nothing but "God give you good." So we saw that the members who have their own posts were not more than 1.34% of the total number of members. And the ones who placed comments after these, were approximately 21% of total members. And of those 21%, not more than 0.6% said 132 something useful. I wished to give a message to those brothers suggesting that they put all of their "God bless you," together in a single post – i.e, this brother and that brother and the other brother all say "God bless you" instead of having ten pages of these posts so that whoever is searching can't find anything useful. After this we made another search for those who have placed their own posts (of the 1.34%). We found that 75% post subjects from Hamid al-Ali, Abu Basir or Dr Hani Siba'i. Of the other 25%, 24% posted subjects originally posted by others. This left us with 1%. Half of this consisted of insults. The other 0.5% was Abi Abd al-Razaq and his like. In Al Hisba, they noticed this, and they made a forum specially for Abi Abd al-Razaq. This means that [overall] the forum is nothing more than a place where news of mujahidin is disseminated.

While the general fact that Web forums typically attract large numbers of 'lurkers' as a proportion of active members is well attested, as hard quantitative data, it is questionable as to whether we can take this specific claim seriously. In October 2008, towards the end of its life (and at the height of its popularity), al-Hisba claimed a total membership of 11,474. Based on the figures claimed above, this would suggest that the total number of people on the forum offering original and constructive contributions was less than one. Be that as it may, his recommendation about tiresome repetitive prayers seems to have been implemented: it is now common for the forums to offer a figure next to the number of responses giving the number of 'prayers' that a post has received.

Indeed, if the specifics of Al-Mihdar's research may be at fault, his conclusions seem to have received substantial confirmation by academic research, and by two studies in particular:

The first is a 'sentiment and affect analysis' published in 2008 by researchers at the University of Arizona's 'Dark Web Portal' project, based on data which they had pulled from two Arabic-language Web forums. One was a mainstream news forum. The other, Al-Firdaws, was one of what were then the big four jihadi forums distributing propaganda from Al Qaeda's

Al Fajr media network. The researchers created a system for automatically analysing the strength of the sentiments and affects expressed in the posts on these forums. What they found was striking: on the mainstream forum, the intensity of emotional expression remained more or less constant.[21] On the jihadi forum, it grew stronger and stronger. The mainstream forum, so it seemed, was serving to 'depolarize' or – in the term used by Johnny Ryan, an analyst who carried out similar research in his doctoral thesis – to 'atomise' the most radical discourses.[22] On the jihadi forum, the opposite was apparently happening.

The second, more recent study by Erez, Weimann and Weisburd, amounting to the largest systematic enquiry into jihadist forums yet attempted, found that 86 per cent of jihadi forum threads are complete within a single page, with just 2 per cent going to four pages or more. Overall, the authors conclude:

> In short, Jihadist forum discussions are generally active for a short period of time, represent the activity of a small fraction of each forum's membership (which is typically in the thousands), generate very little response from the rest of the community, and with each required turn of the virtual page, participation in the discussion drops off sharply.[23]

What these results seem to confirm is, first, that Al-Mihdar's fears about the risks of jihadi forums turning into inward looking, increasingly isolated communities are entirely reasonable; secondly that, as he also observes, the sociality of jihadi forums is rather limited. What this suggests is that the forums can be treated – as jihadis themselves suggest they ought to be – as primarily designed around the practical purpose of disseminating jihadi media, and not as vibrant online communities as such.

And yet this cannot be the whole story. First, the idea that jihadi forums are ideal and necessary components of Al Qaeda's organized propaganda effort is not as certain as it might seem. This point is evidenced by recently revealed comments of Al Qaeda ideologue Adam Yahiya Gadahn, as found in a small cache of documents declassified by the United States from those captured during the assassination of Bin Laden in Abbottabad.

> As for the Jihadi forums, it is repulsive to most of the Muslims, or closed to them. It also distorts the face of Qa'ida, due to what you know of bigotry, the sharp tone that characterizes most of the participants in these forums. It is also biased towards (Salafists) and not any Salafist, but the Jihadi Salafist, which is just one trend of the Muslims trends. The Jihadi Salafist is a small trend within a small trend.[24]

What this comment also suggests – in line with the University of Arizona study – is the idea of jihadi forums as closed, inward looking and perceived as extremist even by Al Qaeda ideologues like Adam Gadahn. And yet, for this to be so, it would seem that there must be at least something going on in jihadi forums beyond the mere practicalities of receiving, preparing and disseminating information. Even if it is not represented by extensive discussions, there is clearly an affective dimension to engagement over and above such tasks.

A useful illustration of what is going on behind the scenes is provided by an emergency discussion that took place on Al-Hisba in September 2008. Just previous to this, the reader may recall, the other three 'first tier' jihadi forums (*Al-Ikhlas*, *Al-Buraq* and *Al-Firdaws*) had mysteriously closed down, for reasons which were at the time apparently unknown to the jihadis themselves. While forums had gone down before, given the scale of the loss, and the uncertainty (so it seems) about when and indeed if the forums would ever reappear, the event caused great consternation. Thousands of the members of the now defunct forums attempted to 'emigrate' – to the last forum standing – Al-Hisba. Indeed, such individuals were described as having 'emigrated' or become 'exiled' – using the same word used to describe the prophet Muhammad's *hijra* from persecution in Mecca to set up a new community in Medina. However, al-Hisba was at the time a referral-only forum, which meant that it was inaccessible to these new arrivals. For this reason, a public thread was opened on 22nd September in which members of the forum discussed the important question of whether or not to open registration. The contentiousness of the question suggests that the view expressed by Al-Mihdar and Song of Terror was far from universally held at this time, and in this online place. The thread opened thus:

> It is impossible that we should be unaware of the stopping of our forums, and their delay in returning. And because of that, it behoves us to work with this situation as we find it. Before a time, a long time ago, there was Al-Buraq forum, from among the most active of our forums. And after it was stopped for a long period, many of its active members fled to al-Ikhlas forum, and we said to ourselves: "maybe it is for the best." For Al-Ikhlas was one of our most beloved networks. And it was a trusted site. But now three chief forums have been taken down, and these are Al-Ikhlas, the blue Al-Buraq [as opposed, presumably, to the red one, which serves the Islamic Army in Iraq] and Al-Firdaws. We ask God to reply to them with something good. And at the same time, the time is imminent for the concession of Al-Hisba to the opening of its pages to visitors. What is the solution? Where will members of our networks congregate? And this is no small number. Indeed, the membership of Al-Ikhlas was more than

57,000 members, including the members of Al-Buraq and Al-Firdaws after Ramadan. And the word is that they will be slow in returning. The word is their members despair of their return. And this drives them to search for other forums, possessing of the upstanding spirit of our forums. But perhaps they will flee to forums not known from the lists where it is not known who stands behind them – but perhaps cracked forums – and the list continues – penetrated by national intelligence with a view to placing our brothers, the Ansar, among their company.

What is the solution, in your opinion?[25]

In the lively discussion that followed some members calling for a temporary opening of the forum to registration by new members, others for membership to remain closed, and yet others for some kind of compromise. Ironically, in the light of recent revelations, members expressed fears of penetration not only by 'spies' and 'intelligence', but also by 'malicious individuals' who would cause 'headaches' or 'dissension' – (i.e. *fitna*) in the community. A particular issue here seemed to be regarding the actions of the Islamic State (Al Qaida) in Iraq.

In other words, the protectionist view of the forum taken by Al-Hisba members was essentially the obverse of Al-Mihdar's. For them (or at least for some of them), membership by referral was not about inviting factionalism and contention, but rather about walling out contention, in the service of a tighter community. Indeed, the personal slogan on the profile of the administrator moderator running the discussion (ironic given the subsequent revelation about the true nature of this forum) was as follows: 'the forum is not [made] by the number of its members, but by their closeness [*rabita*]'.

Thus, while jihadi forums may offer neither particularly vibrant debate nor virtual 'safe havens', neither again are they simply reducible to volunteer media projects. For all their limitations, they remain communities which generate a powerful sense of belonging for those who are members of them. Indeed, an interesting aspect of jihadi self-critiques is the way in which they seem at the same time to complain that the forums are devoid of stimulating discussion, but at the same time that they are full of 'distortions, insults and accusations'. Of course, it is plain that neither situation is conducive to an ideal dialogical environment. And indeed when jihadi writers express what it is they aspire to, it is appreciably similar to Western notions of the dialogical ideal. As one such piece puts it:

> The jihadi forums are an inspirational and tragic story at the same time! A journey of self-discover for some, and a journey of solidarity for others and a journey into the fists of others for yet others again!!

The Islamic forums began in all of their forms, ikhwani and sufi and so on, then there came the jihadi forums. And their number did not amount to the figures of one hand. And they were a new thing in the public sphere of the Internet, where a person could feel that he was able to express what was inside him without being observed or judged: he would express his creed and his divine manhaj for which the present order had made an impermissive environment.

And they were an attractive phenomenon, especially because they made it possible for you to set out with a new name and to sail in it with a personality which differed from your real personality!

A new channel, set up from the point of view of freedom of expression of opinion and for setting out thinking and ideology, but there entered afterwards masks and imposters and security intelligence apparatuses . . .[26]

The impression created here is that the reason for jihadi discussion failing to be the civilized, open affair it is can only be attributed to the deliberately disruptive behaviour of intelligence agencies. It would be naïve to rule this possibility out. In the piece just quoted, the author makes plausible (though unsourced) claims about how this works specifically: intelligence agencies divide members into two teams, one with the purpose of befriending forum members and making constructive comments, and another with the purpose of being deliberately disruptive. But such initiatives are certainly not beyond the bounds of possibility. Indeed, as authors such as Evgeny Morozov have chronicled, far more elaborate schemes than these have been attempted by governments as part of a strategy of information war.[27]

And yet the jihadi attitude to penetration by intelligence agencies is curiously Janus-faced. On the one hand, members are repeatedly urged not to assume that people on jihadi forums are what they seem, and to take appropriate precautions. A significant amount of jihadi forum material (e.g. on Shumukh al-Islam's *training camp* section) deals with electronic security. And critiques by Islamist figures outside the jihadi forum community may use the accusation that the forums are essentially intelligence fronts as one weapon in their rhetorical critique. Indeed, in criticizing jihadi forums, Adam Gadahn refers to the work of one such, Dr Muhammad Al-Mis'ari of the Salafist forum *tajdid*. The (as it happens, well founded) criticisms advanced by Al-Mis'ari against the jihadi forum Al-Hisba have been recorded previously by Gabriel Weimann in a paper on online ideological disputes.[28] However, it may be that Gadahn was also thinking of a more broadly focused talk this cleric gave called 'jihadi forums, penetrated to the marrow', which lays the accusation that intelligence agencies have managed not only to crack the forums, but have started to fake their own jihadi content – specifically the output of the imprisoned Shaykh Abu Muhammad al-Maqdisi – via his still-active website, *Tawhid.ws*.

And yet, as Erez, Weimann and Weisburd's study shows quite conclusively, most jihadi forum members are largely relaxed about the issue of penetration by intelligence, to the extent that it is actually quite a rare topic in the overall reckoning of posts to the forums. A likely explanation for this is simply that jihadis are perfectly well aware that their forums are penetrated and have simply got used to it. Indeed, this is precisely the claim made about them in a jihadi document called *A Course in the Art of Recruiting*. Here, the author (who calls himself Abu 'Amru al-Qa'idi) explains the value of the forums thus:

> And ultimately the jihadi forums – and this is what distinguishes them – convey news of the mujahidin, and their releases, and their literature, and this is their breathing space and their place. This is the jihadi forum. You find the agencies of the jihadi organisations and the brothers in the media, who are effectively members of the organisations, and brothers from the Islamic State of Iraq. And you find in them that of someone who used to post with you, they then announce the glad tidings of his martyrdom. And you find in them brothers who have been in the jihad for real previously and then returned, and you see in them workshops, ideas and suggestions for assisting jihad and the mujahidin . . .
>
> The only inconvenience of those forums is that they are – sorry to say it – the target of all the world's intelligence services, and the source for all the planet's researchers. . . . And therefore we urge the brother that he never say anything concerning an operation or not indicate towards that in those forums, or to try to contact someone by private messenger. All of this is dangerous for them. [ie, the two communicating with each other – "them" is given in the dual form] . . . and we urge that the moderators and the members not allow in them the entry of *murji'a*, and the *murjifīn*, and the troublemakers (*muthabatin*), and they must purify their subject threads. They must understand that it is all about *da'wa*, and perhaps a word or a communication from a brother will motivate a new brother onto the path.[29]

A rather fascinating phrase which Al-Qa'idi uses shortly before this section to describe the forums is their *ijwa' jihadi* – the jihadi 'atmosphere' or 'ambience'. The implication being, presumably, that as long as members of intelligence agencies are *presenting* as jihadis, it really doesn't matter whether they are or they aren't.

But of course, this rather postmodern truce does require that intelligence agents behave themselves online, which, as we have seen, is a questionable proposition for jihadis who see them as the root of all dissent.

And yet, as the example of Al-Mihdar above ought to suggest, while the possibility of systematic information war by intelligence agencies should not be discounted, there seems to be good reason for believing that jihadis are capable of creating their own strife unaided. One does not have to look very far into online jihadi communities to find bitter complaints about such routine online misdemeanours as identity theft, sock puppeting or, occasionally, slightly more material forms of corruption, as with this entertaining exchange from *Al-Falluja* forum:

> - Brothers, for years I have tried to register in Al-Hisba forum, and when I am in it, It is of great benefit. But I have not been able to [register]. So I'm asking of the brothers of the place that they accept my request and carry it out, and the benefit is from God. Or if anyone knows a way that will allow me to register – and God bless you, especially in the network which presents juristic rulings on legal affairs which are beneficial, with God's permission, and God bless you all.
>
> - Hahahahahahahahahaha! By God, brother, God almighty, just before a bit, I was talking to someone I didn't know by messenger, and in that conversation he informed me that he got a login to al-Hisba, and he was able to come by it by buying it off one of the companions on the forum. And he showed me the idea, and what my profile would look like if I were to buy a membership, so that he could inform his friend. And the price was three cards for the contact! Hahahahaha! God, I sat down and laughed at that affair. I told him no way – I'll stay with the free forums, thank you very much. With thirty dollars, I'll buy myself a supply of machine gun bullets. By God, it's a strange, funny story.[30]

However, the most serious mechanism for producing disenchantment is likely to be a more fundamental problem: the difficulty jihadis have, *de facto* with tolerating disagreement. An obvious example would be the case highlighted in this complaint from the English forum *Islamic Awakening*:

> - AlSalamu Alaikum
>   Sorry brothers, but these websites are very fanatic I have ever seen, I was a member of al-Eklass, one day I posted a thread asking about innocent people killing in Iraq and Afghanistan because of suicide bombing, they didn't answer me but they kick me out. That means you can not benefit from this kind of web sites because you can not see different point of views, only the administrator point of view and his friends.

But what is of deeper interest is the seeming lack of self-awareness which characterizes even pieces of internal criticism complaining about the very fact that jihadi forums offer insufficient room for the free exchange of opinion. The author of 'Jihadi forums in the balance' objects that:

> ... in the development of the Islamic media and the jihadi media, some of the forums have experienced crises emerging as a result of narrowness of perspective and a superficial image of their work. And this malaise does not differ much from the development of other forums, except that it has an Islamic or jihadi colouring, and those forums did not adopt Islamic or jihadi colouring with respect to the principles of openness and freedom without fetters. But rather, in many of the secular forums and others the freedom of thought and imagination which is enjoined in the principles of shari'a is greater than the freedom of thought and imagination in some of the forums which consider themselves to be Islamic or those that support the jihad and enhance its benefit.

The truth of the matter is that there are some forums which are nothing more than sounding boards for the transmission of the communiques of the mujahidin and the intermingling of communities for the purpose of building themselves by means of specific pictures – not to give the completeness of understanding and imagination and work to the shari'a and the agreement of the requirements of religion and the foundation of Islam. That is to say that some of the managements have not reached the stage of maturity and awareness, and they lack understanding of the nature of shari'a and jihad, and they have not paid attention to the wishes of their companions towards the understanding of Islam as a complete vision [*tassawwur*] leading to work with data and contradictions grounded in reality and far from fanaticism and the partiality of people, and desires, and money and dissipation. And there have returned to us the ills of the old schools of thought in which factionalisation prevailed, and there is manufacture of opinion and decisions preceding the shari'a texts and the *manaahij* of Islam. And there is a reduction of the purity of Islam and the obligation of moving by it and working by its appropriate *manahij*, and the titles which are the adornments of going by these appropriate procedures, and the titles for addressing people and the breakdown of the *manahij* of the order of the heavens which order God almighty wanted there to be to him "His is the creation and the command. Blessed is Allah, lord of the worlds." (Al-A'raf) and the Almighty said: "and who arranges every matter" (Yunis). The words became – those by which God Almighty commanded his prophet Ibrahim, the master of the righteous nation, and by which he ordained the apostle, prayer upon him, and peace on the most perfect face, these words became reduced to individual personalities, and they became the *manhaj*, and they became the *'aqida*, and they became the *tawhid* and the *jihad*, so that the purity of the shari'a and tawhid and jihad and da'wa went away to whims and the learning of the shari'a was misrepresented and the *manahij* of jihad were distorted.[31]

The irony of this plea for greater broad mindedness is that it itself serves merely as the introduction to a savage Zarqawist attack on the scholar Abu Muhammad al-Maqdisi, whom it sees as particularly to blame for this trend.

So far, so human; but if jihadis have a tendency, like all fringe political ideologies, to splinter into minute self important factions, one reason seems to be the extent to which the jihadi forum, as such, is viewed not just as a place to talk, but as a sort of online realization of the utopian community to which jihadis aspire. One indication of this is the sometimes extraordinary amount of detail which goes into the 'terms and conditions' a member is expected to agree to when registering for a forum. In contrast to general injunctions along the lines of 'no flaming', 'no dirty language', 'posts are subject to removal by the administrator', these tend to be dense, multi-page documents, liberally illustrated with scriptural quotations, which regulate in remarkable detail how members ought to comport themselves in cyberspace. Here, for example, are the first three of seventeen rules members are expected to abide by if they wish to remain on the forum *Layuth*:

> First: The member is required to abide by the creed of the People of Sunna and Consensus (with respect to belief, approach and behaviour), and no member whatsoever is allowed to exhibit, in meaning or purpose, any thought or belief which conflicts with the sources of the creed of the People of Sunna and Consensus, and anyone who conflicts in this way will be subject to having his identity frozen without preceding warning.
>
> Second: the conditions for the member's choice of nickname. Members are generally free in choosing a suitable nickname for them. We ask, please, that it be in the Arabic language, and that it not be in two parts, and that it not be longer than fifteen letters, and it is absolutely forbidden for any name to be as follows:
>
> 1 Names of the people of sin and freethinking.
> 2 Sarcastic or satirical names
> 3 Names with a sinful meaning
> 4 Names of contemporary people, except for those who actually have these names
> 5 Names which resemble administrators or moderators in the network

6   Names which resemble names registered previously in the forum (including with the addition of a space or a hyphen, or the two points of the *ta marbuta*, etc., etc.)

7   Names devoid of meaning (letters, or numbers or punctuation marks)

8   Names of the companions, may God be pleased with them, and names of the scholars of the Islamic nation

9   The name of a forum or network for advertising purposes and as publicity for it, except with the permission of the management or the network.

Third: Good opinion must be presented on the part of the writer concerning his brothers, the members and the administrators. And that is by working according to the following texts:

A   The words of the Truth, Praised and Almighty: *(O you who have believed, avoid much [negative] assumption. Indeed, some assumption is sin. And do not spy or backbite each other. Would one of you like to eat the flesh of his brother when dead? You would detest it. And fear Allah; indeed, Allah is Accepting of repentance and Merciful).* (Al-Hujarat: 12)

B   What has been established by Abu Hurayra as upheld: (O you O you and opinion, verily opinion is more false than words) – narrated by the two shaykhs.

C   What al-Muhamali narrated in his *Hopes*, concerning Umar bin al-Khattab, who said: "Do not think that a word that has escaped from my human mouth is Muslim unless you find it to be conveying some goodness."

D   What Al-Bayhaqi narrated in *The People* concerning Muhammad bin Sirin who said: If something reached you about your brother, then try to find an excuse for him. And if you did not find one, then say: he has an excuse.

E   And concerning it also, Ja'far bin Muhammad said: (If there reached you something about your brother, deny it, and try to find a from one to seventy excuses for him. And even if you couldn't find one, then say: perhaps he has an excuse which I don't know).

F   And concerning it also Sa'id bin al-Musib said (it is written about some of my brothers from among the companions of the prophet that you must give your brother's affairs the best possible interpretation you possibly can, and that you must not think evil of a word which comes from a Muslim, but you must find some good in it.

In other words, what jihadis seem to suffer from, online, is a kind of microcosm of the classic tragedy of every totalitarian community. The ideal of a free community established against all the odds and in the face of all its enemies is held onto so passionately that any act that is seen to transgress it can be understood only as treachery. And yet in doing so, the community members lose sight of the fact that the freedom of the community can exist only in the actual freedom of its members.

How far do these contradictions matter? It would seem that the peak of interest in jihadi forums has some time ago past. Aaron Weisburd observes that each time a forum goes offline and resurfaces, some of its membership would seem to have ebbed away. This anecdotal observation would seem to be plausible when one considers that in 2008 the combined membership of just two forums (Al-Ikhlas, admittedly swollen by 'refugees' from Al-Firdaws and Al-Buraq) and Al-Hisbah stood at 67,000. In 2010, for a European Union report, I looked at the membership claimed for the six jihadi forums then extant. Average membership stood at just under 7,000 members, and the aggregated total of every forum combined was only 48,303. And yet, in spite of everything, jihadi forums do persist. At the time of writing, the main forums (*Shumukh al-Islam, Ansar al-Mujahidin, Al-Jihad al-'Alami, Al-Fida', 'Ushaq al-Hur*) are all still active, and new jihadi forums have continued to be established, such as *Sanam al-Islam*. This suggests neither that the form is dead, nor that it has become entirely subsumed as a direct outlet for specific militant groups.

How, then, can we understood the endurance of a form which, as I have argued, seems neither to sustain an obviously vibrant community, nor to play an irreplaceable or even wholly desirable role in the media strategy of fighting jihadi groups? One problematic assumption in assessments of the potential of online communities in general, and of Web forums in particular, would seem to be the idea that the only and proper way to use them is in order to sustain dialogue in the sense of the kind of conversation one might have in the real world. Viewed by this yardstick, the online actions particularly of the more ordinary members of jihadi forums look rather disappointing, with their brief exchanges, use of short, formulaic statements and an extensive tendency to circulate articles by cut and paste rather than to produce original new posts. But this assumes a vision of the potential of the Web forum restricted by the standards of offline interaction. Web forums – as observed at the outset – can also be seen as collective projects, as multi-authored documents not wholly unlike the more specialized form of the 'wiki'. As such, jihadis, in posting, are engaged more in compilation than in dialogue.

As an example of this, we may consider the case of 'Al-Sayf', a relatively small second-tier jihadi forum that ran from 2006 to 2007.[32] During this time, Al-Sayf was dominated by four members, who between them contributed

85 per cent of the posts. Indeed, more than half of all the posts on the forum were contributed by a single member – who was, incidentally, not the administrator. Overwhelmingly, these posts were simply copied and pasted from elsewhere on the Web. In the case of the bulk of posts, this was because they were simply communiqués and reports from jihadist groups obtained from other forums. But most of the rest of the posts were copied and pasted as well, including those on religious or even personal subjects. And yet this did not appear to mean that the forum was merely a dead dump for content. On the contrary, where members did engage with one another on the forum, they appeared to be seriously engaged in the project and to be quite attached to one another. For example, when one member disappeared from the forum for a period, the others expressed concern, and relief when he returned a few months later.

The very fact that Al-Sayf was not, seemingly, a front rank forum with specific organizational connections would seem to rule out the idea that it was simply functioning as a semi-official outlet for mujahidin propaganda. On the contrary, the forum seems to have been a genuine collaborative 'grass roots' project. But what sort of project? Although certain sections of the site were given the titles of 'encyclopedia of preparation' or 'religious library', the forum's posts were too ephemeral, and the contributions to it too individualized for it to function as a semi-permanent archive of material on the model of the major jihadist site *tawhed.ws*. At the same time, however, the lack of structure and recycled nature of the material were neither suggestive of a reading of the site as a serious kind of alternative media project, except in a very loose sense.

Rather, the regular (sometimes very frequent) posting of new online discoveries represented a kind of collaborative reading perhaps more reminiscent of social media such as *Facebook* than of the Web forum or bulletin board as more commonly conceived. And yet neither is this analogy quite adequate. For, unlike a commercial space of this kind, *Al-Sayf* did still represent a bounded online space distinguished, as a whole, by a clear sense of overall purpose.

In other words, it would seem that the cut-and-paste contributions of the members of Al-Sayf need to be seen not as evidence of inadequate commitment, but rather as a form of collective and individual expression in its own right. Al-Sayf was not so much an ongoing conversation, nor quite a multi-authored document, nor simply a crowd-sourced library. Rather, it was a community sustained through the collective consumption and ongoing organization of a particular universe of texts into a certain overall 'jihadi' form. By continuously finding and bringing together different classes of material – the reports of jihadist organizations, information on military 'preparation', Islamic theology and sentimental 'da'wa' stories – the members of Al-Sayf were engaged in an act of continuous creation of the larger-scale discourse of 'the jihadi'.

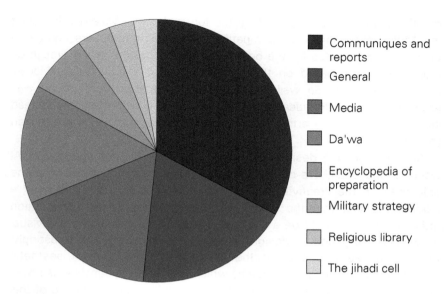

FIGURE 7 *Topics of posts on Al-Sayf forum.*

It is of interest to note here that the idea of a Web forum-based community characterized by an apparently paradoxical combination of intense affect, limited dialogue and a fixation on compilation, collection and comprehensiveness is well accommodated in a typology of online communities set out by Robert Kozinets – an 'ethnographic market researcher' with a strong interest in online audience ethnography, the ethnography of media consumption and particularly in fandom. Kozinets categorizes online communities into four types along two dimensions: the intensity of the relationships formed and the 'consumption or other activity orientation'. Communities characterized by low levels of the latter are primarily concerned with conversational dialogue, whether at a superficial or at a deeper level. Communities with high levels of the latter are either 'geeking' communities (characterized by a strong emphasis on collection and the amassing of information) or 'building' communities, where the members have gone beyond this to use the community (typically, Kozinets thinks, a Web forum) to create and develop things for themselves.

One aspect of jihadi forums which seems to further reflect the relevance of the notion of the 'building community' is the level of value that seems to be accorded, at higher levels of commitment, to the acquisition of media-specific skills such as computing or graphic design. These are of course skills which are in principle sought for the object of assisting the struggle, but there are indications that, in reality, their acquisition may be seen as to all intents and purposes a good in itself within the jihadi milieu. For example, few months ago (at the time of writing) the forum *Ansar al-Mujahidin* launched the '*Ansar al-Mujahidin* Art Competition' – in which members competed to win the most votes for the best jihadi graphic design. In the first three rounds, this was based on the recombination of a group of previously provided elements. So well received was this that a fourth round was launched, in which the idea was developed further, with members instead invited to offer a free artistic interpretation of the music in a pre-chosen jihadi nashid.

Although graphic design is an important skill for the creation of Al Qaeda propaganda, it is difficult not to see in an event of this sort some enjoyment in the creativity and skill of members as a good in itself – indeed, the fact that the event was described as an *art* competition rather than – as would be a more normal term for describing the visual productions of jihadis – 'design' already implies this idea. Interestingly, this would seem to suggest the development of forms of aesthetic distinction rather similar to those by which, according to Jenkins, as noted in Chapter 2, fans construct the 'art world' which is so distinctive of this phenomenon.

To sum up, jihadi forums undoubtedly do function as outlets for the propaganda of militant groups. But whether they can be adequately accounted for in terms of this practical purpose alone is more questionable. Either way, it seems clear that the forums represent collective projects in their own right which generate powerful affective attachments among members – not just to the duty of *jihad*, but to the forum itself, and the practices and sense of presence in jihadi space which it sustains. For some at least, it would seem that participation in the jihadi forum is its own reward – this is, at least, the opinion of the jihadi forum member with whose words I now close.

> First, I would like you to pose some of the questions to yourselves
> Why do you write in the forum?
> Why do you participate with your reply?
> And do you read what is written in the forum?
> Secondly:
> I bring to some of these questions what is seen in reality. Many people participate in the forum for the sake of participating alone. Or they post however many times simply to increase the number of times they have posted. Or there are people who post in order to hear the replies which delight their ears or which please them. And there are among them those

who enter forums and do not even read the thread that has been written and reply to his friend in order to wait for a reply from him. There are places where people want to enter and reply without even looking at the subject. And many of the threads are not read in any case. Or he will know who wrote the post and he will enter flattery for him with a nice reply.

For an activity with as few obvious earthly rewards and as deep an obsession with heavenly ones as online jihadism, the rewards to be found in participation 'for the sake of participating alone' would have to be, we may surmise, significant indeed.

5

Disagreeable disagreements

Jihadi forums, as we have just observed, are not, and arguably do not intend to be, ideal venues for the frank exchange of opinion. They are electronic 'castles', 'towers', 'strongholds', not coffee houses, town halls or street corners. But self-described jihadis are not by any means exclusively restricted to jihadi forums. They are to be found on almost any major Arabic-language forum concerned with current affairs or Islamic matters. In these contexts, it would seem that jihadis necessarily find themselves obliged to engage with those who do not share their world view and therefore to accept the existence of an alternative to it. How do jihadis accomplish this?

On the other hand, Western (and some non-Western) governments have for years now been speaking of 'counternarrative' as a kind of silver bullet against the alleged threat of terrorism and 'violent extremism' on the internet. In contrast to controversial talk of taking down websites or monitoring or filtering content, the idea that it might be possible to simply reason with jihadis (or, rather, with those perceived as potentially 'vulnerable' to jihadism) seems far more civilized, elegant and sophisticated.[1]

Ironically, though, discussions of the need for online counternarrative, much as they aspire to cutting-edge 'information war', often seem to be stuck in a rather antiquated communications model of 'message, channel, recipient',[2] ignoring precisely the dialogical complexities that make the internet what it is.

With regard to 'message', earnest efforts have been made at analysing the so-called 'single narrative' of Al Qaeda[3] with a view to finding weak points in its arguments, apparently oblivious to two rather obvious facts. First, that Al Qaeda's supposedly distinctive 'single narrative' is not really very 'single' at all, but is rather a hotchpotch of Middle Eastern geopolitical 'brinksmanship',[4] Islamic nationalism, millenarian fundamentalism and anti-globalization which is no more ultimately consistent and 'woven together' than Al Qaeda watchers choose to make it. Second, that 'single', identity constituting cultural narratives may not be particularly susceptible to closely reasoned argument.

Having adequately 'crafted' an appropriate 'counternarrative', what is then required (so the standard view seems to run) is to find an appropriate 'channel'. Clearly, governmental and, still more so, non-Muslim voices are unlikely to be 'credible'. Instead, what is needed (so it is argued) is to mobilize and empower the 'grassroots', the 'communities' or, better still, the voices of ex-jihadis in order to undermine the highly virulent ideology which jihadism is taken to represent.[5]

As for the 'recipient', this is typically the least regarded element in the discussion. For all the talk of not reifying or essentializing Islam, discussions of 'counternarrative' seem to be rather uncertain about who the audience is meant to be. Whoever it is – the generic 'mainstream' Muslim, the somehow 'vulnerable' individual[6] or the jihadis themselves,[7] the implicit notion seems to be of a largely passive audience, their minds open to whatever 'meme', 'framing' or other half-understood piece of social science terminology is being thrown their way.

The potential difficulties with 'counternarrative' as thus conceived are easy to enumerate, although actual empirical research on its effectiveness (or, at any rate, its effects) is still very limited. As Lina Khatib observes, in a much-needed evaluation of one relatively long-standing counternarrative initiative, the US State Department's Digital Outreach Team (a small multilingual team dedicated to the thankless task of posting unwanted messages on Arabic, Farsi, Pashtun and Urdu boards and soaking up the torrent of abuse that typically follows), direct attempts at counternarrative on Web forums do not seem very effective at producing rational and constructive exchanges of opinion.[8]

And yet there is, perhaps, a deeper problem with discussions both about 'counternarrative' and the supposed influence of 'violent extremists' (particularly jihadis) which it is necessarily directed at countering. This is the very presumption that some authentic conception of dialogue (whether logical or emotional) is what is really at stake in such encounters. The underlying model remains one in which there are readily identifiable sides, each characterized by an inner, cognitive adherence to a particular set of premises, and in which the dialogical behaviour of each is fundamentally separable both from these issues of identity and of belief. In other words, even in the recognition of a dialogical situation rather than the delivery of an argumentative payload by an appropriate channel into the mind of a passive recipient and even in the recognition of the possible need for more emotional and rhetorical *methods*, the basic notion of a stable messenger, a stable message and a stable recipient remains.

These assumptions would seem to make it impossible to ask in a broader sense what is actually going on when jihadis and those arguing against jihadis encounter one another in Web forums: ought our main concern really to be with how messages are or are not exchanged, and what sort of packaging they come in? Or might the significance of the messages lie somewhere else entirely?

In this chapter, I propose to deal with these questions through a detailed examination of interactions between 'jihadis' and opponents of jihadis in a single Web forum, Muslm.net. I have already made reference to this forum on occasion over the three previous chapters. Muslm.net is a major 'Islamic' Web forum. Hosted in Mecca, this is one of the largest Arabic sites of its kind. As such, it serves as an ideological battlefield both for disputes between conservative Muslims in general (not all of them Arabs) and for conflicts internal to the religious community in Saudi Arabia in particular.

One reason why Muslm.net is a plausible site for such an investigation is that it is explicitly named in jihadi texts as a recommended venue for online 'da'wa'.[9] It is reasonable to assume, therefore, that the site is also a plausible venue for organized attempts at counter-propaganda by states. A likely candidate for this would be the Sakinah project, a nominally independent counter-radicalization initiative mobilizing Saudi scholars and media experts, including in online counter-argumentation against jihadis.[10] Indeed, as will become clear, jihadi members of Muslm.net are convinced – not necessarily entirely incorrectly – that those who consistently critique their positions are employees of one nefarious institution or another, be it the Saudi government, the US Digital Outreach Team, RAND Corporation or similar.

For the purposes with which we are concerned, however, the actual identity of the online opponents of jihadis is irrelevant unless it is openly declared. What matters are how subjective notions about such practices impact on what the relevant parties say and do online. This, in turn, opens out – for the case of those who describe themselves as jihadis – to the more general question of how jihadis conceptualize and talk about other Muslims.

The basic problem here lies with the fact that jihadis, as 'jihadis', must simultaneously account, so it would seem, for three things. First, (obviously) jihadis must present a picture of who they are, and who the others are which shows them as correct and authentic, and other Muslims as misguided and inauthentic. Second, however, they must also negotiate the existence of 'other Muslims' without going so far as to declare them to be apostates. Jihadis – notwithstanding rhetorical attempts to label them otherwise – are conscious and wary of the dangers of being seen as 'takfiris' who are at war with everyone other than themselves. Thirdly (and this issue will be the subject more of the chapter to follow), internet jihadis must account for themselves *as 'jihadis'* – that is, as people who are committed to jihad, but are not currently active mujahidin (i.e. who are not currently practicing jihad in a physical sense).

The solutions which jihadis find to this problem can be seen in the words that they use to describe Muslims who do not adopt their position. A common term, for example, is *qa'idi*, which relates to the classical notion of *qu'ud* or inactivity (literally 'sitting down') in response to the call for jihad.[11] This notion implies that the duty of jihad is one which in reality is generally recognized by all Muslims, and that the fault is not one of incorrect belief, but rather of indolence, moral weakness and excessive attachment to worldly things. This term has a powerful resonance and the rhetorical advantage of framing the issue in exclusively moral terms. And yet it would appear that it is potentially problematic precisely because it denies any distinct subcultural identity to jihadis, thus exposing those jihadis who are not, themselves, presently engaged in violent activity, to the full force of their own uncompromising insistence.

Another term used by jihadis is *inhizami* or, 'defeatist', as illustrated by the following idealized dialogue:

"Mujahid" said to "Defeatist": we are calling for Jihad until victory or martyrdom

The Defeatist said: Your way is rugged and in our path there is delight and happiness

The Jihadi: Fie on the life of injustice and prostration under the pillow.

The Defeatist: This is just poetry and fanatical speech

The Jihadi: With fanaticism and the refusal of injustice unbelief will be banished and polytheism will be left overturned.

The Defeatist: We shall explain by dialogue and reach the truth by politics

The Jihadi: Dialogue with the aggressor is stupidity and a stroke of idiocy

The Defeatist: Perhaps a portion of the infidels are towards us and returning [to their religion], and they have waited passively for the good.

The Jihadi: To trust in the infidels is like leaving your chicken in care of the son of a jackal.

The Defeatist: Politics is the most expedient way, and our path will lead to liberation and the assertion of sovereignty.

The Jihadi: You disobey God and request his victory. By my life, this is a fatuous project. And to work by official channels under the rule of the Jews is unbelief and more.

KNOW THAT JIHAD AND PREPARATION IS AN INDIVIDUAL OBLIGATION ON ALL MUSLIMS AND A SERVANT [of God] WILL BE RESPONSIBLE FOR IT ON THE DAY OF THE RESURRECTION. AND GOD WILL SEE WHICH OF YOUR SOULS IS GOOD WITH PREPARATION AND JIHAD IN THE PATH

OF GOD ALMIGHTY. SO CARRY OUT WHAT IS REQUIRED BY GOD. IT IS INCUMBENT UPON YOU NOT TO BE FOOLED BY THE MULTITUDE OF THE **DOOMED** SO BE HAPPY WITH ADMONITION, AND ITS LIKE.[12]

Here, the stereotyped arguments of the 'defeatist' represent a mixture of both moral weakness and political naïveté. Superficially, the defeatist refuses to take up the duty of jihad not just because it is harsh and difficult but also because he believes that there is a 'more expedient way' – a notion which implies, in turn, that (for him) jihad is a means to an end, rather than an end in itself. Of course, it would seem to be implicit (implicit in the very word 'defeatist') that the defeatist's turning away from jihad, though cloaked in rational argumentation, is in fact caused by the same moral failings as lead to *qu'ud*.

A third alternative commonly used by jihadis, and one which locates the difference between themselves and their opponents much more squarely in terms of differences of *belief*, is the term *murji'ite*. The Murji'ites were an early Muslim grouping who contrasted with another group, the Kharijites, whom jihadis are, in their turn, sometimes pejoratively accused of resembling. Whereas the Kharijites practiced *takfir* extensively, arguing that Muslims who committed major sins were no longer Muslims, Murji'ites went in the opposite direction, insisting that it was not for humans to judge the condition of another's soul, and that such matters should be deferred or postponed (the name of the grouping is derived from *irja'*, postponement) to the Day of Judgement.[13] In reality, of course, as the scholar Joas Wagemakers observes, the deployment of the two terms is primarily rhetorical on both sides. We can get a flavour of this by considering, for example, the following words or the religious scholar such as Hamid al-'Ali, in which he writes that the Murji'ites subscribe to two key errors:

- That regarding the one who is passive with those who predate upon him when the message has come to him and does absolutely nothing in terms of action or self-control, this does not in any way deny for him the name of faith, and it doesn't drive him from the circle of Islam.
- That faith is not to be judged on the basis of an action by an agent, even if what he did was steeped in unbelief and polytheism, unless it is combined with actually denying that it is impermissible then his faith is sound, and he is not to be judged except as dishonest in their opinion.[14]

We can note here that al-'Ali places the issue of whether an individual's unbelief can be read from his actions second – which one might expect to be the central matter at issue regarding the phenomenon of Murji'ism – while giving priority instead to the notion of Murji'ites as passive in the face of aggression, a point of obvious relevance to the specific matter on which jihadis find their more quiescent opponents wanting.

Be this as it may, it would seem clear that the main significance in the use of a specifically sectarian term such as *Murji'ite* is the way that it necessarily seems to express the distinction between the 'people of jihad' and 'people of postponement' not in terms of individual action within a shared framework of belief, but rather in terms of collective action and individual belief. It would seem that belonging to the 'people of jihad' in this formulation entails not immediate action as such, but rather accepting the obligation of jihad, and therefore the need, as a group, to make efforts towards its implementation.

Those (ostensible) Sunni Muslims who seek to oppose the jihadi position have their own problem of terminology in so far as, neologism or no, they are unwilling to concede to the jihadis a name which incorporates the word *jihad*. Terms such as 'extremist' (*mutatarrif*) or 'terrorist' (*irhabi*) are better, but they too have problems. 'Terrorist' is, after all, a label which jihadis have adopted and rehabilitated, arguing that there is nothing wrong with terrorizing the enemies of God. And both terms would seem to smack somewhat of Americanism and partiality. Therefore, the tendency is to describe jihadis narrowly as 'supporters of Al Qaeda'. This designation has two advantages: first, it helps to draw attention to unpopular campaigns such as the mass-casualty suicide bombings of Iraq. Secondly, it helps to isolate the 'jihadis' by suggesting that they are not to be associated with more popular groups such as the Taliban. Indeed, one of the letters released from the haul seized at Bin Laden's Abbottabad compound specifically deals with the problem that the name 'Al Qaeda' does not have any specific resonances with regard to Islam or jihad.

Having quoted an idealized jihadi dialogue above, it is worth noting that Saudi Arabia's Sakinah counternarrative campaign has, in proof of its effectiveness, produced its own example of a model persuasive argument, here quoted from a MEMRI report on the initiative, translated from an original published in the Saudi newspaper, *Al-Watan* in 2004.

> **Al-Sakinah [representative]**: Please don't keep returning to the events in Manhattan and Afghanistan. Let's talk about the central topic of our discussion – the bombings that have taken place in the kingdom.
>
> **Zaman Al-Dajajila**: They are all connected to each other and similar to each other. The issue is clear: There is a camp of belief versus a camp of unbelief.
>
> **Al-Sakinah**: They are all connected and similar?! Was the bombing in Manhattan like the bombing in Riyadh?

Zaman Al-Dajajila: [It was also] like the bombings in Casablanca and Bali. It involves infidels . . . They are arresting and persecuting the sheikhs and jihad fighters because "Mother America" has demanded it.

Al-Sakinah: [These] people have weapons, bombs, and [various] types of explosives. Do you expect the government to applaud them?

Zaman Al-Dajajila: [The weapons] are intended for self-defense. Death is more honorable than the [imprisonment in the] cells of Guantanamo.

Al-Sakinah: Why do they need to protect themselves?

Zaman Al-Dajajila: They are being persecuted.

Al-Sakinah: Why?

Zaman Al-Dajajila: Because they are the group that was promised victory and success, and because they are the ones who remained [loyal to] the truth [Koran]. [Also] because they refused to sell out their religion for a Mercedes and a Lexus.

Al-Sakinah: A group that is promised victory [but] kills Muslims? According to what school of thought do they kill Muslims, or a [foreign] technician or engineer with protected status? Who permitted them to violate the promise of protection? Don't you find it strange that the group that was [recently] captured in Mecca and Al-Madina possessed more weapons [than was required] for self-defense?

Zaman Al-Dajajila: All right. [The weapons] were not for self-defense, but for expelling the polytheists and vanquishing the enemies of Allah. . . . Isn't it true that someone who aids the infidel against a Muslim is an infidel himself? Saudi Arabia helped America and Britain against Iraq.

Al-Sakinah: Saudi Arabia has opposed the war since the beginning of the crisis [in Iraq]. It announced this officially, and proposed many programs to prevent the war. Saudi Arabia condemned the war when it broke out, and announced this officially. Do you have any solid [proof] to contradict this? Or are you talking about statements from [Internet] forums and from communiqués by [Saudi oppositionist Sa'd] Al-Faqih?

Zaman Al-Dajajila: The commander of the American forces said this.

Al-Sakinah: You believe the commander of the American forces, and regard Muslims as liars? What kind of principle is this, and what kind of parallel is this?

Zaman Al-Dajajila: And what about the 'Ar'ar airfield?

Al-Sakinah: . . . . How can you claim that an entire country is infidel [just] because [some] people said that there were [U.S.] forces at the 'Ar'ar airfield? . . . . The Prophet did not declare [even] Hateb [bin Abi Balta'a] to be an infidel, and did not order him killed, even though he conveyed information to the infidels.

Zaman Al-Dajajila [conceding the point]: There is no God but Allah . . .

Al-Sakinah: Then don't remain silent. Speak out, now that the truth is clear to you.

Zaman Al-Dajajila: And what about Osama bin Laden?

Al-Sakinah: Forget Osama bin Laden. That's not the topic of our conversation. Allah isn't asking you about Osama bin Laden or anyone else. The important thing is *takfir* . . .

Al-Sakinah: If you see how the [Saudi] kingdom supports Islam and Muslims all over the world, and how it has influenced the Islamic movement and the Da'wa movement, you would realize that this country is in the crosshairs [of its enemies] . . .

Zaman Al-Dajajila: By Allah, I feel like I'm in a volcano and an earthquake!

Al-Sakinah: It is hard for people to move from one position to another, but for people like you it is easy to follow the path of truth, alongside the *ulema* and the propagators [of Islam] . . .

Zaman Al-Dajajila: Since our first meeting, I have been thinking about the subject. That is, this isn't a decision made overnight. But some of the matters [still] require clarification.

Al-Sakinah: It is obvious from your tone that you are really convinced about many things in this meeting . . .

Zaman Al-Dajajila: I didn't mean any harm. I thought that this was what the religion demanded. You are a blessing [that came to me] from the Lord. Allah knows what is in my heart. Allah will reward you well for your patience and forbearance.[15]

Whether this is really a genuine dialogue or not, it provides a very interesting illustration of what the Sakinah campaign sees (or, at any rate, wishes to present to the Arabic mainstream news media) as an ideal example of what a persuasive exchange with an online jihadi ought to look like.

The first thing to stand out here would seem to be the very narrow ground on which the Sakinah representative chooses to stand, repeatedly refusing to discuss the legitimacy of attacks on Western countries and focusing solely on events in Saudi Arabia (the year in which this exchange is reported to have taken place, 2004, being the height of Al Qaeda in the Arabian Peninsula's campaign in that country). He even seems to imply that the September 11th attacks may have been legitimate and refuses to discuss the status of Osama bin Laden. And yet, when he succeeds in bringing the jihadi over, what we are presented with is not a small, incremental shift in attitude, but a titanic, personally disturbing shift that seems to have identity consequences for the jihadi, who feels himself to be 'in a volcano and an earthquake'.

This is underscored by the fact that the Sakinah representative uses against him the case of Hatib ibn Abi Balta'a. Balta'a was, in the classical tradition, a traitor to the Muslim cause who was nonetheless forgiven by the prophet Muhammad, setting therefore, according to some jurists, a precedent according to which even those Muslims who openly collaborate with non-Muslim enemies cannot be said to have left the fold of the religion.[16] The case is a source of major contention between jihadi and non-jihadi scholars and is therefore indexical of a movement in absolute terms from the jihadi to the quietist camp. The shift 'Zaman al-Dajajila' is making is not just a small change of degree in his position; he is making an absolute change in the status of his allegiance to the Saudi government.

Another point of interest is the way in which the Sakinah representative manoeuvres his opponent into final submission with a move which is, strictly speaking, a logical fallacy. In accusing 'Zaman al-Dajajila' of preferring to trust the infidel Americans over the Muslim Saudi government, he is, of course, begging the question, in so far as the Muslim status of the Saudi government is precisely the point that would seem to be at issue here. The jihadi in this exchange would be perfectly entitled, within the logic of his own position, to announce that, given the choice between the word of an original infidel who openly admits his status and that of a deceitful apostate who lays claim to Islam while serving as the infidels' lackey, he would prefer the former. But in so far as this exchange is to be understood as representing an ideal of effectiveness, we surely must presume that what is being presented here is not so much unwittingly shoddy argumentation, as successful rhetorical footwork. Much as it might be logically correct for the jihadi to prefer the word of Americans to that of Saudis, the contrast, presented thus starkly would seem to imply that such as response would be a violation of an underlying emotional structure which, for this individual at least, would be a step too far.

In the idealized jihadi dialogue, by contrast, the issue is widened as much as possible, such that the conversation is presented not as a fine-grained choice between specific political alternatives, but rather as an absolute one about whether or not to do *jihad*.

The style and even the genre of this dialogue is, of course, different. In contrast to the Sakinah piece, which claims to be a genuine exchange, here we have what is clearly a stylized piece of rhetorical literature. And yet, oddly, the exchange is in some ways less one sided and more properly dialogical than is the Sakinah example. Indeed, if we parse out the actual arguments deployed, it would seem that the 'defeatist' actually has the best of it. Basically, the proposition being advanced by 'the jihadi' here is 'we ought to do jihad'. The 'defeatist' seeks to counter this proposition by advancing two arguments: (1) jihad is a high-cost activity and (2) there is an alternative: politics. The jihadi counters this with two claims. The first of these is to express contempt for the defeatist's actuarial concern for the material costs and benefits of jihad. The defeatist (appropriately) observes that this is mere 'rhetoric', since the jihadi has not actually advanced an argument as such. The jihadi responds, interestingly, by observing that the rhetorical statement is itself a performative argument, since it is intended to illustrate the necessary spirit that will be required to achieve victory. The jihadi's second argument is that negotiation with the enemy is pointless, because the enemy are unbelievers. The defeatist's response, quite appropriately, is to demand that his opponent provide some evidence for this claim, which is not provided. Since the matter is not settled as to whether the enemy can or cannot be negotiated with, the defeatist goes on to observe that the political approach is more expedient. After all, politics, like jihad, may or may not deliver the desired result. But politics will definitely not incur the same costs. At this point, the jihadi effectively abandons the parameters of the argument, by simply announcing that God demands jihad regardless of issues of apparent expediency. And yet, as we may note, this is plainly not the intended effect of the piece.

What is going on can usefully be analysed in terms of more general theories of argumentation. According to Van Eemeren and Grootendorst, the leading exponents of the 'pragma-dialectical' school of argumentation theory, an argument is to be understood as 'a verbal, social and rational activity aimed at convincing a reasonable critic of the acceptability of a standpoint by putting forward a constellation of propositions justifying of refuting the proposition expressed in the standpoint'.[17] A protagonist and an antagonist meet, have a 'meta-discussion' about the basic ground rules for the argument and then proceed. If their argument is to proceed coherently, then it will have to correspond, more or less, to an idealized, normative model for argumentative discussion, aimed at avoiding fallacious reasoning or unfair tactics. In reality, of course, arguments are not purely conducted by cold logic. Proponents and opponents will naturally wish to present their arguments in the most powerful way possible – meaning that arguments also incorporate *rhetoric*. However, if, in seeking to improve rhetorical effect, the discussants overstep the normative boundaries of what constitutes a reasonable discussion, according to Van Eemeren, they 'derail' the procedure.[18] Therefore, real-life arguments are subject to extensive attempts a 'strategic manoeuvring', in which the discussants try to maximize rhetorical effect without overstepping the requirements of reason. Another point about real-life argumentative encounters is that the 'meta-discussion' which sets the ground rules is likely to be implicit: arguments usually fall into culturally pre-established 'argumentative activity types' such as courtroom adjudication or parliamentary debate in which the rules are already understood by participants.[19]

We may observe, however, that the two pieces we have just considered seem to challenge Van Eemeren's faith in the assumption that, as he puts it: 'in practice, argumentative moves that are considered rhetorically strong by a critical audience will almost certainly be in accordance with the dialectical norms applying to the discussion stage concerned'.[20] In each, we are presented with an *idealized* vision – offered up to a wider audience – of just how an argument ought to be conducted. And in each case, the argument advanced by the victorious protagonist is either fallacious or utterly devoid all but the barest semblance of an attempt at logic. In other words, it would seem that both cases presume an audience which will be so affected by the rhetoric that the weakness of the reasoning will be rendered either irrelevant or actually attractive.

How can this make sense? An interesting question which make move us towards an answer is how far it is possible to observe, for the case with which we are concerned, the existence of a distinctive 'argumentative activity type' governing the dialogue, and what the particular characteristics and ground rules of this might be. According to Marcin Lewinski, the structural nature of Web forums is such that they can be seen as affording a kind of 'argument activity type' unto themselves. Of course, Web forums do not resemble courtrooms in the sense that there are specific rules and expectations (but explicit and implicit) governing arguments, or even ensuring that arguments take place. This is because, so he insists, built-in features about the way Web forums operate (such as pseudonymity) help to ensure that the preference for agreement which psychologists have observed in face-to-face interactions in everyday life is suppressed. Additionally, the mainly textual nature of Web forum discussions, and the openness of the format tends, all things being equal, to ensure a heterogeneity of opinion and the making plain of grounds for disagreement in claims advanced. And yet, as observed in the previous chapter, specifically jihadi forums have complex and mixed feelings about open debate which, when it occurs, tends to be interpreted as intolerable and disturbing strife. Thus, it would seem that the dialogical possibilities of Web forums are also 'cultured' by the assumptions of participants about what kinds of dialogue and plurality are permissible within the Islamic framework to which they lay claim.

If we turn to the two examples here, we may note a striking commonality between them. In each case the argument is ultimately won (or claimed to be won) on the basis of an assertion of identity which, in itself, would seem to function not so much as an actual argument in favour or against the proposition being debated, but rather as a 'meta-argument' (i.e. an antagonistic meta-discussion) which is itself constitutive of the possible grounds for debate.

Thus, the Sakinah representative basically insists on the Islamic identity of the Saudi regime (cunningly contrasting it with the identity of the US Army) and dares his opponent to claim otherwise. Once established, it seems ineluctably to follow from this point that jihadi violence in Saudi Arabia must be wrong. But were this point not accepted, it is questionable what grounds there would be for discussion, since the Sakinah representative, by defending the Saudi state would, otherwise, be an apologist for apostasy.

By contrast, 'the jihadi' insists on the shared Islamic identity of both himself and his interlocutor, the duty of jihad that seems to follow from this and the corresponding wrongness of any attempt to reach out to the unbeliever. What is interesting, however, is that whereas, in the Sakinah dialogue, the jihadi is clearly presented as lying outside the circle of correct Islam, meaning that the dialogue must end with a moment of crisis, in the jihadi-defeatist dialogue there is no such sectarian issue. We have a discussion between two Muslims – one better than the other, no doubt – but although the defeatist may be flouting God's command, there is no sense that he is on that account outside the sphere of Islamic dialogue. And yet, in making his case, the jihadi depends, as we have seen, almost entirely on rhetorical arguments premised on the idea that the question of whether to implement jihad is not really up for debate. Thus, the 'dialogue' has an ultimately paradoxical quality. On the one hand, the 'defeatist' must be invited as a partner into the dialogical sphere of Islam. On the other hand, any actual dialogue that then occurs must be treated as tantamount to sin.

On the basis of this anatomization of idealized dialogical exchanges, as imagined respectively by internet jihadis and by critics of jihadis, it would seem that there are fundamental obstacles lying in the way of any genuine argumentative exchange between the two sides: the rhetoric of each depends, so it would seem, on constructing a vision of the opponent which must necessarily be alien to the actual reality. Moreover, there is an important ambiguity as to which issues are up for debate, and which – as religious fundamentals without which no debate can proceed – are not.

Thus it is, perhaps, unsurprising to observe that attempts by jihadis' opponents to engage them in argument tend to be rather limited in their ability to generate genuine dialogue.[21] Typically, it seems that jihadis, when challenged, refuse to accept their opponents as appropriate interlocutors or find other ways to evade extended discussion.

Indeed, it would seem that there is quite a specific range of ways in which jihadis, in particular, avoid entering into arguments with those dedicated to critiquing them is worth setting out.

One thing which jihadis commonly do – not, as I have suggested, necessarily without justification – is to label their detractors as government agents employed to sow dissent. Of course, it is very difficult for jihadis to prove this conclusively. However, their character assassinations may also involve attacks on specifically observable aspects of a person's *online* persona. For instance, a common accusation thrown about is that a person's command of grammatical Arabic is too weak to qualify them as an authentic Arab or Muslim. Or again, on at least one occasion on Muslim.net, a member who started a thread entitled 'Letter from a Muslim mother to Al-Qaeda' was told to take her sensitive feelings back to the 'mother and child' section of the forum.[22] While reflecting highly conservative social norms the rejoinder is also, obviously, sarcastic.

Another approach is to read the treachery of the critics simply from the fact that they dare to criticize the mujahidin in the first place. As one wrote:

> I become paralysed with pain every time I see my brother from the companions of the jihadi media entering polemics and replies fomented by that dirty clique. O brothers, believe me the lack of reply to their posts and leaving them to the removal of pages sends out a stronger message and is more destructive than the reply which you will write, if it is a reply which will make you think that you have put it in its place, but rather the opposite - these people are practicing a good exercise and they have sold life for a number of dirhams.

Another common tactic is to contest the epistemological basis of the evidence brought against them, by denying the reliability of all information deriving from mainstream media. Indeed, so important is the question of what media sources are morally worthy of being believed in that, we may note, even the Sakinah exchange just discussed employs basically the same method.

A third type of online response used by jihadis against critics is to act as if both sides know full well that the jihadi position is correct, and that attempts to argue the converse are simply cover for underlying cowardice and laziness. Based on this formulation, the jihadi approach is to act as if what is needed is not intellectual persuasion, but rather moral 'goading' or 'incitement', through exhortations such as the following:

> . . . . Sit down and ask yourself: Have you denied yourself like them? Have you brought victory to this religion like them? Have you left your family and your children like them? Have you left your house and your possessions

and your self like them? Have you given yourself every day to God like them? Do you have dust on your feet from the path of God like them? Have you been wounded a wound in the path of God like them? Have you, some days, slept in fear like them? What is greater than the decadence of the present time!!![23]

Or again . . .

. . . .When you lie down on your mattress and put your head on your pillow, call on your unconscious mind to ask your conscious mind: is what we do right, or falsehood? Is what we do of benefit to our friends or our enemies? Is the encounter in which we reap worth what we put into it? What we do – how long will it last? O conscious mind, after my sleep, will I wake to this? And if I don't wake – then where is my money for me? Naturally these questions and their replies concern you personally. As for me, I have no need of them.[24]

And yet, as has already been observed, while tactics of this sort are, at one level, ways of evading dialogue, they can also be seen as meta-arguments which, by the very fact of delegitimizing their opponents, have the effect of rendering their arguments null and void. For in each of these three tactics what is really being achieved is the deconstruction of the space for permissible dialogue. In the first, there is a challenge to the critics' eligibility to enter into Islamic debate, in the second, there is a challenge to the admissibility of the information they wish to present. In the third, opponents' attempts at advancing arguments are reclassified as speech acts of a different sort.

Because of the meta-argumentative nature of these claims, however, they are susceptible to counter-arguments at the same level. For, however much jihadis may refuse to admit their opponents arguments as legitimate arguments in specific instances, they are bound to accept the ideal of reasoned Islamic dialogue under appropriate conditions. For this reason, it would seem that a particularly problematic issue with which jihadis may be confronted is the question of under what circumstances they *would* be prepared to debate, as we can see from an analysis of the following discussion.

Al-Mustanir 10

Between the lovers and the haters of Al Qaida, can we find any solution? Please post.

Brothers, I would like to start by saying thanks to God and prayer and peace on His messenger. God's blessing on every brother which is a true monotheist who writes in this forum to support Islam and the Muslims, and not for hatred of a person or the desires of a troublesome personality, but rather as a Muslim who loves Islam and what is good for them in what God almighty ordained and who longs for the establishment of an Islamic state which I ask God the Most High, the Omnipotent that my eye should witness it and that I should live under its shadow before I pass away.

I am a believer, brothers, that the beginning of the path to an Islamic state is unity in a single rank, governance and mind in which there are no disputes about law. Honoured brothers, I have read a number of threads posted on this forum and seen new splits between brothers, which is a small window when we live it in reality. By way of an actual example, [there are] the haters of Al Qaeda and those who insult it and cast aspersions on the mujahidin and consider some of their works to be corrupt, and in no respect resembling Islam, and accuse it of distortion of the shari'a; and [on] the opposite side, [those] who see in Al Qaeda the sole ray of hope which fights in the path of God, and thus, at the hands of the mujahidin, shall establish a caliphal state.

O brothers, all of us know that the first plan of the enemy is to initiate difference as an obstacle, so till when shall we take this food and sleep biting each other? Thus I implore you by God to pull together under the same words without insult and cursing and accusation, and if we all think together with one loud voice to find solutions, then this will become real, and I ask you that you remember that the first caliph of the Muslims, our Lord Abu Bakr used to say on the day of his oath of allegiance:

"O people: I have been placed over you, and I am not the best of you. If I do well, then help me. And if I do badly, then resist me."

We must learn and get to know what the mistakes are in every party and try to find solutions to bring together the different parties among the brothers. What is your opinion, brothers in monotheism?

From the outset, it should be clear that Al-Mustanir's neutrality here is purely a rhetorical tactic from the fact that he chooses to frame the issue in terms of a debate between lovers and haters of Al Qaeda – the preferred phraseology of the jihadis' critics, thereby closing off the preferred jihadi frame of support or opposition to 'jihad'. And yet, by presenting the issue in terms of strife within the Muslim community which Muslims have a duty to resolve through honest dialogue, he would seem, nonetheless to be laying down a challenge that is difficult to resist – as evidenced by the response that follows.

Abu Wa'ad

Honoured brother al-Mustanir. . . . God bless you. As for those who hate Al Qaeda, they are of various species, and among them are those who are influenced by the preaching of vanity which is promoted by those media that have gone astray, or believe the words of the shaykhs of the Sultan, trusting in them, and so we ask God to grant them clear sightedness to see the truth.

And among them are the employees of the intelligence agencies and the organisations which can't attack jihad directly, so they find thus a way to mount an attack on Al Qaeda. And [in] the most recent episode, after the field opened for registration in this forum, and when it had a good reputation, we saw these attacks from many identities, and exchange of roles in coordinated and persistent attacks, and it was of the form of calling it [i.e. jihad] by names other than its names, and the Islamic State of Iraq al-Qaida, and the al-Shabab movement in Somalia al-Qaida to make the identities easier for their attacks, and the Taliban of Afghanistan al-Qaida. Talk, my brother, and no discomfort, but the important things were that they distorted and insulted and elevated vanity from its low place. And if it is necessary to offer advice to the people who love jihad and the mujahidin, comradeship is comradeship. Do not surrender yourselves, and do not exchange for the people of the words of snakes with their like, and make your intention the defence of the *manhaj*, not about personalities, except for those who are not able to reply because of having died or being engaged in jihad with a post in this forum or another, and God preserve you.

Al-Mustanir 10
Brother Abu Wa'ad, God's blessing on you, and thanks for your point of view. What, in your opinion, is the solution to agreement between the two sides, so that we can oblige that everyone on the two sides has shari'a proof for the lack of faithfulness of the other party, and perhaps there are points of truth on both sides. What is your view? God's blessing on you, and on every monotheist who loves the good of the Ummah of Islam.

At this point in the discussion, Abu Wa'ad has attempted to retake control of the framing of the discussion by proposing that those who claim to oppose 'Al Qaeda' are actually opponents of jihad more generally. This point – which in and of itself relates to a purely discursive matter – is of course allied to his claim that the opponents of Al Qaeda are, in reality, imposters and therefore unworthy debating partners. But Al-Mustanir is able to block this attempt at re-framing by calling for 'shari'a proof of the lack of faithfulness of the other party'. By doing this he is achieving two things: first, he is pointing out that even if the jihadis are not prepared to reconcile with the opponents of Al Qaeda, it is, at least, reasonable to expect them to engage in a meta-discussion about why they will not. Secondly, by calling for things to be resolved according to the proper standards of 'shari'a proof', Al-Mustanir is calling for a form of dialogue the legitimacy of which the jihadis cannot well refuse.

Ibn al-Badiya 8

Brother, you live in a fantasy. Al Qaida will go extinct, God willing, as the dinosaurs went extinct before. The manhaj of Al Qaeda, which is to kill everyone opposed to it, and everyone who gets close to who is opposed to it is a false manhaj. They blow up bombs in public places and kill thousands of Muslims in markets and places of worship and general offices, train stations, etc. Mullah Umar says regarding these organisations:

"And obey your responsibility in the matters of jihad, and take care to preserve the general and specific restraints in carrying out your operations, and concentrate in martyrdom operations on the enemy occupiers and their operations, and targeting them is the important thing. And avoid killing and injuring ordinary people; this is the responsibility of every believer, for general targeting of people for killing and injuring is a matter which is not permitted by shari'a in any situation, and it is a matter which our upright religion does not love by any means."

Where is al-Qaeda with regard to what Mullah Umar is talking about? Have they not sworn allegiance to him? Hypocrisy, hypocrisy, hypocrisy!

Al-Mustanir 10

Brother, ibn Al-Badiya, thanks for your point of view. Brother, there is no one who is immune from mistakes, and there is room for improvement. Why not present their jihad as it would be according to the shari'ah of God and His sunnah? Have you any suggestions to improve the matters, rather than vilification?

Abu Wa'ad

Esteemed brother, whoever has shari'a proof then let him come now and present his proof and distance himself from insults and slander, for there will not be found among the lovers of Al Qaeda anyone whose heart is not open for debate and arriving at the truth by what God has said, and what the Messenger of God has said (prayer and peace of God upon him), but what we read is sweeping claims of accusation and fabrication and implication of the mujahidin based on the presentation of personalities, and if it issued from the scholars or the students of knowledge, but in fact there are those who cast aspersions then flee and do not enter debate, and among them the one who enters our thread to derail it from its path, and among them the one who communicates lies and builds upon them. Jihad is a long path and some people will fall from its path, and some people will be overturned by its difficulties. And just as there are companions of good, so are there of evil. Thank God, who has made me one of the companions of jihad and the mujahidin in every place, and if he has made me inactive on account of weakness in following them, I ask God that He place me in their ranks by means of my pen, and I seek refuge in God that he preserve me from the idolators and their followers, and those who work in searching for the mistakes of the mujahidin. . . . God bless you, and forgive me and you and the monotheist Muslims.

Ibn al-Badiya 8's rather crass intervention here provides a perfect foil for Al-Mustanir by taking advantage of Abu Wa'ad's hesitancy about the possibility of a legitimate debate against the opponents of Al Qaeda to strike a blow for free against the jihadis' position – in effect entering willy-nilly into precisely the debate about the worthiness of Al Qaeda which Abu Wa'ad refuses to have.

What we may note here is that a dynamic has now been set up between two debates: a meta-discussion about whether an argument between the 'lovers' and 'haters' of Al Qaeda is actually possible, and an actual discussion about the merits and demerits of Al Qaeda. This puts Abu Wa'ad in a rather complex position. Simply engaging in the latter argument means, in effect, conceding the former. Abu Wa'ad's answer accordingly struggles to negotiate these points. He continues to reject a debate, citing the unacceptable practices of the opponents of Al Qaeda, but recognizes that a debate, appropriately constituted, is theoretically possible. At the same time, however, he concedes that 'jihad is a long path, and some will fall from its path' – which comes close to responding to Ibn al-Badiya's criticisms without quite overstepping the boundary of actually mounting a defence of Al Qaeda and the jihadis. Finally, he also stresses his claim to be 'in their ranks by means of my pen'. In doing so, he is stressing the worthiness not of jihad and of Al Qaeda, but specifically of those who seek to defend it online.

Al-Mustanir 10
God bless you brother Abu Wa'ad for this fine initiative and may he enter you into heaven, O beloved. Let us work together in singleness of ranks towards the good of our Ummah in what pleases God, and God is our help.

Abu Sa'ad al-Bahili
Our solution is to use the shari'a and intellect, rather than thin air.

Al-Mustanir 10
What do you mean, brother? I wish you would clarify your reply more. Thank you for your view.

Abu Wa'ad

Brother al-Mustanir, thanks to God, prayer for you and God's blessing on you. The Abu Sa'ad al-Bahili is a clear example. He gave us a single line and he makes it blink like the writing of prayers.[25] If the jihad and its people don't know the shari'a in every step they take – by God's grace – then who does?

Al-Mustanir 10

Brother Abu Wa'ad, I hope that you are well and in good health

Do you think, brother, concerning what you wrote that some of the people of jihad do not know about the Shari'ah and therefore the mistakes perhaps are present which they make on some occasions to a summit which is agreeable to those who contest them, and how, by God, is it possible to be aware of these so that they don't taint the jihad, or are they simply commanded and doing what is ordered of them? Please give us useful advice.

Abu Wa'ad

Esteemed brother, it is not possible rationally to deny that in every work of jihad and da'wa there will be mistakes. But the mistakes do no justify in the slightest the weak spirited perspective that draws the sword against the mujahidin.

And these writings of the esteemed brothers who love the jihad and the mujahidin, will one of them deny the presence of mistakes? Will one of them refuse to offer advice for the good? And you have a diversity of those who hunt for mistakes of the mujahidin, and if they don't find them, they search in the archive and if they don't happen on anything, they aren't shy of inventing what is found past the door of slander and insult of the mujahidin . . .

Brother al-Mustanir, are these sorts people to debate with?

Do you think that the one who debates with them benefits at all?

Brother, the mercy of God on your parents, do require of Hanzala[26] that he should cultivate grapes?

Ibn al-Badiya

When these mistaken people show kindness and they recognize their mistakes, then I will believe them. As long as a respected shaykh carries out a jihadi operation and kills children by accident and women and does not issue or present any excuse to Muslims in general or compensation to the family of the killed.

Yes, they do not deny and they do not acknowledge and the ambitious youth sees them as an example of jihad.

Al-Mustanir 10
Brother ibn al-Badiya. Thank you for your point of view again. This is what Mullah Umar advises and confirms and what the mujahidin in Afghanistan practice.

Ibn al-Badiya
God bless you. Some people are unable to climb down from their obsolete ideas.

Abu Faris 1
Brother Abu Wa'ad . . . you are the first brother who has this idea . . . there is not one of the mujahidin or of the ansar of the mujahidin in this forum who decides or recognizes some of the mistakes of Al Qaeda in this forum or others than it, and there is not one of them who likes to take advice. For example, have you seen one person decide that Bin Laden's going beyond [his pact with] Mullah Umar in his blow against the Americans caused the suffering of the Afghani people, and was a mistake, and that the ill was much greater than the benefit, or acknowledge of any of the mistakes which happened in the bombings?

Now that Abu Wa'ad has staked his right to continue to refuse debate with the opponents of Al Qaeda, he finds his position undermined by the apparently fortuitous intervention of another jihadi member of the forum, Abu Sa'ad al-Bahili. Since the online jihadis' claim to superior virtue is behaviourally indicated by their observable commitment to the proper standards of Islamic dialogical propriety, the violation by even one jihadi member of this norm is sufficient to refute the meta-argument against engagement with their opponents. And moreover, it is interesting to note, defeat in this meta-argument seems automatically to lead to defeat in other argument as well. For the very acknowledgement that the online jihadis might be mistaken in their belief that they are necessarily superior to their antagonists in the integrity with which they apply Islamic epistemological standards naturally invites the possibility of the falsity of the entire project they support.

Having examined the underlying 'meta-argument' which seems, in general, to stand in the way of meaningful argumentative exchanges between jihadis and their critics, it is interesting to consider an exception to this case by examining an online exchange which did, so it seems, fulfil the criteria of a genuine argument, with a recognizable standpoint being defended against specific criticism.[27]

The encounter which I propose to examine dates from December 2009, and concerns the release of French and Spanish hostages by Al Qaeda in the Islamic Maghreb. The interest in the example lies primarily in the fact that, unlike most attempts at online critique of jihadism, which seemingly characterized by insults, evasions and obvious irrelevancy, the argumentative content of this exchange is – or at least appears to be – of a relatively high quality, with genuine attempts being made by both sides to advance arguments for or against the propositions of the other.

The exchange opens with the following post:

The release of hostages for seven million dollars: jihad or business?

The Organisation of Al Qaeda in the Islamic Maghreb received seven million dollars from the Spanish government for the release from captivity of three detainees held by them according to news sources from the Spanish newspaper *El Mundo*, and the French newspaper *Le Monde*.

I am not an *'alim* or a shaykh, but this deal seems to go beyond the teachings of Islamic shari'a for the following reasons:

- Those captured were *civilians* and not combatants
- These civilians were *abducted* after they had entered a Muslim country and taken a security contract (*'ahd al-aman*) from the Muslims
- The reason for abducting them was to obtain money.

It can be observed from the outset that the arguments being advanced here are, if one assumes a thoroughly jihadi world view, not particularly troubling. First, the source of the news is the Western media. Second, the distinction between 'civilians' (the poster specifically uses the Arabic word *madaniyin*, which is a direct gloss on the English), a category which jihadi scholars do not accept as relevant to Islamic law. Third, jihadis do not accept the right of the apostate regimes of Islamic countries to issue contracts. And indeed, arguments along these lines formed the main lines of the jihadi response. Specifically, it was suggested that the Spanish tourists in question were not tourists at all, but actually spies; that Spain, through its involvement in the occupation of Muslim lands (including Ceuta and Melilla), is at war with Islam; that there are clear precedents in the life of the prophet for violent operations purely aimed at acquiring resources, as demonstrated by his raiding of caravans, as well as for the ransoming of hostages (as happened after the Battle of Badr).

What is more significant here, however, is the extent to which this post did in fact attract focused attempts at rebuttal, as opposed to personal insults and generalized calls for support for the mujahidin (although comments of this nature did appear on this thread as well). By reconstructing the thread according to Van Eemeran and Grootendorst's four 'transformations' of *deletion* (the removal of those elements irrelevant to the reasoned resolution of a difference of opinion), *addition* (inserting into the argument moves or claims that are otherwise only implicit), *substitution* (replacing ambiguous formulations with clear ones) and, finally, *permutation* (rearranging items within the text in order to clarify the role they play in the resolution of the argument), it is perfectly possible to discern an argumentative structure to this exchange with successive layers or argument, counter-argument, counter-counter argument and so on.

The real question which the existence of such a structured argument seems to raise is why this particular post seems to have been so successful in attracting this level of engagement. And as we can infer from the explicit meta-argument of the exchange above, this question can be recast in terms of an underlying meta-argument which must, implicitly, have been won as a result of the speech act performed by the initiator of the thread and the way in which it was subsequently conducted.

A plausible reconstruction of this may perhaps be seen in the specificity of the criticism being advanced (a specificity which seems to resemble that seen in the model Sakinah exchange as well). By asking the question 'jihad or business', the poster is implicitly framing his intervention in terms of support for jihad. Nor is he even directly expressing opposition to Al Qaeda in the Islamic Maghreb as such: he is simply querying a specific incident. In other words, notwithstanding his obviously un-jihadi arguments, his textual performance presents a level of reasonableness to which at least some jihadis apparently feel the need to offer a concrete response. Finally, however rationally defensible the actions of Al Qaeda in the Islamic Maghreb may be from a jihadi point of view, the claim that they were prepared to release the hostages does not present them, so it seems, in a very noble light. Indeed, this is plainly the most problematic part of the jihadi case here, since it is difficult to square with the idea of an absolute lack of engagement with the forces of unbelief. As such, it is the source of the largest contradiction in the jihadi case in the argument that follows. In claiming that the people captured are in fact spies, or that they are belligerents because of their nationality, it is difficult to explain why they would be ransomed rather than killed. If they are innocent, then it is difficult to explain why they would be captured in the first place. The point is not logically irresolvable, but the jihadi points raised with regard to it are somewhat confused and ambiguous.

Thus, underlying any rational structure to arguments involving jihadis, it would seem that what is really at issue are more emotional considerations and, specifically, the issue of moral worthiness. Moreover, the moral worthiness

DISAGREEABLE DISAGREEMENTS

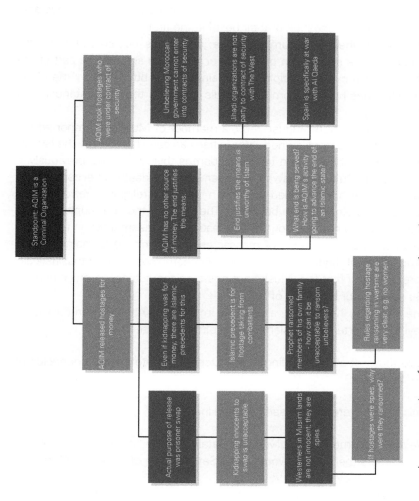

FIGURE 8 A diagrammatic representation of an argumentative exchange between supporters and opponents of Al Qaeda on the forum Muslm.net. Arguments in support of the standpoint are in light grey, arguments against it in dark grey.

with which jihadis are concerned is of two kinds: the moral worthiness of the mujahidin, their virtues of courage, self-denial and simple piety; and the moral worthiness of the jihadis, as reflected in their Muslim virtues of politeness, restraint, rationality and diligence as well as loyalty and devotion. Where the first is called into question, jihadis must answer the insult. But in doing so, they are continually at risk of violating their second claim to worthiness and, with it, the sound foundation of their belief in the first.

As a result, the equilibrium of online jihadism is not so much directly threatened by the suggestion of ignoble or forbidden acts on the part of the mujahidin, which can in principle be explained away, but rather by the effect such insinuations have in prompting jihadis to violate their own standards of *online* decency.

For example, on 13th August 2009, a member of Muslm.net reported the good news that two Yazidi-owned cafes in Iraq had been bombed by the Islamic State of Iraq. The background to the incident is this: two years previously, a Kurdish Iraqi girl, Du'a Khalil Aswad, had been stoned to death by her community, in the belief that she intended to convert from her religion – Yazidism – to Sunni Islam and elope with a boyfriend. The video of the community stoning was captured on a mobile phone and spread across the internet. In response, terrorists carried out a series of massacres and enormous bombings which killed hundreds of random Yazidis.[28] The 2009 bombings were enthusiastically interpreted in the first few Muslm.net posts on the subject as much-needed further revenge for the killing of Du'a.

One member, however, was not so impressed. As Abu Harun, a logo-displaying supporter of the Islamic State of Iraq objected:

> Have they not stopped killing them? Does the State intend a genocide of the Yazidi sect?

His misgivings were met by sarcasm and insults:

> We are concerned with servants of Satan. You say "does the State intend to massacre them!!!" Is worshipping Satan a form of unbelief? What, Abu Harun – are they breaking your heart?
>
> You fawning dog. (*kalb al-ibtah*). Are Yazidis of innocent blood!!! Are Yazidis innocent of killing Du'a, or were they complicit? Did you see the video you dog, and how many participated in the killing of Du'a? Fawning dog, I ask God that he kill you like the Yazidis before, dogs, dogs dogs. You are dogs and in the state of a dog, O dogs, Islam will come back. Your councils and your fronts are nothing but dogs and fawners, the banner will not be raised for you. People of the world (*dunya*), may God kill you.[29]

But these responses in themselves exposed the purity of the jihadis' intent: as one contributor to the thread commented:

> This is the condition of many of those who call for jihad on the Internet. They use support for the mujahidin as an attempt to claim manliness and false strength. Abu Harun is trying to discuss the matter and its religious basis and there is no reply to him.

The tension between simultaneously upholding the virtue of the mujahidin and the ethics of Islamic dialogue is something which online jihadis seem to be very much aware of. Indeed, the disillusionment resulting from excessive and un-Islamic online behaviour appears to be a significant reason for bringing an end to a course of online jihadi engagement. As one jihadi posted, bidding farewell to his forum colleagues and announcing his retirement:

> I've written a lot on this forum, and I wasn't being mindful of God in much of it. I got wrapped up in pursuing my own interest. And I spoke in God's name without knowledge in many posts. And that is very wrong. I even swore, and I ask God to forgive me for that. My entry into this forum hardens my heart because of the frequency of arguments and the way that some opponents go beyond the bounds of what is permitted. And it leads me to seek victory over myself.

Most of this jihadi's colleagues expressed their dismay at this decision, expressing their affection for him, insisting on the important work he was doing in 'defending the honour of the mujahidin' and his importance to the online community. 'If you go', said one 'then who's left?' Another was more accepting, however, quoting an interesting hadith 'if the water is lower than two feet, it carries dirt, and one cannot become purified from it'.[30] Throughout the exchange, the central point at issue seemed the same, however: the business of actually doing jihadi disputation on the internet is often a rough, dirty affair, and one inconsistent with the standards to which jihadis aspire.

What does all this tell us? Reflecting on the actual nature of jihadis' arguments with antagonists may not, after all, tell us very much about the potential value of 'counternarrative' initiatives. One conclusion we may draw is that counter-argument is likely – rightly or wrongly, for better or worse – to achieve its effects by disruption rather than by persuasion as such. Another point is that concerns with credibility may, accordingly, be less relevant on the internet than they are seen to be. In the end, people in Web forums are what their words make them – and this is reflected not just in the content of what they say, but in how they behave.

But in studying these encounters, there is a good deal to learn about how the affective relationships that underlie online jihadism are structured. Internet jihadis, so it would seem, have a foot in two different worlds. On the one hand, their emotional relationship with the idealized object of the mujahidin gives their online activities a gravitas which enables them to escape from the pettiness and mundanity of mere chat. To quote one jihadi, responding irately to what he saw as the disruptive influence of critics on the forum:

> Leave us and go far away from us, for there is no benefit from you except polemics. As for us, we turn our gaze far away, there where our gaze rejoices in the sight of the Al Aqsa mosque. There in Baghdad where we raise our banner – "there is no God but God. . . . Muhammad is the prophet of God" . . . there in the mountains of Khurasan . . . in the Caucasus and Bashkortostan and Tatarstan, there, rather than towards the Kremlin and the White House.[31]

And yet jihadis cannot, after all, turn their backs on the world of the forum, since it is after all their own action of 'joining the ranks with the pen' which creates the very connection to the nobler, truer world of the mujahidin on which their own subcultural capital depends. They are trapped, therefore, in a paradox. The regulative rules which normally govern rational dialogue are hopelessly tangled up with the constitutive rules about what dialogue means *for a jihadi*. To understand how this paradox is negotiated is to understand how being a jihadi works.

6

Being a jihadi on the internet

Do you believe the RAND report?

They say that Al Qaeda has hundreds of websites if it doesn't have thousands on the Web. And some of these are for the purpose of distributing its releases, and their manhaj, and you would not realize from their words that Al Qaeda has failed to get its ideology across to most people, or to the American Muslim youth and they rely on the figures and the statistics about the number of imprisoned jihadis in America from September 11th to the year 2010, and these statistics do not concern me, and they are not important to me what they derive from them, but it did cause me to realize one thing, and that is that their words are about the psychology of the cyber or virtual-mujahid which is me and you and us alone in the incitement of others to carry out jihadi operations on the ground without exposing myself or yourself personally to danger. And we have been fooled by the words of Al Qaeda when it said that the media makes up 90% of the jihadi project, and we take this claim as a valid excuse for inactivity and for holding back from the field of jihad or implementing jihadi operations on the ground. And therefore the virtual mujahid becomes content with posting his opinions of the forum and how much he loves the jihad, and the creed of tawhid, or that he says that he intends to do this or that. Or he publishes terrorist threats to this or that. And he thinks on this account that he has discharged his duty of jihad in so far as Al Qaeda says that the inner intention to is sufficient to action and that because you intend to do something you get reward even if you haven't done anything how not, and you are doing jihad on the net! So according to what Rand says, you are preparing simply by disseminating your intention to do an operation on the network, and that this discharges your obligation of jihad in real life.

And when you have grown up a bit and matured in the world of the Net or with the world of the Net, you cannot distinguish between the virtual world and the real world. And you jihad on the net is a jihad on the ground, and you jihad on the net without a weapon resembles to some extent the personal satisfaction which you experience when you play a video game.

And he says that you are not committed in the way that an individual is committed in a jihadi group, because you are a member in a virtual group whose members cannot influence you as would be the case it you were a member of a real group, where the mujahid influences by goading into advancing into terrorist operations. Therefore you do not feel that you are committed, according to what he says, if you are in a network where each person does something or doesn't, and the existence of the personalities who work with them is virtual and you do not feel the same shame which one would feel if he were a member of a real group which is working on the ground.

And just as cyberjihad is easy to get into, so too is it easy to get out of!!! Didn't you understand? I shall explain to you. It means that you become a mujahid behind your computer and when you log out of the jihadi forum no one knows who you are, and no one is requiring of you. . . . Anything![1]

In the first chapter, I remarked on Anthony Giddens' ideas about the crucial importance of reflexivity to the experience of modernity. Increasingly, fewer and fewer people are so cut off from the wider world as not to be forced to confront other societies and therefore to reflect on the meaning and value of their own. This is strikingly true of online jihadi culture. Internet jihadis watch their watchers every bit as keenly as their watchers watch them.[2] The extended quotation above is a summary and paraphrase of Brian Jenkins' Congressional testimony on Al Qaeda's use of the internet which was posted on the jihadi forums *Shumukh al-Islam* and *Ansar al-Mujahidin* in 2012.[3] But the questions it poses are in any case hardly alien to the militant jihadi project.

For example, Omar Hammami (better known as Abu Mansur al-Amriki), an American-Syrian fighter with Al-Shabab Al-Mujahidin in Somalia, and also, so he says, an internet jihadi who has participated under the name 'Abu-Jihad', makes a rather similar point in his memoir, recently published at the time of writing.

> I suppose it's like they say: "Every little bit counts," but I prefer to impress upon people the fact that it's less about the tangible victory and more about a victory over our own Nafs. Jihaad is an opportunity to obtain Jannah, and that is priceless; whether we manage to see victory in our times or not. The victory has been promised, and it will come, but the real question is: Will you be a part of bringing it about? What good will it do on the Day of Judgment to say you witnessed a victory you had no part in?[4]

These two quotations serve to illustrate the fundamentally paradoxical status of the internet jihadi. Indeed, the paradox is encapsulated in the very fact that one might describe one's self as a 'jihadi' at all. On the one hand, internet jihadis recognize the fundamental obligation of taking part in the militant activities they see as *jihad fi sabil Allah*. On the other hand, they are, as they recognize, not actually taking part in them directly themselves.

And yet, as I have argued thus far, not only do internet jihadis continue to exist, but their existence, and the types of activity they engage in, are not fully to be accounted for in terms of the rational and strategic needs of militant groups. There is, in a sense, an independent online 'jihadi culture' which offers practices, forms of satisfaction, forms of value which, though theoretically premised on the goal of supporting the mujahidin, are not wholly reducible to it.

How do jihadis resolve this contradiction?

One clue as to how this works is already present in the (second hand) words of Jenkins above. To some extent, the ideological space in which internet jihadis build their culture is actually an artefact of the very 'strategic' discourses which are in principle supposed to provide wholly rational and instrumental accounts of such action. By giving their blessing to online activism to any degree at all, jihadi ideologues and leaders necessarily offer a set of rationalizations which are available to *any* internet jihadi.

Ironically, this fact arises from the very ideological mechanisms by which contemporary global jihadism seeks to solve the theological problem of calling Muslims to militant jihad in a world where there is no official political authority willing or (in the jihadis' view) legitimately entitled to do so. The solution to this, for pioneering jihadi thinkers like Sayyid Qutb and Abd al-Salam Faraj, and the one inherited by contemporary jihadist thinkers, is to declare what is, in effect, a global state of emergency.[5] Such accounts draw on the tradition that states that if a Muslim country is invaded and no authority exists within to organize resistance, then a state of 'defensive jihad' comes into being. Under such circumstances, participation in violent jihad is now an individual obligation required of every Muslim in the affected area, who must, on pain of mortal sin, join the resistance even in the absence of an effective coordinating authority. If these Muslims are, in turn, unable or unwilling to repel the invader, the obligation falls on those nearest to them and so on until it falls on every Muslim in the world. In a situation where every Islamic government has fallen, and therefore in which the whole world has, in effect, been taken over by hostile forces, this situation doubly pertains.

In principle, this rationale for action seems to be utterly unambiguous. And yet its very lack of ambiguity would appear to imply ambiguities of its own once it is applied to the indeterminate situations that occur at the individual level in real life. Either one is doing fighting, or one isn't. If one is, then well and good. If one isn't, then one has fallen into serious sin at the very least, commensurate with abandoning any other core Islamic commitment, such as prayer or fasting in Ramadan. At worst, one's very status as a Muslim may be in doubt.

But in reality, the question of whether one is fighting or not is not quite so clearcut. Indeed, two quite different and contrasting views seem to be possible on the matter. Viewed from one perspective, it can be argued that even if there is an individual obligation on a Muslim to join the fight, there is a collective obligation on Muslims to fight as effectively and strategically as possible.[6] This means that resources must be husbanded and deployed to best effect. Rather than send unequipped, untrained recruits to carry out uncoordinated attacks on any target within range, it might be better to establish training facilities, to amass financial resources, to develop better weapons and so on. But if this is the case, then what is the status of those who are engaged in such activities? If what they are doing is not jihad, then they are still failing in their obligation and – from an individual perspective – it is difficult to see what incentive they have to carry on. But if, on the other hand, what they are doing is jihad, then what is to stop them from carrying on indefinitely with such activities, always being on the point of action but never quite reaching it? In order to avoid such a situation, it would seem to be necessary to constitute some kind of overarching authority to decide which particular actions do and which don't count as meaningful contributions to the overall programme of military action. But the need to act in the perceived absence of such authority is precisely the problem which global jihadist ideology is supposed to be premised on solving!

Alternatively, one might argue that overarching strategic considerations are irrelevant. Muslims (from the jihadist point of view) simply have a ritual and spiritual obligation to do whatever actions count as jihad, and the actual *effect* of such jihad is a matter to be left in the hands of God. But if this formulation is accurate, it potentially creates a problem of a similar order. For if there is any basis (as it happens there is an extensive basis, which jihadis fully recognize) for saying that actions other than direct, bodily violence might count as jihad, then these actions are just as legitimately jihad as is anything else. Moreover, even if jihad were restricted to doing direct, personal physical violence without any regard to the consequence or effectiveness of the action, this would create an equally thorny problem. After all, the political diagnosis upon which the whole global jihadist argument rests necessarily assumes an enemy which has occupied Muslim lands by a wide range of methods, including complex military operations, financial muscle, political subterfuge and ideological influence. Therefore, if this latter interpretation of participation in jihad is upheld, it seems tantamount to saying that if, for example, diplomats persuade a government not to implement the *shari'a* in its entirety (whatever implementing the *shari'a* actually means), then the only appropriate response for Muslims is to randomly shoot, stab or bludgeon any legitimately targetable unbeliever they can immediately lay their hands on, and that any other response is sinful indolence.

A final possible alternative would be to accept that there is somehow a condition in between doing and not doing jihad – a kind of limbo in which jihad is being 'assisted' or 'prepared'. And yet it is *a priori* rather unclear what the meaning or status of such a condition might be.

It is interesting to observe that contemporary jihadi ideologues – and indeed, so it would seem – even those elements the classical Islamic tradition on militant jihad upon which jihadist ideologues draw – seem to countenance all of these possibilities without being able (or perhaps willing) to find any clear resolution among them. And nowhere is this clearer than in the things which jihadist ideologues have to say about engagement in jihadi activity by means of the internet.

Indeed, jihadi writing about the status of those whose contribution to the jihadi project is itself to use verbal means to encourage others to accept and take up the duty of action seems inherently to be productive of some of the very ambiguities which, in order to be successful, jihadism must confront.

On the one hand, as long as literature aiming at *tahrid* (incitement) to jihad is addressed to those who are not engaged in jihad, and may not be fully convinced of its obligatory nature, it is apparently important – as it would be for any similar attempt to draw people into 'risky activism' – to offer lower-cost forms of action which might serve as a way of building commitment. Thus, in much circulated works such as *39 Ways to Serve Jihad and the Mujahidin*[7] and Anwar al-'Awlaqi's adapted English version, *44 Ways to Serve Jihad*,[8] 'electronic jihad' is offered (along with activities such as boycotts, writing letters to prisoners, fund-raising and media activism, prayer and simply making up one's mind to do jihad) as what seem to be plausibly readable as a series of escalating commitments, culminating eventually in physical participation in violence.[9] And yet, in offering these activities as ways of 'serving' jihad, there is a constant ambiguity as to whether these actions also amount to a form of jihad in their own right.[10]

This ambiguity is especially in evidence with regard to the entry in *39 Ways* on 'electronic jihad'. In contrast to most other activities suggested in the text, this is specifically described as a form of jihad. Electronic jihad is in turn divided into 'the forums project', which entails visiting non-jihadi Web forums (a list of potentially promising Islamic forums is supplied) in order to distribute propaganda and try to persuade people to join the cause and 'the true electronic jihad', which consists of computer hacking in order to take down and deface enemy websites.

The notion of hacking as 'true' electronic jihad, in particular, seems to pose some interesting questions relevant to electronic jihad in the wider sense. Is it more truly 'electronic', or more truly 'jihad'? If the latter, is this because it can be interpreted as a form of violence in its own right? The text does not resolve this issue either way, but intriguingly it does describe jihad by hacking as 'the language of power'. Normally, in Arabic, this means much the same as it does in English. Bashar al-Asad once said, for example, that Israel understands only the 'language of power'.[11] But in this context it seems almost as if the phrase might be intended to mean power or force exercised literally by the use of language (or computer code). If so, it would seem that hacking occupies a grey area in jihadi thought between actual fighting and support for fighting.

The question of whether 'electronic jihad', whether by hacking or by other online activities, is genuinely or only metaphorically a form of direct participation in jihad is one which 'Isa al-'Awshan, the author of *39 Ways*, seems unwilling to fully resolve. Indeed, jihadist ideologues seem to have adopted at least two distinct stances on the issue – sometimes simultaneously in one and the same text.

Perhaps the most typical line of argument regarding online jihadism is to consider it directly equivalent to other forms of support activity regarded as jihad in the classical literature. Indeed, following classical precedent jihadist authorities such as Abu Muhammad al-Maqdisi define jihad as 'fighting to make the word of God supreme, and assisting in this'[12] – a definition which inherently assumes that certain support activities (without certainty as to precisely which ones) can indeed be considered to constitute actual participation in jihad. The canonical sources provide ample evidence for the idea that materially contributing to fighting – jihad with one's money or possessions (*jihad bi-l-mal*) – is a legitimate way of doing jihad.[13] Indeed, the jihadist writer Anwar al-'Awlaqi said on one occasion that contributing one's money rather than one's body to the fight may actually be preferable (his argument is that native Afghans, Chechens or Somalis are better at fighting than weak and pampered Westerners, but that Westerners are more readily able to obtain cash by staying at home).[14]

The sources are seemingly less convincing, however, with regard to a third way of doing jihad – jihad with the tongue (*jihad bi-l-lisan*). There is no direct reference to this form of jihad in the Qur'an, and its status as a form of jihad is rather based on indirect statement in the Qur'an and the hadith literature.[15] Moreover, there is a tradition of scholarship which suggests that this form of action is reserved specifically for Islamic scholars, with its Qur'anic justification in the verse:

> . . . it is not for the believers to go forth all together [*kaffatan*]. For there should separate from every division of them a group to obtain understanding in the religion and warn their people. (Al-Tawba: 122).[16]

Another precedent for the importance of verbal action is provided by the Qur'anic injunction:

> So fight, O Muhammad, in the cause of Allah; you are not held responsible except for yourself, and encourage [*harrid*], the believers [to join you] (Al-Nisa': 84).

This stipulation is enriched by further traditions relating to the virtues of incitement (*tahrid*) to violence. But these seem to relate to the actions of those (such as women) who are not expected to participate in action themselves,[17] and it is therefore not clear that it serves as a satisfactory precedent for actions by able-bodied men of fighting age. Moreover, it is also at the very least unclear as to whether it is itself a form of jihad or not.

An alternative interpretation of online action suggests that it is to be understood not simply as support for action, but as a form – albeit an auxiliary form – of jihad in its own right. An example of this claim is to be found in the complex and often contradictory work of 'Abd al-Rahman Salum al-Rawashdi, a thinker apparently associated with the Islamic Army of Iraq (which may explain why his work has been generally neglected in the literature). In introducing his book on media jihad in the Iraq war, al-Rawashdi draws on the familiar traditions about jihad of the tongue, *tahrid* and the need for the believers to not all go forth *kaffatan*, so that a portion can remain to study and warn.

However (and indeed within the space of the same few pages, both of his own work, and of the Qur'an) Al-Rawashdi also makes what seems to be the opposite point. Citing the verse of the *Surat al-Tawba* (28) where it says:

> And fight against the disbelievers collectively [*kaffatan*] as they fight against you collectively.

Al-Rawashdi takes this *kaffatan* to mean something like 'comprehensively' and understands it as calling for a 'total war'.[18] Since, so he argues, contemporary 'full spectrum warfare' as practiced by the United States calls includes the use of the media as part of an information war strategy, corresponding activities by media mujahidin can similarly be viewed as a type of combat.

A somewhat similar perspective is offered by the highly influential jihadi thinker Abu Mus'ab al-Suri in his best-known work, *The Global Islamic Resistance Call*. In contrast to Al-Rawashdi, Al-Suri's general approach in outlining the role of media activity in his overall programme for global jihad is to try to insulate the theological justifications for action from the strategic plan for advancing it through recourse to a 'technical' *istilahi* vocabulary within which it is possible to set out ideas without the need to provide an exact theological foundation for each one (though Al-Suri does offer the same general theological arguments as other jihadist thinkers do).[19] For Al-Suri, jihadi actions in general fall into what he (in common with other 'strategic thinkers' such as Abu Bakr Naji) calls the 'jihadi current', which is a subset of a wider modern phenomenon he calls the 'Islamic Awakening' (presumably distinct from the primarily Saudi non-violent movement of the same name).[20] Members of the 'jihadi current' are more or less equivalent to 'jihadis' (*jihadiyun*).[21] Because the Islamic Awakening is a distinctly contemporary movement within Islam, activism within it is not a prerequisite for membership of the Islamic religion. Thus, Al-Suri is not – as jihadists are often accused of being – a radical *takfiri* who thinks that all Muslims outside a specific sectarian movement are in fact apostates or unbelievers.[22] Likewise, while jihad may be an obligation in general terms, the 'jihadi current' does not possess an automatic monopoly on legitimacy. It is ahead of other groupings in its implementation of the *jihad* part of the programme of awakening in Islam, but not necessarily ahead in other important areas such as correcting the manners and practices of

Muslim (*adab*), or calling others to Islam.²³ It is better understood as having what Marxists would call a 'correct analysis' of the global situation than as having a radically different set of principles or beliefs. Nor does the jihadi current even have a monopoly on *jihad*. Just as one may be a Muslim without being an activist in the Islamic Awakening, so too one may be a mujahid (e.g. if one is an ordinary Afghan or Iraqi who has taken up arms to defend his country), without being as such a member of the jihadi current. Nor indeed does membership of the jihadi current automatically entail practicing jihad.

For Al-Suri, then, *Global Islamic Resistance*, 'individual terrorism' and 'organisation without an organisation' all exist under the overall heading of jihad, but certainly don't exhaust the possibilities of that term. And while jihad may indeed be a religious an obligation upon Muslims, the actual practice of resistance in the present day is better seen in pragmatic terms. Within this overall programme, media work is as essential as to any other kind of 'terrorism' (which is what Al-Suri specifically calls for), but only as part of a properly worked-out overall strategy. Al-Suri stresses the point that if his strategy is to work, many will have to participate in acts of self-organized violence. On the other hand, only relatively few are actually needed to do media work.²⁴ And yet, practically speaking, these media cells, once set up, are actively discouraged from becoming involved in violence, on the grounds that their media duties will have compromised their security from an operational point of view.²⁵

The obvious problem with all this is that, while Al-Suri's programme may make sense from an overall strategic point of view, it seems to clash directly with the pathways to action which are set out in documents such as *39 Ways*, and *A Graded Course in the Art of Recruitment*, where media activism is apparently seen as an incremental step towards deeper engagement. Taken together, the injunction to get involved in media work as an initial step towards developing one's intention towards jihad and the injunction not to seek to take part in violent action if one is already active as part of a 'media cell' seem to provide a very convenient set of justifications for those active online not to engage further. Of course, Al-Suri is aware of this and therefore includes a specific statement to the effect that involvement in media work is no excuse for not engaging in violent action – on the contrary, the media activist has less excuse than anyone else because he is fully aware of the ideological need for action.²⁶ But this general injunction ignores the necessarily time-bound nature of individual activism – the media jihadi may well (must in fact) recognize the obligation to join the violence one day. But that day cannot be today, as long as the media jihad activity continues.

And yet, as we saw at the outset of this chapter, internet jihadis are hardly unaware of these contradictions, and it is hard to credit that they can be *consciously* satisfied by such casuistry in rationalizing why they have not engaged in actual violence. How then do they justify their actions? A neat place to start this enquiry is with the actual responses to the jihadi summary of Jenkins with which I opened the chapter. Here is a selection from *Ansar al-Mujahidin*.

. . . We are just communicating the voices of the mujahidin to people by any means available, but the intention increases the act, with God's permission. And we must give everyone his due, and overcome the intelligence. Abu Dujana was a writer in the jihadi forums. Likewise the martyr as we reckon by Abu Al "Ayna" al-Muhajir was a writer likewise, when it is not possible for them they will write, but if jihad becomes possible then they will leave the computers to the inactive and emigrate and this is what history has recorded.

. . . By God while you have made the skies happy, let you make God happy with you or let you come down to us in virtual jihad at the stage of intellectual and cultural preparation and sterile knowledge to our hidden enemy who is behind some disputes. Then we shall set out to military jihad, even if it were on the jihadi boards, or in the police state, we shall fight the Ziono-Crusaders if they local operations, and we shall see whose promise is true and to be believed. And God is great, and glory be to God, may God bless you beloved brother.

. . . The Randi[27] ought, before he starts talking about his masters the mujahidin and their supporters to look at himself as follows: Who carries out the crime of killing a person in America is still sentenced to execution in many of the states. And if what he were lucky and he did what he did in a state that does not implement the judgement of execution, then he would be in prison for life: that is the one choice before him. Here we ask what is the judgement upon someone who has killed 1,400,000 people in Iraq alone and that is before the manipulation and the monitoring and the fabrication and the lies to whitewash what he has done? And what is the judgement on these crimes, and the expiation for them? I think that there is not one Randist who is able to open his mouth

. . . Sit in Macdonald's and poison yourself with a hamburger – that's the best thing for you. Even where you are in the land of unbelievers, America, they say "don't talk about things you don't understand." Enjoy your time, for the hour is coming when those who do jihad with words will mobilise, by God, may he be struck with death, this idiot who produces and analyzes and writes. As if the jihadi networks did not have a role in the war and did not represent a great matter in their hearts, Rand would not have been founded in the first place. Therefore shut up you imbecile and keep to your hamburger.

Even within these four short paragraphs, we can see a substantial variety of different attitudes, values and positions, all of which, as it happens, seem to be of larger significance in explaining the meaningfulness of internet jihadism to those who partake in it. Among the most important themes here seem to be:

Jihad – one day, when God wills it

Internet jihadis often seem to express a kind of fatalism about the possibility of involvement in violence. They present themselves as – for whatever reason – currently unable to partake in jihad, and apparently unable to advance the moment at which they the opportunity to arise by means of their own action. They must simply wait until the moment when, God willing, the road to jihad is opened for them. A very interesting motif of this is the figure of Abu Dujana al-Khurasani. Abu Dujana al-Khurasani was the adopted name of a Jordanian medical doctor. Humam Khalil al-Balawi. Al-Balawi was, under this name, a well-known online jihadi until his arrest, in 2007, by Jordanian authorities, to whom he volunteered his services in infiltrating Al Qaeda as a double agent. In 2009, al-Khurasani turned out in fact to be a triple agent when, at a meeting where he had promised to offer information on the whereabouts of then Al Qaeda no 2 Ayman al-Zawahiri, he killed himself and eight intelligence officers in a suicide attack.[28] Abu Dujana al-Khurasani is, quite understandably, a source of enormous admiration for internet jihadis. And yet, as an emblem of the possibility of making the transition from online activism to real-life violence, he would seem to be rather an ambiguous one. For instance, in admiring discussions of Abu Dujana among jihadi members of the Islamic forum Muslm. net, much emphasis was placed on his supposedly extraordinary talents – so far, in fact, that one member specifically cautioned others against believing that they had what it took to follow in his footsteps:

> . . . The hero-brother, the martyr, we reckon him, and God is his reckoner to have been from among the most intelligent men, and his level in the standardised test was 97%. And this indicates something. It indicates that his intelligence was outstanding.
>
> Before I get into this subject, my warning to the brothers is that I would like to pose some questions far from the outcome.
>
> 1   Were the Jordanian Intelligence and the CIA involved in planting the brother Abu Dujana, may God accept him, among the mujahidin?
>
> 2   Were the mujahidin involved in planting the brother, may God accept him, in the American and Jordanian intelligence apparatuses?

3 Was the brother from the beginning trying to be in control of himself and who then was in charge of coordinating with the mujahidin and who then set up the operation?

If it was the first of these, then the brother rendered unsuccessful these intelligence services in changing the opinion of a person and this also compels us to pay attention.

We have warned those who participate in forums in general, and in jihadi forums in particular, because it is the goal of these intelligence services thus.

We advise the brothers not to trust anyone of the participants on the forums and at the same time not to doubt them, because it is easy to get involved.

As for if it was the second, this indicates towards the extension of the information which arrives to the mujahidin to the domain of the security and intelligence services, and this is would mean to them that the war has begun to take on a trend of a security dimension with the penetration of the strongest intelligence apparatus in the region and the world, and we ask God to bring them victory in this war of intelligence.

If it was the third, and this is the most likely in my opinion, and God knows the truth, this is the aim of my post, and I would like to warn the brothers about it.

Concerning the operation of penetration, it is imperative that the brother who wishes to penetrate a security apparatus not try to penetrate it on his own.

The brother Abu Dujana, of whom we do not know the details of his penetration into the security apparatus, possessed a stock of information which we cannot estimate and intelligence which he was able to employ in order to arrive in the position he arrived in, in addition to logistical and information support from the Taliban of Pakistan, and the coming together of these two facilities helped bring about success in the cracking of great security which was gained by an unparalleled media blackout. Therefore we advise the brothers not to improvise work like this unless it was coordinated with specialists from the mujahidin and their organisations.[29]

Indeed, if we consider the trajectory of al-Balawi's engagement, based as it was on his clever exploitation of a chance event he turned to his advantage, it would seem to offer a nearly perfect example of the idea that the pathway to jihad is regulated by the whims of fate, and that God will or won't open it as he sees fit. The other figure mentioned here – Abu 'Ayna' al-Muhajir, a Saudi by the real name of Muhammad al-Tubayhi who died in Iraq and is much admired for the engaging smile with which he read out his martyrdom statement – represents in some ways a not dissimilar model. Both of these stories are interestingly double edged in their ultimate morals: on the one hand, they underline the ultimate responsibility for involvement in violence. On the other, they stress that the spatiotemporal distance and contingency associated with that moment.

Role in the war

The second rationale we see here is more instrumental in character, and attempts to reassert the idea that online jihadism is indeed an integral part of the overall progress of global jihad. What is interesting though is that how this is supposed to be so is expressed rather vaguely. On the one hand, we see hints at the idea of online activity as its own virtual war. Indeed, one of the arguments made within this set of responses is that it is obvious that internet jihadism is important, because if it were not, the United States would not be so concerned about it. And yet, ultimately, this is obviously not a wholly satisfactory response. Jihadism on the internet must cause someone to succeed in doing some kind of real-life violence *eventually*. Thus, we see a larger-scale version of the fatalistic idea above: the fruit of internet jihadi activity will not just be eventual physical engagement by individuals, but an entire mass uprising at some point in the future. Indeed, oddly, this is actually an inverted version of the same argument used by Omar Hammami *against* internet jihadism: the mass revolution is coming at some point in the future. When it comes, the choice between joining the mujahidin and joining the forces of unbelief will be unavoidable. But the real merit will accrue to those who already mobilized beforehand. The point is that this is a double-edged claim: if the apocalyptic battle (and it seems that there is a real ambiguity here as to whether it is a man-made revolution, or the coming of Judgement Day that is intended here)[30] is on its way, then the case can be made for behind-the-scenes work laying the groundwork for the eventual Muslim victory just as much as the case for heroic battlefield participation here and now.

Reaffirmations of moral binaries

The third response here may seem to be missing the point. After all, the fact that Brian Jenkins is a wicked infidel and the slave of brutal American imperialism has nothing, in principle, to do with the validity of his arguments. Nor is he engaged in a moral critique of internet jihadis such that accusations of hypocrisy represent a coherent response. But this is to take such outpourings too literally. Words of this sort are not to be understood simply as arguments, but rather as speech acts – specifically, speech acts of a particular kind: declarations of support for the mujahidin. We see something similar in the fourth response as well. Here, the stereotype of the McDonald's burger franchise as a symbol of Americanism, capitalism, ill health, greed and indolence is used to highlight the inherent nobility of the mujahidin against the inherent baseness of their opponents. Jihadis need not even bother to engage with the opinions of such people, because they partake in the glory of their heroes. Indeed, as we shall see, a common riposte to attempts to critique the merit of *online* jihadist is to reiterate the perceived physical virtues of the mujahidin. There, irony of such cases – as we see also here – is that the very mobilization of arguments about the moral worthlessness of the enemy and the moral worthiness of the jihad actually serves as an argument for the legitimacy of (behaviourally non-violent) internet jihadism.

What we see here, in short, are the three major types of subjectively conceived practice by which – in principle – internet jihadis justify their existence, namely, preparation, propaganda and solidarity or, to give them the Arabic words by which jihadis refer to them, *i'dad*, *da'wa* and *nusra*.

It will be noted that the first two of these are, at least in principle, justifiable as instrumental contributions to the jihadist project. And yet it would be a mistake to see 'preparation' solely in terms of material preparation for violence. Jihadist writing places consistent emphasis on the need for spiritual, moral and sentimental preparation aimed at developing correct intention. Without this, even if one actually fights and dies in jihad, it is worse than if one had not done so.[31] And indeed even jihadist texts which are typically presented as almost wholly technical and practical like the 'training camp' magazine *Mu'askir al-Battar* contain substantial amounts of more reflective and sentimentally oriented content.

Moreover, even in the collective amassing of narrowly technical content, it is possible to discern consumption practices that seem to be more oriented towards enjoyment of the material itself, and the idea of 'preparation' than a pragmatic focus on supporting engagement. Among the two thousand-odd posts on the 'military camp' section of *Shumukh al-Islam*, a now more or less unique throwback to the time when recipes for bombs and the like were one of the major forms of content on jihadi forums,[32] it is difficult to separate 'serious' attempts at amassing information of value to would-be fighters or bomb makers from the aggregation of information on war weapons more typical of the military-history enthusiast. Here we find, for example, endless posts detailing the specifications of particular bits of American military hardware, on rocket firing schedules which (presumably) any group with actual access to rockets is hardly in need of, on ingenious ways of making one's self a rather ramshackle machine gun from materials lying one might have around the house (usually copied from videos put up by American enthusiasts). A member posts an English document which he thinks offers a hundred ways of making dynamite (in fact, it is a list of tips for writing a 'dynamite resume'); another wonders whether the 9/11 operation could be repeated by a group of wholly unarmed mujahidin, assuming that they had studied Kung Fu to a sufficiently advanced level. In a hypothetical discussion about (initially) how a dirty bomb might be constructed, a member joins in with a post 'for information only!!!!' providing some basic facts about some nerve gases. 'We are not talking here about one of those crime stories made famous by Agatha Christie!' he feels the need to insist about his proposed project to 'begin an important stage in the project of Al Qaeda organisation'.[33]

Moving on to jihadi da'wa and media jihad it is, again, possible to see indications of the emergence of a close community of practice which, in its emphasis on mutual support and the development of personal skills, would seem to have something to offer independent of questions of instrumental effectiveness. Indeed, in calls to action such as the following, the notion of 'being a jihadi' as an online identity in its own right seems to be taken more or less for granted:

> *The object is the complete transmission of experience to the Internet.* It is true that one of our brothers is missing, and by God he has left a profound influence in the heart. But it is necessary that jihad not rely on any single person. And if we have experienced a loss, then I say as a media mujahid that we have not joined except so that we can experience imprisonment. We ask God for mercy and forgiveness. I ask God to accept us for recruitment to the lands of jihad and martyrdom. Right now, your duty is to have conveyed all your experience and all your information to others, whether in a manual, or forum threads, and you will have a reward, God willing, which will reach you after death and martyrdom. A brother who is inventive in the field of **graphic design** of videos or banners, if he were to present a study, and try to summarise the essence of what he knows would, God willing, complete the preparation of ten others beside himself. It is true that every brother has skills and creativity. But the transmission of information remains necessary, and it influences many. Another example: a brother who is a *munshid*, if he mentioned to us the programmes he uses and the useful programmes, and ways to record (but with the **condition that this does not implicate him, or constitute a security risk**), and this **munshid** brother has a voice and an outstanding way of singing nashids, but by this means there become known, and we see, twenty munshids who did not know how to get started. And always the words of the **one who works** in a certain field will have a place in people's hearts.[34]

In this piece (the emphasis reflects text highlighted in the original), we could readily forget that the *real* object is supposed to be the continuation of jihad in the path of God. The writer's expressed aspiration is, after all, not for one munshid to inspire twenty people into *jihad*, but rather twenty more people into the production of jihadi *anashid*! The object of ultimately benefiting jihad is, of course, implicit throughout the text – but it is only at third remove that any such ultimate benefit is supposed to emerge.

Something rather similar can be found in a more substantial piece released by *Shumukh al-Islam* and entitled 'The Strategic Theory for the Second Generation of Jihadis: Foundations and Practice':

The war on Iraq and Afghanistan contributed greatly to the spread of jihadi awareness so that the brothers became active in setting up jihadi websites and forums for incitement. Their importance was that they communicated the emerging reality and the brilliant thought to the service of the crystallization of these factors which were injurious to the news of the mujahidin and their operations and their preparations.

And the first generation of jihadis displayed the influence of awareness and brought vision to it, and it concentrated on information which was harmful to the enemy and attacks upon him by means of what he possessed and what he had invented.

The war on Iraq began and with it began other wars in the sphere of electronic war involving the destruction of the enemy and the elimination of his economy and resources.

A media war involving the dissemination of the massacres of the enemy and his crimes.

And the jihadi forums were in the vanguard of these advances towards this work, and some of the pulpits were publicizing this but in a restrained way and with much massaging of the truth and the works of the enemy.

And the war in the field consisted of harming the enemy's combatants and the destruction of his foundations and harming his bases.

And the da'wi war consisted of da'wa to jihad and resisting the enemy and inciting against him and da'wa to fight him.

And the individual war depended on the single individual for its completion, such as the killing of cartoonists and the plums and Zionists in America, and the Israeli soldiers in Egypt and this is the most complicated of wars and the hardest of them to predict and to govern at the enemy's extremities.

And this first generation founded a complete arsenal of methods with which to destroy the repose of the aggressor Americans and the criminal Jews. It was a generation with a programme which laid the first bricks in the new citadel of global jihad. And we do not forget how our great books contributed to building this citadel and inciting people to become active.

And it was the articles of the inventive writer-analyst Lewis Atiyatullah may God almighty preserve him which were a special flavour in the liberation of a walled in situation in the Iraq war and the articles in support of the blessed Al Qaeda organisation. And from here and there the articles of the analyst "Lion of Jihad 2," the warhead of the mujahidin may God preserve him, and his articles resembled a practical and theoretical course of action for every event and derived from his case studies, and he gave them a political colouring besides what is called reading what is behind an event. And so on and so on.

It goes on to say:

... this was the first generation which did not pass a door towards an opportunity for support without going through it.

It went through the door of media and there emerged the dangerous terrorist star Irhabi 007, and he was in truth one of the greatest if we don't say that he was the greatest of those who benefited the mujahidin in this area, and he dizzied the international intelligence.

Then Abu Dujana al-Khurasani, the martyrist, entered the door of the jihad to which we have sworn, who gathered up the Americans in a single operation unimaginable to the human mind.

Then was entered the door of individual jihad and a Moroccan established for us in the West the killing of the one who insulted the Lord of Creation the noble Muhammad, prayer and peace upon him.

It was the generation of *nusra*, it was the one that built the citadel, it was the one that irrigated the jihad with its dear blood and its life.

It was the first mujahidi generation of this age.

But we walk about and wander about in the buildings of that great first generation.[35]

It is interesting to note that, by the time of a recent piece such as this, written at a stage when jihadi forums and online jihadism are now sufficiently mature for it to be possible to suggest that idea of a 'second generation' following on from a heroic age, it is essentially taken for granted that one can speak of a jihadi movement and of jihadis as a distinct grouping, not wholly equivalent to mujahidin in general (the use of the term 'mujahidi', as opposed to *mujahid* like 'jihadi' does not necessarily weaken this interpretation). Moreover, in positing a heroic age for the jihadi movement with its own distinctive heroes it is notable that we are not talking about the likes of Bin Laden, al-Wuhayshi, Mullah Umar, Abu Mus'ab al-Zarqawi, Abu Umar al-Baghdadi, but rather about distinctively *jihadi* figures, who contributed to the movement in a variety of ways, some violent, but others not. Finally, even the non-violent forms of engagement seem to be presented not only as contributing to the ultimate goal of violent jihad, but of having the effect of 'destroying the enemy's repose', 'building a citadel' and so on. Indeed, when the author goes on, later, to diagnose the weaknesses of the present generation of jihadis, and propose solutions, nearly all of his suggestions relate to improving the movement's capacity to engage in *verbal* and confrontation with its *ideological* opponents – identified, typically, as the 'murji'iyun' rather than ways of engaging more effectively in the production of violent action. These include efforts to improve the jihadis' knowledge of theology and Arabic grammar, and they generally become better at pooling their education and expertize.

Notable among the role-call of jihadi heroes in the source above is the name 'Irhabi007'. Indeed, in the previously quoted post, where it says 'it is true that one of our brothers is missing', it seems to be Irhabi007 and the hole he left in the online jihadi movement that is being referred to. Irhabi007 was the online handle of, as it turned out, Younes Tsouli, a young Moroccan living in London who prior to his arrest in 2004, had been an administrator of *Al-Ansar* forum, where he associated online with members of Al Qaeda in Iraq, a founder of *Al-Ikhlas* forum, a small-time hacker (his much revered *Manual on Hacking Zionist and Crusader Websites* is basically script-kiddie stuff),[36] a graphic designer, a website creator, a credit card fraudster and generally an online jack of all trades.

The true story of Irhabi 007, if and when it comes out, is likely to be a mixture of genuine spy thriller and farcical, *Four Lions* style comedy. For our present purposes, however, it is not the true 'Irhabi 007' we are concerned with (if asking for the true story of an online persona is not a contradiction in terms), but rather the myth that has developed around his name. For, along with figures such as Abu Dujana al-Khurasani and Abu 'Ayna al-Muhajir, Irhabi 007 has become yet another member of the very select pantheon of heroes specific to *jihadi* culture – a role model for everything an internet jihadi (as opposed, in this case, to a real-life mujahid) can be. Indeed, alongside a similarly revered figure, less well known in the West, who went by the nickname of Muhibb al-Shaykhayn al-Tunisi, Irhabi 007 would seem to have become a hero precisely because of, rather than in spite of the fact that he never fired a shot in anger. As such, he shows that purely online activity can be a worthwhile activity in its own right.

Some of the regard in which Tsouli and Muhibb al-Shaykhayn are held can be found in the online poems that have been written celebrating their careers and lamenting their imprisonment. These poems are interesting not only because they are, so to speak, jihadi media about jihadi media, but also because of the way in which, as such, they help to represent in a broader sense the ways in which online activity is meaningful for those jihadis who participate in it.

Indeed, what seems particularly remarkable about the way these poems achieve their effects is the way in which they seem to invert notions of virtual and physical presence, such that the material practices of online activity are presented as vivid and embodied, while acts of physical violence is given a dreamlike, abstract quality. For example, in the following lament by 'poet of Al Qaeda', it opens:

> The letters scattered for missing you
> And the sadness started to move in my clothes
> As if I hadn't talked to you for nights
> And I hadn't read the *Sahab* posts
> As if you were like a candle playing in the wind
> And the sun doing a magical disappearing act
> Ah Younis! I did not feel upset or miserable
> With the colours of problems, with being away from home
> And I couldn't be away from terrorism
> But your disappearance from among us is the reason for my torment
> If you went to *Ikhlas* one day, your steps were crying "O best of youth!"
> For you is the increase of longing
> And *Ikhlas* is yours– in the best of places
> And every day is a memorial to you
> Remind us of colours and shades of torment
> You made terrorism a practice for us, and you terrorised the pagan dogs[37]

Or again in a work called 'Tears of the Two Eyes for the Lover of the Two Shaykhs', the poet recounts how:

> Al Ansar fell
> But *the* Ansar did not fall
> And moved, flying like a hurricane
> I remember the day we met
> In Al Ikhlas
> In the second citadel of the media
> I remember the day we made a date
> With the esteemed, the leopard, the terrorist 007
> With the esteemed Abu 'Umar 'Ali
> May God release you from imprisonment
> We were four people

> I remember the day I tired
> Both of us with Shaykh Abu Mus'ab
> If only he and you and Abu Mus'ab
> Returned to me so I could be happy
> And I wrote your name in the search bar
> And when I pulled my eye away from the piece
> I found the *shahada* on the pages
> The pages of glory and pride[38]

Here the ordinary, everyday acts of Web browsing are transmuted. Text becomes something material – blown by the winds of sadness. The internet is even the site for miraculous – or near miraculous happenings, as when the Muslim declaration of faith is retrieved by a search engine when the poet queries the name of his missing friend –the voice of God Himself is speaking through the algorithm.

If we wish to understand how jihadis can explain their own practices to themselves, it is surely more in these intense affective moments that we find the answer than in the more rational accounts surveyed thus far. And it is here that we must turn to a deeper examination of the third core category jihadi online practice: *nusra*.

Jihadis tend to use three Arabic words, *nusra*, *munasara* and *nasr*, in ways which are roughly interchangeable. The former two are typically translated into English as 'help', or 'support', while the latter, while also conveying the notion of 'support', is ascribed the primary meaning of 'victory'. However, the distinction between 'support' and 'victory' is largely one imposed by the needs of English translation. In reality, the Arabic seems to operate on a fluid continuum between the concepts. 'Supporting', 'helping' and 'bringing victory to' are not, so it seems, separate ideas, but rather part of a continuum. The authoritative Arabic-Arabic dictionary, *Lisan al-'Arab*, defines the word '*nasr*' as follows (the extensive use it makes of context means that the relevant words need to be left untranslated):

> *Nasr* means helping the wronged person to achieve his *nasr* against his enemy. He *nasr*-s him, and *nasr*-ed him, and he *nasr*-s him to *nasr*. And a person who is a *nāsir* is one of a group of *nusar*, like a *sahib* is to *sahb*. *Ansar*. God said "call those who give you *nasr*, and God will influence you with his influence thereby." In the hadith it says *nasr* your brother whether he is wronged or wrongdoing, and in the interpretation, it means "forbid him from wrongdoing if you were to find him doing wrong, and if you were to find him wronged, help him against the one who wronged him. And the word *nusra* is the son of its master . . .[39]

In other words, bound up in the lexical space occupied by *nasr* and *nusra* seems to be the assumption that *supporting* someone in a moral and intellectual sense, *helping* someone, materially, achieving group *solidarity* and achieving *victory* over ones' enemies are somehow equivalent. By countering the forces of atomization and dissolution, by keeping one's personal resolve strong, one is achieving victory *by that very fact*. Indeed, this point is made quite explicitly in a popular jihadi text by Yusuf al-'Uyayri, entitled *Constants in the Path of Jihad*.[40] Some indication of the influence of this text is provided by the fact that the great English-language jihadist ideologue Anwar al-'Awlaqi chose, as his first properly 'jihadi' work, a commentary on this text.[41] Indeed, in the quotation by Omar Hammami above, we can see, in all likelihood, another reference to it where the value of jihad is given as primarily relating to the victory of the *nafs* over one's sinful inclinations. In *Constants in the Path of Jihad*, Al-'Uyayri sets out, in a series of concise rhetorical passages, to refute the idea that jihad is to be understood primarily as a rational, strategic endeavour. Jihad, he insists, will continue to the Day of the Resurrection, and victory within it is 'not to be reckoned in terms of overcoming militarily'. Rather, the mujahid wins his victory simply by the moral strength he demonstrates by fighting.

The *nusra* of the jihadis – meaning the ways in which they declare their commitment to jihad, to the jihadi movement, to the *nasr* of the mujahidin – seems, in a sense, to represent the inward-looking face of the practice of jihadi *da'wa*. Like *da'wa*, it is represented in practice by activities relating to the consumption, production and distribution of jihadi content. But in contrast to the latter, the apparent purpose of such material is not to convince others of the rightness of the cause, or to spread the news of the mujahidin, but rather to demonstrate the strength of feeling among the jihadi community itself. Indeed, we can see explicit evidence of this division in jihadi thought in online episodes such as the following post submitted to a thread on *Ansar al-Mujahidin*'s 'questions and answers' section dealing with the important matter of ordering one's online 'signature' on the forum. In this case, the member is ordering three distinct signatures from the relevant specialist:

> With respect to the banner – the State of Islam, may God bring glory to it. You could use a horseman who carries the banner of the state, rather than the banner on its own. Likewise, the logo of the organisation of Al Qaida in the Islamic Maghreb, may God bring them victory if you could find a clearer picture of it.
>
> The second: The name, Abu 'Ali al-Sadiq.
>
> And behind, the picture – my Shaykh the lion of Islam, Usama. And the governor of the Ummah, Zawahiri, and the mark of Abu Yahya al-Libi. And our commander, the leader Abu Musab Abdul Wudud, with the writing:

preferably, if these words were to the commander Abu Musab Abdul Wudud [whatever happens in our darkest hours, as long as the lions are running . . . however tyranny and corruption domineer . . . whatever the dwarves and the slaves do, if they pine for killing and they threaten, will they stand in the way of the victory of Islam??? No!!! We shall remain always singing hymns to its dawn, and without doubt, tomorrow will come'].

The third: And this one is *da'wi*
The name: Abu 'Ali the Somali Jihadi Salafi
Embellish this signature with the best appearance you can see.[42]

The two *nasri* signatures here are clearly militant in their imagery and display affiliation to specific groups and specific (albeit in three cases generic) mujahidin. The last, however, is markedly different. It lacks specific mandated image content, but declares its 'jihadi-salafi' orientation explicitly.

It is abundantly clear that online jihadi communities value artistic, rhetorical, musical and technical abilities for the way in which they contribute to the community as well as for any concrete contribution they make to violent jihad as such. It is also, however, fairly clear that jihadis also take specifically aesthetic pleasure in the content they produce. For example, consider the following posthumous panegyric of the writing of Abu Dujana al-Khurasani:

. . . he was a creator in every field, indeed he was a complete encyclopedia who carried in his pockets every kind of knowledge and art, so where there are those who flaunt Shakespeare and his detective novels and imaginary stories they should look to Abu Layla [Abu Dujana al-Khurasani], who made his words about actual truths and their implementation in the real world so that they could be studied by the inactive dissenters so that they would receive exhortation and outreach so that every one would rise up from among them from the writing of his story and his sketching out of the path with his hand to make clear the penetration and we do not want it that he master the art of "representation," but rather we want him to master the art of "torment" of the enemies of God from among the unbelievers and the apostates.

And where there are those who flaunt Picasso – that great, famous painter and obscure creative artist, look to that remarkable canvas upon which Abu Layla drew with interest and finesse at every stage of drawing on that artistic canvas and finished it in the most splendid condition. And if Picasso was drawing on his canvas – rigid with oil paints, then Abu Layla drew on it with his blood and his intelligence so that he painted it with these colours of technical red. And his pieces were stretched out on this canvas: a canvas of glory and nobility and honour and self respect. I speak here not of

"Abu Layla," the insubstantial lover of wine and women, but rather I speak of Abu Layla Al Khurasani, the lover of jihad and martyrdom, and if there was a war, the felon and the estranged ones, it would reveal the insubstantial one, and the war between unbelief and faith revealed Al-Khurasani, so he true when he said: {{record my name in the first page of the notebook of Al Qaida}}. And your name will be recorded in the notebook of Al Qaida and in the first page of the pages of glory, heroism, honour and manliness.[43]

While the writer here makes the expected arguments about the practical power of Al-Khurasani's words to deliver real benefits to the mujahidin, and about how his ultimate actions spoke louder than any visual representation, it is striking that the comparison he seeks to draw in assessing their excellence is specifically with art. In his writing, Al-Khurasani is evaluated, certainly, as an artist with a practical purpose, but as an artist nonetheless, and it is in this that a portion of his excellence lies.

In moving from paradoxes of jihadi practice to notions of aesthetic and performance, then, I am reprising the conclusion of the previous chapter. Again, I reiterate that jihadist actions online should not be seen as wholly irrelevant to a project of political activism. But the very insistence jihadis make on the specific need for *violent* action adds a paradoxical dimension to their engagement over and above that of other online activists, and therefore invites us to give closer attention to the less instrumentally rational aspects of jihadi online practice. Indeed, the point is not that one can simply separate out those online jihadi actions which are rational, strategic and practical from those which are 'exuberant', excessive and even playful. Rather, the two necessarily coincide, with the former being, in a sense, inhabited by the latter. Internet jihadism is like a *trompe l'oeil*. Looked at one way, it is all about moving from thought to physical action. But looked at in another way, it is all about how thinking about physical action can give meaning and purpose to virtual actions. Indeed, in a sense, the doctrines of jihadism serve to rebuild a kind of 'Islam within Islam'. In 'traditional' forms of the religion – those which jihadis themselves would dismiss as 'murji'ism', it is typical to argue that it is not for humans to judge whether another person who claim to be a Muslim is, in fact, telling the truth. As the Islamist thinker Abu al 'Ala Mawdudi himself said in his piece 'the mischief of takfir':

> As to the question of a person being in fact a believer or not, it is not the task of any human being to decide it. This matter is directly to do with God, and it is He Who shall decide it on the Day of Judgment.[44]

For Jihadi-Salafism, it is a point of quite specific doctrine that this view is not correct, for if it were, it would not be possible to definitively declare the rulers of Muslim lands apostates, and the whole notion of a global, individual defensive jihad would cease to be defensible. Thus, the theologian Abu Muhammad al-Maqdisi has gone to some trouble in his major work, *Millat Ibrahim*, to refute the shari'a basis for the view.[45] And yet, having denied the sufficiency of the mere declaration of one's status as a Muslim as a sufficient condition for membership, jihadism then apparently reinstates something similar: the mere insistence that one is intent on involving one's self, in one way or another, with 'jihad', becomes, in effect, the new boundary for the community of the virtuous.

In other words, internet jihadism would seem to work, affectively, through an interesting paradox. Through an imagined communion with the noble ideal of the mujahidin and the lands of jihad, the internet jihadi is provided with a powerful emotional resource which, by the very fact of its seemingly irreducible embodiment,[46] gives substance and meaning to online actions which otherwise might seem to be frivolous or empty (the jihadis' dismissal of their opponents by use of the typical Islamic term *hawa*, which means 'idle fancy' or 'whim', but which is cognate with the word for 'air' may possibly have interesting resonances here). As such, at this emotional level, it may be that jihadism functions in some ways as what Hebdige called a 'magical solution' to the day-to-day doubts and concerns of those who participate in it.

It is interesting, for example, to note that in those sections of jihadi forums not exclusively reserved for content dealing directly with news and productions relating to militant groups, it is common to find posts dealing with issues of lifestyle uncertainty, religious doubt (invariably refuted of course) and misgivings about the meaninglessness of modern, commercialized culture such as the following example:

> We are still here, we are still in a body, with a heart that beats, with life remaining in us – so why do we live without life, and die without death? If life has stopped in our eyes, it shouldn't stop in our hearts, because the real death is the death of the heart. Imagine that you have a cup of tea with no sugar in it, and you add sugar to it, and you don't stir it. Will you find the taste of sweetness in it – surely not. Keep looking into the cup for a minute, and then taste the tea. Did anything change – did you taste the sweetness? I guess not. Did you notice that the tea has started to get colder and colder, and you still haven't tasted the sweetness in it? So one last try. Put your hand on your head and go around the cup of tea and wish that it become sweet. All of this is crazy, and it can be also ridiculous, because the tea won't become sweet, it only got colder, and you haven't drunk it yet. And this is what life is like- a cup of unsweetened tea. And the abilities that God gave you – the goodness that is inside you is the sugar, and if you don't stir

it yourself, you won't taste the taste of sweetness. And if you pray to God with your hands folded, if you pray for him to make your life better it won't become better unless you work hard yourself, and stir the talent that you have. Therefore, work so that you can reach success – so your life becomes better, and so you can taste the sweetness of your accomplishment and your work and your talent, and your life will become better. A good cup of tea that makes you feel good. But now there is a very important question: why? Why is it hard for us to say the truth while there is nothing easier than to say what is false? Why do we feel sleepy while we are praying, and we wake up suddenly and feel energetic right after the prayers finish? Why are the words of God hard on us? Why is it hard to talk about religious issues, and easy to talk about all the other things? Why do we get bored when we read a religious article, and we feel curious reading about anything else. Why do we delete the emails that talk about religion, but we forward other emails? Why do we feel that mosques have become haunted, and cabarets become full? Did you give up? Think about it? Will you forward this letter to your friends? Or will you ignore it and deal with it like any other religious letter? Put one thing in your head: God, who is observing you. Let's see if Satan could stop that. When this letter reaches you, pray for the person who sent it to you – prayer [du'a] won't be heavy on you, but it will bring you great benefits, and don't forget to forward this letter to all of your friends so they can pray for you. Let us keep praying for each other. Sibhan Allah – copied for the benefit of your brothers in God.[47]

The fact that this seemingly heartfelt piece is 'copied' is itself of interest. Indeed, it would seem that a piece of this sort would fit quite easily into a more widespread genre of Islamic text called *raqa'iq*, literally meaning 'subtleties' but often translated as pieces intended 'to soften the heart'. While *raqa'iq* are to be found originally as a subcategory of Islamic hadith, the term also refers today more generally to highly sentimental, morally improving anecdotes, which are apparently supposed to produce a collective emotional release, as evidenced by intense images of the audience of sermons containing *raqa'iq* openly weeping as they listen to them.[48] The notion of *raqa'iq* has also been classically invoked in a more metaphysical sense as referring to those 'subtleties' which fall between the explicit words of the text and are therefore inaccessible to direct intellectual inquiry.[49]

In so far as jihadism aspires to be an Islamic ideal, the concept of *raqa'iq* plays an explicit role in specifically 'jihadi' texts. For example, in *The Global Islamic Resistance Call*, the supposed bluff pragmatist Abu Mus'ab al-Suri devotes a number of pages to the importance *raqa'iq* and the allied notion of *zuhd* (asceticism) as crucial to the all-round Islamic education needed to produce the virtuous mujahid.[50] Moreover, the notion of 'fine feelings' is a regular motif in accounts of the character of martyrs and (even before martyrdom) of heroic figures such as Osama bin Laden.[51]

With regard to the specific matter of online jihadism, however, the situation is further complicated. We may analyse what has happened for the case of posts such as that provided above stepwise as follows:

- A concept is set out regarding the notion of underlying subtleties within the scriptural system of Islam which are inaccessible to reason, but may be touched on through the cultivation of appropriate emotion
- A performative, oral genre develops with the purpose of stimulating collective expressions of emotional sensitivity within the scriptural framework of Islam
- Texts along these lines are published in digital form online
- These texts are then copied and pasted, as part of larger compilations of similar texts, as contributions to specifically *jihadi* Web forums.

It would seem therefore that, in such textual performances, what we are witnessing is a sort of cyclical movement from affective, communally rooted performance to text and back to performance again: a text originally charged with affective power is stereotyped for instant reproduction. However, by virtue of being pasted by a self-conscious internet jihadi (as the poster was in this case), as a contribution – a gift – to a jihadi forum, the text would seem to be recharged with emotional significance all over again. Moreover, the emotional significance can be observed to derive from the interaction of at least three sources: the text itself (which of course incorporates within it both explicit references to other sources of meaning and also generic implications about its likely original performative context); the community of online jihadis to whom the text is being offered and, finally, the heroic mujahidin whose actions give the jihadi community its source of meaning and significance.

Two more general observations seem to follow from this. First, the standardization of value which this sort of move seems to make possible implies that online jihadi actions can be analysed in terms of the accumulation of distinctive forms of subcultural capital. Indeed, in a sense, the relationship of the online jihadi to the mujahidin is perhaps not entirely unlike the distinctly un-Salafi notion of *baraka* associated with saintly figures and relics. By amassing and constructing digital jihadi content, the jihadi can obtain at least some share of the salvation stored up by the noble collective project of jihad. Thus, online jihadism can be thought of in terms of an internet subculture in which action is motivated in an immediate sense by the availability of its own forms of subcultural capital, achievable by writing, design, nashid music, technical services or even simply display and collection of material.

Second, however, the value of this 'capital' is ultimately produced not just by this one imaginative relationship, but by a complex series of interactions between three overlapping but distinguishable systems of text and action: the world of ordinary Muslim life (i.e. everyday life and what Islamic texts have to say about it), the world of jihad and the mujahidin, and the world of 'cyberculture' as represented by online practices and communities, and by Manovich's notion of the 'language of new media'. Thus, despite the apparently extremely rigid and generic structure of the texts themselves, taken as a whole, internet jihadism would seem to partake in some of the heteroglossia that Bakhtin identifies as central to the modernist project of the novel. It is through the latent contrasts, ironies and opportunities that result from the continual juxtaposition of these different spheres with their different media 'languages' that online jihadism seems to acquire its significance.

The complexity of the cultural moves that give value to jihadi subcultural capital (rather like the almost untrackable complexity of the transactions that give value to modern-day financial capital) is such – so it may be surmised – that it may be fairly stable in the face of the paradoxes and contradictions on which it is ultimately premised. Jihadis can escape from the meaninglessness and vacuity of the material world through their pious adherence to Islamic values. In turn, they can break free from the emotional rigidities of this textually constructed world through their imagined contribution to the jihad. At the same time, however, they are shielded from the world of actual violence through the constraints imposed by a compromised, infiltrated and tainted world of cyberspace.

The subcultural capital of internet jihadis remains, and jihadis are of course aware that it remains, ultimately built on flimsy foundations. And yet, ultimately fragile as it may be, the construction of distinctively online forms of jihadi practice does imply that it is untenable to see 'being a jihadi' as simply a form of 'violent radicalisation' that merely falls short of actual participation in violence. Rather, it would seem plausible to view non-violent jihadism as a state in its own right, maintenance of which depends on the development of a certain tactical skill, a cunning, unspoken and unspeakable way of operating of the sort theorized by Michel de Certeau. While the internet jihadi's position, from an absolute, scripturalist point of view, may ultimately be untenable, from the time-bound, day-by-day point of view of actual life, it may be possible to prolong it indefinitely.

7

Some other 'jihadi' consumption cultures: Crusaderism, war porn, shock

In Chapter 3, I started out with the conceit of asking what comes up if one simply keys 'jihadi' (and variants thereof) into a search engine. As I went on to show, even as seemingly naïve an exercise as this actually appears, on closer examination, to give a surprisingly accurate snapshot of 'jihadi' culture as it appears in Arabic content on the Web. What would happen if we tried the same in English? Let us consider, by way of introduction, the results of this exercise from Friday 13th 2012.

At hits number three and four, we have a story about a radical cleric giving his permission for mujahidin to sodomize each other if it will make it easier to insert explosives in their anal cavities.[1] The story, as it happens, is based on a total misunderstanding at best, and a deliberate hoax at worst,[2] arising from a video in which an anti-'Wahhabi' Sunni cleric, Abdullah al-Khallaf, reads out (apparently in earnest) a question and answer along these lines from a (genuine) forum called *Usud al-Sunna*, for the purposes of exposing the jihadis' supposed moral corruption. It would seem, however, that the story actually originated as a satirical joke rather than a serious inquiry, coming from a forum post written in imitation of the studied archaism of the jihadi style, as supposed extract 'from the battles of the Shaykh Muhammad al-Munjid with Mickey Mouse'.[3] Ironically then, what is supposed to be an instance of online extremism is the precise opposite: a humorous critique of the jihadis' tendency to make ends justify means.

Hit number five is a blog called 'jihadi du jour'. The entry 'du jour' is 'a very short story that reveals a truth about the nature of Muslims living in civilized countries. And to be fair, not all Muslims, just most of them'. It consists of a joke about a group of scrounging Muslims freeloading on a barber's good will.[4]

At hit number seven, we have an article by a Dr Babu Susseelan, writing for faithfreedom.org in which we are told:

> Ideas expressed in the Koran provide all the justification necessary for Jihadis to carry out deadly terrorist activities. Jihadi terrorists are primarily afraid of freethinking, liberty, pluralism, secularism, and co-existence. They are defensive, capricious, and conditioned by their outdated irrational fanatic religious dogma.[5]

In other words, if it is relatively easy to track down 'jihadi' content items on the Arabic Web, it is at least as easy to find ignorant, prejudiced and indeed hateful content about Islam in its English pages. But what exactly does this tell us? Today, concerns are growing over the rise of a new kind of globalized right wing movement, focused not on Jews or other ethnic minorities, but rather on Muslims. The casual availability of online material like this is hardly comforting in that regard.

And yet if, as I have argued in so far in this book, it is extremely risky to assume that online militancy translates in any simple way to offline violence for the case of *jihadi* content, it seems only fair to approach the case of a possible wave of anti-Islamic violence, focused on the figure of the 'jihadi terrorist' with the same degree of scepticism. Indeed, as I shall argue in this chapter, analysis of the possible emergence of a new 'crusaderist' ideology in Europe and the United States actually helps not only to show why this threat may be more limited than it appears, but also to further illustrate the gap between online rhetoric and offline reality for the case of jihadism as well.

This is not to say that there is not a serious general problem with Islamophobia in Western countries, that there is not a specific problem with Islamophobic violence, or that seriously Islamophobic rhetoric is not rife online. Rather, it is to say that, as with jihadism, it is far from obvious that the specific properties of the internet make the problem worse, or that there is an obvious link between distinctively online practices in relation to this phenomenon, and its other manifestations.

To be clear about where we stand, let us begin with the rise of militant Islamophobia in a more general sense. The idea that there exist, and have long existed generalized, Western forms of antipathy towards Islam is hardly new. As Lopez notes, the word 'Islamophobia' dates back to at least 1925, where it is used in the book *Orient vu de l'Occident* by Étienne Dinet and Slimane Ibrahim to denote a hostility to Islam that goes beyond criticizing the religion to present it as an opponent which must eventually be eliminated.[6] Indeed, a passage he quotes at length from another early work of anti-Islamic prejudice, L.G. Binger's (1906), *Le Péril d'Islam* seems astonishingly relevant to the 'War on Terror' era:

> If the Muslim defends his country, his home, his independence, his liberties, he is neither a patriot nor a man sacrificing himself for the sake of a noble and lofty sentiment, he would be a fanatic. Does he regularly say his prayers, does he simply follow a religion? .... He is a fanatic .... Do we find him reading his Qur'an, the only book he possesses? He must also be a fanatic. Does he refuse to serve your interests? That would be fuelled by fanaticism. Does he meet his co-religionists to discuss the Pentateuch or the Gospel, perhaps simply to learn to read his prayers properly? This is for the purpose of later exercising his fanaticism. Has he allied himself with other Muslims in a war? This will always be driven by fanaticism and hatred of Christians. In a word, all the Muslim's actions, especially those that run counter to our policy or our interests, can be ascribed to fanaticism. And, stranger still, we at home would consider most of these hostile acts inspired by this so-called fanaticism as highly commendable qualities, as highly patriotic acts or even as highly political acts. If Vercingetorix were to appear among the Muslims, we would treat him as a fanatic.

Nor, again, is Islamophobia a purely Western phenomenon (even taking the broadest possible definition of 'Western'. For example, India also has its own distinctive forms of anti-Muslim prejudice.[7]

However, serious attention is now increasingly being given to radical Islamophobia not just as a discursive phenomenon with deep roots in Western culture, but as an increasingly important and specifically identifiable oppositional ideology, something which, in Western countries (particularly in Europe), is coming to be seen as a domestic security issue of a similar kind to that which is supposed to be presented by jihadism.

And yet, in the very oppositional nature of this emerging ideology lies, perhaps, some indication that we may be concerned not solely with a wave of unprecedented anti-Muslim hate, as the increasing manifestation of prejudices once so deeply institutionalized as to be almost invisible at the wider public level.

In the United States, for example, the victory of the Obama administration and, with it, a rhetorically (if not 'kinetically') softer approach has meant that the most extreme 'war on terror' language is now more readily identifiable with hardline conservative movements such as the Tea Party than with the American state. Similarly, the increasing emergence of shocking discoveries about how institutionalized anti-Islamic rhetoric has been within US agencies reflects precisely the *discovery* of pre-existing truths, not the emergence of new trends. For example, it was of course profoundly disturbing when it was revealed in a report in *Wired Magazine* that an officer training course on offer at an American military college had defined Islam as an 'enemy ideology' and discussed how an all-out war might be fought against it by suspending the Geneva conventions and, if necessary, by destroying Mecca and Medina and 'taking war to the civilian population following the historical precedents of Dresden, Tokyo, Hiroshima, Nagasaki'.[8] But if the news was new, the existence of such courses wasn't. Specifically, courses teaching US military and law enforcement officials that Islam is evil, and is the enemy as such, have been taught for the whole decade since 9/11.[9] Moreover, the cultural roots of this notion go much further. For example, the idea of a nuclear attack on Mecca as a strategic response to an act of nuclear terrorism on US soil was part of military strategic thinking at least as early as the 1990s.[10]

In continental Europe, the emergence of radical anti-Islamic political figures calling, as the Dutch politician Pim Fortuyn did, for a 'Cold War against Islam'[11] predates 9/11. It is true, however, that in some countries, such as Holland and Denmark, political parties hostile to Islam have increasingly been able to move, to some extent, into the political mainstream. Alternatively, as with bans on the full-face veil in France or the minaret ban in Switzerland, the mainstream (or sections of it) has moved in their direction. Moreover, events such as the assassination of Theo van Gogh have perhaps caused proponents of such views to be seen more as objects than inciters of violence. Factors such as these may have contributed to what Arun Kundnani sees as a 'blind spot' with regard to oppositional far-right violence, particularly with Muslim targets.[12]

In the United Kingdom, while counterterrorism strategies such as Prevent have had the effect of systematically securitizing Islam and Muslims,[13] and while there are important and influential public figures who have made outspoken accusations that the government is pandering to Islamic extremists and allowing an Islamization of British society,[14] the political mainstream has perhaps been somewhat more resistant to such discourses. Here however, for a complex set of reasons which deserve more thorough investigation (but which are not necessarily simply reducible to the lack of a mainstream political opportunity structure), a formalized and quite well-organized social movement has arisen relatively recently in the form of the English Defence League.[15]

Another event which, obviously, has helped to crystallize attention on the idea of radical Islamophobia as a domestic security threat to Western countries has been the attacks in Norway on 22nd July in which Anders Behring Breivik killed 77 people with a car bomb at a government office in Oslo, and a shooting spree on Utøya island. While this – the largest terrorist attack on a Western country since the Madrid bombings, and the second largest since 9/11 – is the sole outright example of a large-scale terrorist attack by an individual professing specifically 'Western nationalist' or, perhaps best, 'crusaderist' ideology, there are, as Githens-Mazer and Lambert observe, other examples of bomb plots in the United Kingdom for which there is some evidence of English Defence League material (as well as content relating to the old racist extreme right) having been in the possession of the perpetrator.[16]

These authors also observe that there seems to be a growing trend in the United Kingdom of violent hate crime directed specifically at religious Muslims, including assaults and incidents as arson attacks on mosques. It is difficult to quantify this phenomenon exactly, partly because it is likely (so these authors argue) to be under-reported, partly because of limited research in the area, and partly because it is difficult to disaggregate from other types of hate crime.[17] For example, the United Kingdom already has a history of specifically racist violence against minorities such as Pakistanis where it is the ethnicity of the subject, rather than religion per se, that is the reason for the attack. The authors suggest that violence directed at Muslims may to some extent represent a shift in the targeting of racist violence, which possibly suggests (not that this makes it any more acceptable, of course) that in a sense it represents the continuation of a pre-existing forms of violence rather than a wholly new form of violence by an altogether new category of perpetrator.

What this still implies, however, is that even if we restrict ourselves to the specific material practice of violence, Islamophobia is still very far from being a monolithic phenomenon in the West. At present, violence actually directed at Muslims seems to a significant degree to betray influences of older forms of more straightforward racism, while the only clear example of an act of serious terrorism in which a specifically Islamophobic agenda was clearly articulated did not, as it happens, actually target Muslims as such (although it did have Muslim victims) but rather members of the Norwegian centre-left. The English Defence League, while its demonstrations have been associated with acts of violence and intimidation, is at least rhetorically committed to non-violence.[18] It is of course also the case that the major form of violence which Islamophobic discourse tends to align in support of (although even this is not exclusively true) are the official military operations associated with the war on terror, which is often interpreted, even against the claims made by the governments responsible, as part of an existential conflict with Islam as such.

Trying to find a coherent intellectual discourse for this putative movement is, naturally, even more complex. If all that unites it is an intense hatred and fear of Islam, one might locate within it militant atheists, conservative Christians, ultra-nationalists, staunch Zionists, 'ex Muslims',[19] militantly secular former Islamists[20] and so on. And even this is to dramatically oversimplify the case, since it is questionable whether even 'hatred of Islam' is the most appropriate defining characteristic. For instance, as Fred Halliday has influentially noted, 'Muslimophobia' might be more appropriate than 'Islamophobia', implying a concrete hatred of actual Muslims, rather than an abstract concern with Islam as a religion.[21] On the other hand, as Kundani points out, actors who might be labeled 'Islamophobic' may be skilful at positioning themselves within existing monolithic state security narratives about a unique threat from Muslim extremists,[22] by calling for what they consider to be 'extremist' Islam to be still more heavily securitized, while making forthright demands that Muslims make it very clear which side of the arbitrary line they are on, but all the while claiming that they are not against Islam or Muslims as such. Similarly, as Githens-Mazer and Lamber observe, Islamophobia may also manifest itself by presenting radical Islam as synonymous with *observant* Islam, implying, for example, that simply wearing Islamic clothing is a problem.

Thus, even if Islamophobia could be robustly defined in the abstract, actually locating it would still often be a difficult task, requiring, as it does, close attention to irreducibly specific matters of context and emphasis. For example, it is presumably not Islamophobic for a gay rights campaigner to criticize homophobic discourses from certain Muslim sources, as well as from other religious groups, and miscellaneous 'cultural conservatives'. But it might be Islamophobic if an undue amount of attention were focused on the former, in such as way as to imply that Islam *as such* is uniquely problematic in this regard. But how much attention is too much attention here is in principle a criterion to which no hard-and-fast rule can be applied.

One potentially promising starting point for siting a discussion of 'anti jihadism', 'militant Islamophobia' or 'crusaderism' for the specific case internet is the 'manifesto' which Anders Behring Breivik disseminated online some time before his attacks under the anglicized pseudonym of 'Andrew Berwick'.[23] If there is, after all, a truly distinctive new form of violent 'Crusaderist' *practice* to be concerned with, then this is the sole unequivocal instance of a corresponding example of online content.

Another reason for finding Breivik's manifesto of interest for our purposes is that, quite apart from its discursive content, there are also features of the document itself and the manner of its dissemination which, with regard to form, are of specific interest in terms of the structural features of new media. Breivik's document very clearly exhibits the specific properties which Manovich, for example, sees as defining properties of the form. First, what Breivik presented was not a document as such, but rather a database. As he states in his introduction to his main document, titled 'A European Declaration of Independence', about half of it is not his own work.[24] Indeed, if we concern ourselves primarily with the specifically political and ideological sections of the piece, rather than with book three, which deals with operational matters, including Breivik's personal account of how he prepared for his attacks, then it is clear that considerably more than half of Breivik's account is simply cut and paste.[25] This fact becomes all the more significant when we consider two further points: first, the enormous length of Breivik's 'compendium', as he calls it, at 1518 pages and, second, the practical purpose which Breivik envisages for it. As he writes:

> I am 100% certain that the distribution of this compendium to a large portion of European patriots will contribute to ensure our victory in the end. Because within these three books lies the tools required to win the ongoing Western European cultural war.[26]

The dissemination of a 1518-page document on the understanding that it is to provide a practical guide to action makes sense only if we accept that Breivik assumes a reader who is likely not to attempt to read the work in its entirety, but rather one who will treat the work – as Breivik describes it – as a compendium of sources, to be accessed or not accessed as he sees fit. Indeed, Breivik himself invites this form of reading when he urges recipients of the document to 'distribute the book or some/all of its content'.[27]

This in turn demonstrates another of Manovich's principles regarding new media artefacts – the fact that they never exist in any final form. Breivik himself released sections of his compilation both in the form of a text document, and also a 'movie presentation of the compendium', consisting of a video montage, which in turn was made up in large part of images which he had subsequently altered digitally, for example through the addition of speech bubbles or graphics. He also notes that he 'originally planned to add a database of high-quality graphic illustrations and pictures. However the document (file) would have been unpractically large'.[28] Indeed, there is something perhaps a little revealing in the way in which Breivik instinctively seems to conflate 'document' and 'file' here. Breivik very clearly declares that the manifesto he says he has spent three years of his life researching and writing, which is the culmination of nine years of preparation, which is the culmination of a project that has consumed all of his financial resources, is an open text, which he expects to be dismembered, altered and rewritten as the reader sees fit. Indeed, Breivik quite specifically recognizes the fluidity of the position he stands for in the self-interview which takes up pages 1349–1356 of the compendium, as when, for example, he observes:

> Justiciar Knights are not an ideologically homogenous group. Many Justiciar Knight Commanders would probably reject some of my personal views as I would with theirs. Some are deeply Christian while some are Christian agnostics or even atheists. Some are individualists while others not so

much so, some puritans. The primary factors that unites us is that we are all nationalists, anti-Marxist, anti-Islam(isation), we support indigenous rights and we are revolutionary, willing to martyr ourselves.[29]

And yet, on the other hand, Breivik is profoundly concerned about the material and legal obstacles to the dissemination of this fluid, unfinished, montaged hypertext. He includes a legal disclaimer which he hopes, presumable if copied and pasted to the head of the document, will enable the reader to circumvent European laws with regard to terrorist content.[30] He further recommends that, just in case, the reader should make any alterations she sees fit. He minutely discusses his decision to release the work as a word document (for its smaller size and ease of editing) rather than a PDF and give extensive information on the media and networks by which it may be disseminated.

Indeed, even aside from the Breivik's admission that some 'justiciar knights' would reject his views, as he would theirs, Breivik's views, as he presents them, are quite clearly incoherent. The best illustration of this is not in his vast, heterogeneous compendium, but rather his inability to summarize his position even in the twelve-minute video montage which is clearly supposed to serve as an arresting call to action.[31]

Here he presents what are, in effect, three (possibly four) separate enemies – the sinister menace of cultural Marxism, the vicious, but vital barbarism of Islam, and the weak, degenerate 'suicidal humanists'. While it is fairly obvious that the weakness of the suicidal humanists provides a mechanism for the imminent Muslim takeover of Europe, the cultural Marxists – with whom Breivik begins, and who would appear to be the primary villain of the piece – are much harder to understand. The brutal, genocidal, totalitarian and yet curiously intangible threat they represent is, in and of itself familiar from a whole range of anti-modern political ideologies of both left and right. They reflect both that sense of 'taint' which seems to be innate and primal in human moral reasoning[32] combined with the general sense of dread and loss of control which Giddens and others associate with the experience of high modernity. The obvious reading of them is in the familiar role of the evil puppet master, pulling the strings from on high, slowly, unerringly working out a perfect and long-planned conspiracy. And this reading is helped by the fact that the cultural Marxists are also (somehow) allied to capitalist globalists as well. But Breivik does not, in fact, allow this conclusion. The sinister, all-controlling cultural Marxists are actually fools. They will not achieve their communist totalitarianism, because they, through their own policies, will actually themselves be destroyed by the coming Islamic caliphate.

The point is complicated further by the fact that radical Islam, as such, is not really the enemy. On the contrary, it is potentially a part of the solution. Not only does Breivik have a certain, grudging respect for the strength, unity and perceived vitality of extremist Islam but further, as he outlines on page 958, where he discusses the possibility of obtaining weapons of mass destruction from an Islamist group, he notes that there are in fact common goals between radical Islamists and his proposed cultural conservative movement.[33] The former aspire to a caliphate on historical Islamic territory, the latter to a culturally purist European federation. As long as the one does not intrude on the territory of the other, there is a theoretical possibility for accommodation between them. More threatening are the ostensibly moderate Muslims, who threaten to gradually subvert Europe not through out-and-out war, but through demographic jihad.[34] These moderate Muslims are likely to be radical Muslims in disguise, concealing their true beliefs through the principle of *taqiyya*.[35] But actually, Breivik accepts (or at least, he accepts through some of the authors contributing to his compilation) that the situation is more complex than this. Many Muslims are simply unaware of the true nature of their religion. They honestly believe it to be a religion of peace and are as surprised as anyone when they are informed about what it has to say on the subject of jihad.[36] It is worth pointing out that this does not, of itself, render Breivik's position incoherent – presumably the implication is that these Muslims, like it or not, will ultimately find themselves ineluctably bound to accept the true nature of their religion in the caliphate to come. But it does seem to inject a perhaps rather surprising note of doubt in the work of someone so certain in his convictions that he was prepared to commit mass murder for them.

The key point in all this is that it is risky to assume that, because Breivik carried out an unquestionably extreme action, he must also have a clear ideological position. Indeed, as the scholar Max Abrahms observes, the presumption that there the extreme actions of terrorists necessarily coincide with equally extreme ideological positions is, as a general point, not necessarily true.[37] Extremely violent terrorist groups have often held ideological positions which are either inchoate or essentially in line with relatively mainstream non-violent groups within the overall political context in which they are operating. With specific regard to Breivik's 'manifesto', one searches in vain for any clear explanation of how the action he proposes to take will plausibly achieve the goals he seeks to attain. Indeed, if such an account is to be found within the work, it would seem to lie less in its intellectual content than in Breivik's romanticization and fetishization of violent action itself as a response to the decay, as he sees it, of these martial virtues in contemporary Europe. Ultimately, Breivik's 'manifesto' is not a manifesto at all, but a distinctively digital compilation of 'likes'. Breivik likes epic history. He likes *The Lord of the Rings*.[38] He likes military hardware. He likes computer games. He likes working out. He likes cultural conservatism. He likes the notion of a pan-European Western civilization. He likes knights. He likes certain pieces of music – particularly *Lux Aeterna* from the soundtrack to the film *Requiem for a Dream*, which he proposes as the national anthem for a future European federation.[39] He dislikes political correctness. He dislikes (though he has a certain respect for) Islam. What is his overall ideology? Aside from the idea that Europe as he knows it is doomed, and must be redeemed by violent heroic action, Breivik is not wholly sure. He leaves the matter deliberately open. Any attempt to formalize things further is the reader's imposition, not the inevitable consequence of Breivik's text.

A point which it is important to stress here is that Breivik's 'compendium' approach seems to go beyond the idea that the internet increasingly tends to deliver individualistic, idiosyncratic and bespoke identity commitments – although clearly this is the case as well. Breivik is not just constructing his own particular ideological outlook (primarily by cutting and pasting the views of others). He is also open to the idea that others will do the same – and this in spite of the profoundly and extremely detailed vision of a totalitarian order he imagines coming into being premised on the notion of 'cultural conservatism'. Thus, not only do Breivik's heterogeneous ideas bear witness to the montaged nature of new media content, but they also seem to inform a kind of reflexive and meta-ideological edge to his thinking, whereby he recognizes that while he may be totalitarian, he cannot force his totalitarianism on the other totalitarian sympathizers he hopes to reach out to, each of whom will, he knows, be thoroughly totalitarian and intolerant in his/her own way.

Compared with Breivik's, a somewhat more plausible and coherent account of potential violent action by Islamophobic terrorists is to be found in the work of a contributor to one of the sites which Breivik identifies as one of the 'well known and relatively moderate contributors to the Vienna school of thought' – the writings of 'El Ingles' on the website *Gates of Vienna*.[40] El Ingles has produced a number of works which, in contrast to most other writers namechecked by Breivik, more or less directly advocate violence. These take the form of extended hypotheticals about future violent confrontations between Muslim minorities and the citizens the European countries in which they live, with titles such as, 'The Danish civil war'[41] or, 'Genocide, Surrender or What?' However, perhaps the most disturbingly detailed of 'El Ingles's' musings is a series of five posts, later made available as a single PDF e-book.[42] El Ingles insists that his work is 'descriptive' rather than 'normative' and that he is merely predicting what is inevitably to come.[43] However, the actual content of what he writes makes it fairly clear that what he is actually trying to do – rather analogously to the 'jihadi strategic study' is to provide guidance in the hope that what he writes about will in fact occur.

The conceit of 'Our Muslim Troubles' is the use of the author's analysis of the troubles in Northern Ireland as a guide to how a comparable episode of extended and violent community strife might be managed on the UK mainland.[44] The basic argument, however, is only quite loosely based on any strict comparison with this case, which, for all sorts of reasons, he acknowledges not to be strictly applicable to the situation he envisages. In summarizing his argument, certain points stand out. First, while he takes it as a more or less eternal given that there will always be a threat of mass-casualty terrorism from Muslims, he is actually quite sanguine about this issue.[45] He accepts that only a very small (albeit effectively constant) minority of Muslims will attempt to carry out attacks. He also thinks – based on a detailed and rather impressive outline survey of the challenges of making home-made explosives – that Muslims are unlikely to succeed in reliably producing effective large-scale bombs.[46] In other words, the threat he is concerned with is not terrorism, but simply Muslims as such. Why Muslims are inherently a problem is a matter he gives little space to, although it seems reasonable to assume that this is because the reader is already supposed to have come to this conclusion from other works on this subject. Having accepted the premise that Muslims must be largely eliminated from the United Kingdom, he then outlines the following strategy for doing this:

First, we are supposed to assume the existence of a highly organized and capable terrorist group with units all over the British mainland. This group will begin by systematically and violently harassing those Muslims who live in what he calls 'zone c', that is, those rural areas of the United Kingdom with very small and scattered Muslim-minority populations.[47] Once these have been harried into shutting down their businesses and leaving, ethnically cleansing these areas of their Muslim population, the struggle will then move on to 'zone b', where larger populations of Muslims will be forced out of places like Cardiff by a mass bombing campaign into 'zone a'. At this point, the British government will lose control of the situation and effectively collapse.[48]

The major point to be made in relation to this, admittedly chilling document, is that it seems to require, more or less as a first step, the existence of an organization of a level of sophistication and resolve which, realistically, it is extraordinarily difficult to imagine coming into being in the United Kingdom, particularly given the level of surveillance and the effectiveness of the internal security apparatuses which 'El Ingles' pays great tribute to with regard to their ability to contain Islamic terrorism.[49] This requirement means that, as a direct incitement to a terrorist campaign, El Ingles's plan seems to suffer from a problematic catch 22. However, and perhaps of more concern, the author does also propose a number of violent actions which he suggests could trigger the situation he envisages. These include an incident such as a car bombing of a mosque, or the assassination of a radical Muslim such as – he specifically suggests – Anjem Choudhary.[50]

While these threats are still, of course, only bits of data in a PDF document, they are to that extent plausible, and it would be foolish to suggest otherwise. But the plausibility of these, and not other elements of the plan is in itself interesting and gives an insight into the limitations even of a particularly well-thought out and militant document in this genre. El Ingles's larger scheme depends, contextually, on the accuracy of his wider apocalyptic narrative of total violent collapse in British race relations, combined with a prone and helpless state. The document is intelligently written, carefully thought through, and plausible in part because it avoids having to make the argument for its premises. Indeed, as the author states at the outset, it would be quite impossible to make the kind of case it makes without keeping certain 'parameters' constant.[51] It is, whatever else it is, an elegant counterfactual game – indeed, its grotesque, chilling and poisonously hateful nature aside – there is something diabolically, perversely pleasurable about reading it: as if the author thinks he is writing a Tom Clancy scenario, instead of a plan for how a group of imaginary thugs could carry out a genocide on their own countrymen.

There are two well-known jihadi publications to which it seems interesting to compare these works. In certain underlying respects, *Our Muslim Troubles* seems to resemble the 'jihadi strategic studies' literature and, particularly, a book by Abu Bakr Naji called *The Management of Savagery: The Most Dangerous Stage Which the Ummah Will Pass Through*.[52] The basic argument of this book is that the way to establish a caliphate is for jihadists to systematically exploit conditions of anarchy or 'savagery' which, because of their own superior ability to survive and thrive in such conditions, will enable them to outcompete alternatives and emerge in dominant positions. Naji's argument has, it has to be said, an advantage in terms of plausibility over that of 'El Ingles', for the simple reason that Naji is speaking from hindsight and present reality, rather than simply projecting into the future. There are, of course, plenty of cases of failed states and regions with effective Islamist militias which he can refer to. (On the other hand, one might counter that El Ingles' ambitions are at least more constrained that Naji's since what he wants is not a universal caliphate, but simply the ethnic cleansing of a minority population from a particular island.) However, at a deeper level, the two books have certain rather interesting things in common. First, both books are written in what seems to be a deliberately dispassionate, matter of fact and quasi-scientific tone. They are not really trying to make the case for their overall ideological position, but rather trying to plot a course from 'a' to 'b'. As already noted, this actually functions as a rhetorical device in so far as it creates a compelling sense of logic and clarity which disappears only when one begins to step back and consider the overall 'parameters' within which the argument is located.

This rhetorical device also helps, so it seems, to conceal a certain romanticism underlying the argument. Both portray an idealized situation of anarchy as the backdrop for the emergence of a heroic, highly organized and ruthless group which will emerge as saviours. Moreover, in both cases, there is what seems to be a deliberately unsentimental and unflinching emphasis on the types of brutality which this group will have to engage in.[53] Again, there seems to be a rhetorical dimension to this. It is as if the very tough-mindedness of the author is itself intended to create a sense of clarity. Finally, in both cases, the redemptive effectiveness of the organization is clothed in the impersonal language of scientific management. Just as El Ingles stresses the high level of internal order, unity and tradecraft, his imaginary militias will have to have, Abu Bakr Naji urges the mujahidin to study management theory, so as to be better able to administer the populations over which they will assert their control.[54]

And yet, in both the Islamophobic case, and the jihadist one (at least in so far as it relates to grander plan of establishing a caliphate over the entire Islamic world), it is precisely not the highly rationalized, highly strategic visions of action that provide a plausible rationale for individual action, but rather the visions of violence relating to the moral act of the isolated, kamikaze (not necessarily suicidal) of an individual entrepreneur who is prepared to carry out violence even if the fruits of his action may well not materialize in his lifetime. In other words, just as the 'strategic' vision of jihadi literature has more of an ideological than a genuinely strategic purpose, so too the grand strategic vision of an 'El Ingles' really seems to serve best not as a strategic vision in its own right, but rather as an imaginative backdrop for the actions of a Breivik.

There is, it may be noted, quite a good parallel in the jihadi literature for Breivik's 'manifesto' as well – albeit one which experts in jihadist militancy are likely to find rather surprising and, perhaps, controversial. This is Abu Mus'ab al-Suri's *The Global Islamic Resistance Call*. The comparison seems unlikely at first, because whereas Breivik is a loner and social outsider who may in fact be mentally ill,[55] Abu Mus'ab al-Suri is a respected jihadi fighter with a long career of militant activism and service in mujahidin training camps. Moreover, Abu Mus'ab al-Suri is generally known to specialists through the biography written of him by the Norwegian military college professor Brynjar Lia. Here, his work, and particularly *The Global Islamic Resistance Call*, is specifically appraised as a brilliant strategic document laying the foundations for the decentralized strategy of 'global jihad'.[56]

There are, however, two fairly clear problems with this work. First, as I argued in the first chapter, the strategy of individualized action would appear not to have been so brilliant after all. Successful or even near-successful acts of jihadist terrorism have not been carried out by self-sufficient cells, but rather have required significant amounts of more formal support. Moreover, the problems with the approach are, as I argued in the fifth chapter, to some extent inherent in the nature of Al-Suri's plan itself. However, a bigger problem with Brynjar Lia's treatment of this figure is that precisely by offering such a masterful analysis of what is original and interesting about what Al-Suri has to say, it necessarily fails to convey just how unfocused, how meandering, how unnecessarily comprehensive Al-Suri's 1604-page book actually is, when viewed as a whole. Indeed, ironically, the snappy translation of some of the most direct and to-the-point bits of Al-Suri's book provided in Lia's own biography seems to be one of the only parts of the book that get circulated in English-language jihadi contexts online. In reality, while Al-Suri's book is not quite the straightforward cut and paste of Breivik's compilation, it is similar both in the way its content essentially repeats vast swathes of more or less identical material available on jihadist and Salafist websites, but also in the paradox of a dauntingly encyclopaedic work being presented as supposedly a straightforward manual for action. In both cases, it is as if the author, in the course of producing a brief 'how to' guide, felt driven by an irresistible urge to write down *absolutely everything* that might explain that action – essentially, to invoke an entire hypothetical social order, to build a whole parallel world. Indeed, even the order in which the material is presented, and the overall structures of the works have quite a lot in common, with universal histories and contemporary political analyses being followed by final sections dealing with more concrete and practical military issues. While it is true that some of Breivik's more outlandish moments are certainly not replicated in Al-Suri's analysis, at least part of what makes Breivik seem mad and Al-Suri seem brilliant would seem to have less to do with content per se, as intersubjective context: Al-Suri writes for a wider milieu who take his words seriously. Breivik wishes he did.

Thus, while Western Islamophobia is no doubt worrying as a general phenomenon, and while the specific prospect of radical 'anti-jihadi' or 'crusaderist' terrorism is not one to be ignored, and more than the prospect of jihadist terrorism, it seems perilous to overstate its coherence and political meaning. It is questionable whether Breivik's action can really be explained by the beliefs he espoused. And there is a real risk that by exaggerating the coherence of his ideology, we will end up creating a new, artificially coherent, bogeyman analogous to that which jihadism was supposed to represent over the past ten years. If anything – as I have suggested with my perhaps mischievous comparison to one of the supposedly great, canonical works of jihadi literature, we do better to consider how far the example of highly idiosyncratic works like Breivik's might help us to treat jihadi ideological work less reverentially with regard to its supposed ideological and strategic coherence.

There is another, quite different way in which we can seek to site an enquiry into specifically online dimensions of the privatized war on 'radical' Islam of which Breivik represents a particularly extreme case. This is by considering the phenomenon as yet another online consumption practice analogous to jihadism – indeed, one which, like jihadism, is substantially premised on a certain set of subcultural relations to 'jihadi' content. Over the years of the 'war on terror', many sites have grown up, such as *Jihadwatch*,[57] *The Jawa Report*[58] and *Internet Haganah*[59] which revolve, to a greater or lesser degree, around the core activity of reporting on online jihadi content. While these sites tend to have (or in the case of the latter, had) a politically conservative, strongly pro-Israel outlook and report on jihadi content for the purpose of promoting and, as they see it, raising awareness of an existential threat posed by jihadist radicalism, ultimately to Western civilization itself, it is interesting to note that there is no firm line between the activity of sites of this kind and those of more formalized research projects.

Thus, for example, Aaron Weisburd, of Internet Haganah, while he has been styled by some as an online 'vigilante',[60] has also worked on serious academic papers on online jihadi phenomena. He is also part of the community associated with the site *Jihadica*, a collective blog run by Will McCants – a major scholar of radical Islam, and featuring regular work by leading figures in the area like Thomas Hegghammer and Nelly Lahoud.[61] On the other hand, some of the professional institutions offering access by subscription service to the translations of the latest jihadi and Islamist content to serious researchers, such as MEMRI or the SITE institute, would seem to be perceptibly pro-Israeli in their general orientation, whatever this may or may not imply for the overall balance of their reporting.[62]

There is, in short, as uncomfortable as some may find it, no absolute line to be drawn between the consumption of jihadi content by 'counter-jihad' activists, typically motivated by strong, broadly conservative and pro-Israel convictions, and those of more professionalized and formalized institutions – including academia; an area which, of course, includes the present author.[63]

However, a line can be drawn between those who engage with jihadi content for purposes of research or political activism, and those who take things further, striving to actively 'combat' jihadism online via 'asymmetric' information operations waged online. Indeed for some, this notion of virtual 'combat' seems to have sustained vividly imagined enterprises strikingly similar to their 'electronic jihad' equivalents. A grouping calling itself the 'Internet Wolf Pack' (now seemingly defunct) dedicated itself to a 'YouTube smackdown' project, based on crowdsourcing the identification of jihadi videos on this site which YouTube would then be asked to remove via its built-in procedures for flagging content in possible violation of community guidelines.[64] Somewhat ironically, perhaps, this involved advertising the very content which was to be removed. In an even bigger irony, the Wolf Pack site linked directly to another (so stylistically similar as to appear to be part of the same enterprise) called *Got War Porn?* which displayed videos of American forces engaging 'terrorists' in Iraq and Afghanistan and 'kicking their a**' (the asterisks are in the original).[65] Another example would be a figure who calls himself Th3J35t3r. This computer hacker rose to a certain amount of prominence when he engaged in an electronic exchange with members of the Anonymous movement in relation to actions surrounding the leak of US diplomatic cables by Wikileaks. However, up to that point his skills had seemingly mainly been devoted to taking down jihadi forums.[66]

The fact that the consumption of violent content from both sides of the 'war' between 'the West' and 'Islam' led to rather analogous online practices on both sides is brought into particular focus by one forum in particular: Infovlad. Infovlad, established by the anonymous, eponymous 'Vladimir' began life as a 'clearing house' for content relating to the War on Terror. Its founding members (the second after 'Vlad' was Aaron Weisburd, who very kindly allowed me access to his archive of the site) were broadly devoted to the project of investigating and combating jihadism. But since the forum was open to anyone to join, since it was in English, and since it offered excellent access to jihadi content items, it wasn't long before it attracted members who presented themselves as, not to overstate the case, Muslims with a distinctly critical stance on the war on terror.[67] Indeed, some of those who had been active on the forum were later implicated in jihadist terrorism cases in the United Kingdom and elsewhere.

Over time, Infovlad became so popular with its Muslim members (many of whom did in fact present as active supporters of jihadi groups including Al Qaeda) that some, at least, came to treat it as a jihadi forum, almost unaware of its origins, as posts like the following serve to indicate:

> I'm a new member here and I've been reading some stuff. However, it seems to me that there are a lot of non-Muslims here. So can someone please tell me which of these people are kufaar, as it is getting very confusing. Just their names will do. Jazakallah khair.

This new member's confusion was understandable. Structurally, infovlad was almost identical to a jihadi forum, being organized around a main section dedicated to 'Video, Audio and Images from Islamic Militants', while other sections dealt with more general news, technical issues. Another section on 'military video' paralleling those providing material from Islamic Militants was entirely devoted to Western military footage of the kind which elsewhere would be called 'war porn'. Moderators and senior members of the forum included both those with militant Islamic and those with militant anti-militant

SOME OTHER 'JIHADI' CONSUMPTION CULTURES

Islamic stances (as well as some with more difficult-to-classify agendas). And the terminology used reflected the multiple ideologies of the site's members. For example, the news section was described on the main page as offering 'news articles related to Islamic resistance, insurgency and terrorism'.

This is not to say, of course, that relations between different members were entirely harmonious, and, given the anonymous nature of online interactions, interesting misunderstandings were bound to arise. For example, the member who commented on the existence of 'another even more dangerous net crusader named Aaron something or other' was presumably not aware that the person he was talking about was the second most senior member of the forum on which he was writing. Interestingly, neither, does it seem was pro-Islamic resistance moderator he was discussing with, who offered to check up on the status of this mysterious Aaron. But for the most part, the basic business of the forum was conducted with, so it seems, a shared seriousness. After all, the ultimate goal of the members was the same – to find and disseminate content produced by the warring parties in Iraq, Afghanistan and other conflicts involving jihadist groups. As with jihadi forums, this business was conducted with a minimum of conversation. Most of the posts on the main sections of infovlad had few, if any, replies, and most of these replies were terse and factual. Actual discussions happened only on the more generalized, relaxed sections at the bottom of the list of the forum's chat rooms, particularly in the miscellaneous section which was called, invoking the carnivalesque humour inherent in the Jerry Springer-like possibilities involved, 'Hatebox a-Go Go!' Here, discussions unfolded on questions such as whether Allah is the biblical Satan, whether Americans attached a fake beard to Saddam Hussein's face, and which Islamic countries would do well in Olympics.

What the example of a site like Infovlad helps to illustrate is some of the anarchic complexity that actually undergirds the emergence of phenomena such as 'jihadism' or 'anti-jihadism'. It would be naïve to assume that Infovlad's members all entered the forum simply as curious observers of the war on terror, whose framing of the significance of its events was purely the result of their online participation. Certainly it would appear that some members of the forum fell into this category. However, others who came to the forum no doubt did so with clear ideological opinions, and specific instrumental intentions, whether to monitor online 'terrorism' or to conduct electronic jihad. But even with regard to the latter, what is striking is how the materiality of the forum, that nature of the practices involved in distributing and consuming both jihadi material and US Army 'war porn' led to a remarkable and, by and large, harmonious symmetry within the forum environment itself, not so much through actual dialogue, as through shared (albeit opposite) interests in terms of collection. The overall ideology of infovlad, so it seems, was ultimately the ideology of the internet: of the unfettered collection, compilation and consumption of digital content.

We can examine a yet more extreme example of this by considering a case of a forum in which substantial amounts of similar kinds of content were collected and consumed, in principle not out of any political interest, but rather for reasons of curiosity and entertainment: shock sites specializing in gory footage such as Ogrish.com. This particular sited had started out in the late 1990s with the portrayal of graphic gore obtained from such sources as *The Colour Encyclopedia of Pathology*. As the site (and the internet) developed, however, fresh images started to be sent in by people such as crime photographers whose professions gave them access to fresh shock material. However, a major development came with the emergence of a new phenomenon altogether, in the form of live execution and torture videos from the Chechen war. Starting with the earliest examples such as Chechclear and Ofex, this trickle of material swelled considerably with the wars in Afghanistan and, particularly of course, Iraq. And a growing community of seemingly very ordinary people gathered on the site to consume graphic footage of this kind.[68]

What is interesting about this case, however, is not so much the notion of gore content as pure entertainment, unfettered by any deeper intellectual considerations, but rather the insight it seems to offer about the ideological processes at work even where the relationship with the content is apparently purely about entertainment, curiosity or shock for its own sake. While Ogrish began, according to the recollections of Hayden Hewitt, who was asked to take on the role of managing the site around 2003, the project began primarily as an act of youthful rebellion, of 'sticking two fingers up to the world'. Before long, however, the site's founders began to find this unsatisfactory and 'wanted to go in a much more serious direction'. For Hewitt, the practical implications of this meant taking care to research the videos and images being uploaded, given them serious rather than flippant titles, and avoiding humour or mockery as well as the advertisements for pornography ubiquitous on underground sites. But there was, he thinks, a deeper rationale as well. He insists that the second half of the twentieth century saw a removal of representations of death and gore from news-stands which amounted to a collective act of denial. This in turn means that the violence that was to be seen, in action films for example, became 'incredibly glamorous . . . a polished and sanitized version of nastiness'. For him, Ogrish was about restoring that balance, bringing people into touch with some of the 'nastiness' which mainstream media was determined to shield them from.

According to Hewitt's observations, the vibrant online community that built up around Ogrish was strikingly normal and diverse. People from both genders and a wide variety of backgrounds seemed to congregate on the sight. And their

SOME OTHER 'JIHADI' CONSUMPTION CULTURES

conversations typically had little to do with the material which nonetheless he had 'no doubt they were watching'. And yet, as we can see from his comments on the attempts to move the site in a more serious direction, the dissemination of gore footage did, at least for the managers of the site, raise moral issues which seem to have made them increasingly uncomfortable. Indeed, Hewitt notes with dismay how beheading videos, in particular, seem to have become increasingly shocking. As he observes:

> . . . there was some horrific, absolutely genuinely horrific media that came out of this at the time, [from Chechnya] that was easily as horrific as the far more known media from Al Qaeda and Iraq at the time. They were showing some horrific . . . not just murdering but torture as well and mass murder, and it seems like it moved from there when that all stopped to the Iraq war, and once Al-Zarqawi was informed "this isn't helping us" . . . you only saw the execution of Arabic people after that. There were no more execution videos. And now it all comes from Mexico. So we've gone from, if we look at the broadest possible strokes without getting too, which side the fence you might stand on, a small country fighting a huge country, and using the propaganda, an insurgent movement, fighting what they perceived to be the invader, and now you've got the Mexican cartels just trying to outdo each other in what brutality they can show on tape, so we've gone from these massive conflicts things where the idea seems to have been adopted by these criminals just trying to frighten other criminals and the general public into being terrified of them, so all different types of terrorism. Uh, but now it's almost as if we've currently living through a time of the cheapest form of it. This is the closest it's ever been to snuff.

What is interesting is the apparent parallel between the disquiet which seems to have been ultimately felt by the management of Ogrish over the value of their actions and the role of ideological narrative in injecting an albeit slight element of justifiability to extreme violence. Hewitt takes similar umbrage at the levity of Mexican drug cartel beheading videos compared to the more ritualized nature of Al Qaeda ones (which is not of course to suggest that he finds the latter somehow acceptable) as he does with the levity with which some other gore sites treat their material. And the only alternative to levity is it seems to move in a more political direction. And yet, based on Hewitt's reading of audience, there seems to be a tension here. For when he speaks of the typical audience of Ogrish, the language he uses is of normality and restraint. But when he comes to address more politically motivated consumers of violent content such as, particularly, jihadi material and military footage from the 'war on terror', the impression is created of a generally less polite and restrained kind of viewer.

Here too, though, Hewitt's observations greatly emphasize heterogeneity and the difficulty of ascribing clear motivations. He observes – in keeping with the comments about infovlad forum above:

> . . . as unsettling as certain viewpoints might be, because on Liveleak at a previous point, the guys that love the warporn, we see it from another side – the guys that love watching the American soldiers get potted. They love it. They love it to bits and it's the same thing. That's why I drew the parallel between the militant atheist and the extremely religious person. They're practically the same. Interchangeable. The way they put their points across, the way they attack each other, certain kinds of language they use. It's almost the same. Every other day on Liveleak I'll get an IM saying "you want to look into this member I'm sure they're a terrorist." They're acting the same as them, just from the other side.

By contrast, those who maintain more distance on this content type are, he thinks, less likely to take part in online discussion.

> They are the exception in so far as they don't tend to post to begin with because if you're ever on the fence you tend to get attacked by both sides. Cos you can never make both sides happy, so the least vocal people are either the ones who take nothing from it, or who can see both sides. Who, even if they might agree with one side more than the other they can see what one side or the other believes to be a valid issue or valid political point. But they're the least vocal. The most vocal are the ones that are firmly in one camp or another.

What Hewitt's observation seems to suggest is a certain equivalence between being 'serious', being engaged and being ideological which would appear also to apply to his own journey from Ogrish to Liveleak and from 'shock' to 'citizen journalism'. While, in principle, fascination with death is presumably a human universal, something which requires little explanation, over time, the need to provide some kind of moralizing account for the kind of content provided by Ogrish seems to have been irresistible. Just as real-life violence is always ultimately hemmed in by social norms and taboos, so too for the dissemination and systematic consumption of mediated violence. Gore cannot be presented simply as gore. Sustained engagement with it must be justified within some sort of larger moral system.

The fate of Ogrish.com can, therefore, be contrasted interestingly with the case of Infovlad. Whereas those in charge of Ogrish.com ultimately struggled with the need to find a satisfactory account for their activities, on Infovlad, senior members with diametrically opposed, but reasonably clear ideological outlooks were seemingly able to work together relatively harmoniously, united by the values associated with a common set of online *practices*. For both supporters of the War on Terror and supporters of the mujahidin, the technical demands of obtaining, disseminating and organizing militant content produced a project remarkably similar in form and style to the jihadi forums to which some members at least were radically opposed. Practically speaking, for both sides, Infovlad was, one might suppose, potentially a rather dubious project. For anti-jihadis, the site was clearly helping some ostensibly quite radical Muslims to obtain propaganda material. For radical Muslims, the risks of being on a forum run by the enemy might seem to be cause for concern. And yet it would seem that the ideologies of members played a stabilizing rather than disruptive role, by offering precisely the sort of clear justification for the consumption behaviours in question that the Ogrish management began to feel the lack of.

The consideration of how ideology seems to emerge, more or less inevitably, from consumptive relationships with jihadi content, with 'war porn' and with graphically violent material more generally, juxtaposed with the complexities of a solitary incident of real-life terrorism such as that carried out by Anders Behring Breivik serves, perhaps, as a good summary of this book's overall arguments so far. It is natural for humans to look for narratives, to try to construct social actors, to produce essentialist accounts which link action to group and group to belief. But how far, in the contemporary world, do these accounts really explain actual, embodied human actions? And how far, with regard to the internet, is it the actual practices by which we consume the medium that really shape what we do, as opposed to the terribly important sounding discourses and ideas that we interact with by means of those practices? We may now conclude the book by turning to a deeper reflection on some of these questions, and how they may inform our understanding of terrorism and political violence in the present day.

8

Jihadism between fantasy and virtuality, a tentative conclusion

A recent piece (at the time of writing) by Maura Conway, a long-standing scholar in the area of terrorism and the internet, whose work was mentioned frequently in the first chapter, serves usefully to place the task this book has undertaken in context. Drawing on the recent work of Stefan Malthener, Conway begins with the notion of the 'violent radical milieu' and proceeds to argue that the internet supports violent radical milieus of a distinctive kind.[1]

The idea of the violent, insurgent group as isolated, marginal and eccentric is one which the powers opposing it will naturally wish to insist on. But the reality will almost certainly be more complex. Not only is it a matter of tautological necessity, built into our very understanding of what it means to be 'political' that the practitioners of an act of political violence are not wholly isolated and idiosyncratic; but in practice it is also likely that there are many more who sympathize with the group than make their sympathies public. Moreover, such sympathy may exist not only as something latent within society, but even within individual members of it. At least until circumstances force a choice, sympathy and even admiration for a group and its specific members may coincide with condemnation of its means or even its ends in one and the same person.

Indeed, as fascinating research by the psychologists Sophia Moskalenko and Clark McCauley seems to indicate, there may be fundamental distinctions to be drawn between those who are, rhetorically at least, predisposed to involvement in political violence and those who are predisposed to be involved in political activism generally. Using questionnaire-based studies in three different settings (American students, Ukrainian students and American adults), they found that readiness to carry out acts of conventional political activism and readiness to carry out acts of violent or illegal activism were not on a single continuum, but independent of one another, with those who identified most with their country being *more* ready to carry out peaceful political activism, but those who identified less being more sympathetic to the idea of protesting in ways which broke the law.[2]

And yet, the notion of 'violent radicalisation', much as it has entered the vocabulary of policy, is one which mainstream scholarship on political violence is still uneasy with. As scholars such as Anthony Richards[3] and Mark Sedgwick[4] have pointed out, the notion seems to suffer from major problems. For example, it seems to focus counterterrorism on supposedly problematic ideas, rather than illegal behaviours; it begs the question of a connection between certain sorts of public discourse and certain sorts of violent action. Indeed, by shackling together 'radicalism' and 'violence', it implies that there is some kind of intimate relationship between the two. This is despite the fact that, as Max Abrahms has brilliantly observed,[5] contrary to popular belief, terrorist groups have often had political ideologies no more 'radical' than those of their non-violent peers.

It is over issues of this kind that I part company with Conway's analysis. In attempting to further explore the internet as a 'violent radical milieu', she presumes that what is at issue in speaking of the internet as a 'violent radical milieu' is necessarily the relationship between online interactions and actual violence. That is, she seems to identify the 'violent' bit of 'violent radicalisation' in violent *behaviour*, while leaving the 'radical' bit to cover the discursive phenomena that are considered to be candidates for bringing this about. More specifically, in pursuing this question, she posits the idea that the internet may substitute for antecedent phenomena to political violence that would otherwise take place through face-to-face interaction.

Amidst this debate about the salience of the notion of 'violent radicalisation', and the question of whether it takes place to any significant degree on the internet, there is, I would suggest, a point that is being missed. This is that 'violent radicalisation', if it means anything, must surely mean a process leading not to violence as such, but rather to a condition of 'violent radicalism', that is, to a certain sort of engagement with 'radical' discourses about violence. Now of course, it might also turn out to be the case that there are significant links between violent radicalism and actual violence. Indeed, in certain circumstances, it would have to be the case: since political violence must, almost by definitional necessity, be violence in which those parties constituted as the actors responsible have access to some kind of generalizable and rational account of their actions, the very existence of 'political violence' would therefore necessarily also require the existence and, furthermore, articulation of a 'violent radical' discourse. However, in such cases the question of whether this discourse represented an actual effective cause of the violence would still remain.

This observation brings us to my second main objection to Conway's recent argument. While she is clear (at least in general principle) that the internet, as a site for violent radial milieus, is likely to have some distinctive features, in practice, she treats online violent radical milieus as more or less equivalent to what she sees as their offline alternatives. Indeed, she specifically addresses the problem of whether the internet might serve as an alternative to 'violent radical' practices (assumed to be related to actual violence) that would otherwise take place through face-to-face interactions.

Political 'radicalism', political violence and political ideologies with specifically rebellious, insurgent or 'counterhegemonical' things to say about when violence is appropriate are certainly not new. Moreover, the ideas and discourses of this sort which are to be found on the internet may not differ in any fundamental way from those that have been disseminated previously by other media. And yet, it may nonetheless be so that the properties of the internet make it capable of facilitating the emergence of forms of 'violent radicalism' quite different in the overall natures from those which have existed before, not by virtue of any change in the nature of the content, but rather by effects produced – nodding of course to McLuhan's famous adage – at the level of the medium.

In other words, in speaking of an 'online violent radical milieu', we may in fact be speaking of a substantially new phenomenon, which cannot adequately be understood or dealt with reference to existing assumptions about political violence and its relationship to media and to ideology.

In this book, I have attempted to explore this assumption in relation to one such, particularly high profile, case. Of course, online Jihadi-Salafism hardly represents the only case of an online violent radical milieu, and it seems very likely that others, presently unimagined, will come into being in the future. Other examples would likely include White Supremacism, certain material relating to sections of the American Christian Right and, as we saw in the preceding chapter, the emerging phenomenon of extreme 'Counter-Jihad' or 'Crusaderism'.

And yet, as should by now have become clear, global jihadism, at least in its starkest formulation, does in fact represent rather a useful paradigmatic case for a discussion of the violent radical milieu as a putative class of phenomena. Indeed, if we were to devise a way to test the proposition that 'violent radical' beliefs disseminated online, in the absence of material support structures, are capable of causing actual violence, it would seem that the case of internet jihadism offers about as good a natural experiment as could be imagined.

First, compared to its alternatives, jihadism would seem to be more *explicitly and specifically focused on violence*. While the main elements of jihadist thinking (an essentialized, polarized vision of a virtuous in-group locked in eternal struggle with an irredeemably evil enemy; a millenarian belief in an imminent apocalypse; a fetishization of violence as something ennobling, beautiful and spiritual in its own right and, simultaneously, a doctrine capable of justifying the most seemingly brutal means in terms of the perfection of ultimate ends) are none of them unique, whether individually or indeed in combination, the sheer precision with which these things are codified in jihadist thought, and the emphasis on participation in violent jihad almost as a condition of faith seems to exceed anything quite comparable in the various ideologies mentioned. White Supremacism may match or exceed jihadism in the manichaeism of its vision, and in its obsession with violence as part of a warrior ethic; radical anti-abortionist Christian movements may equal it in its notion of violent action as a divinely mandated ethic absolute, and emergent movement of crusaderism may aspire to form its mirror image. But none of these phenomena would seem to match it on all counts.

Secondly, internet jihadism is, in important ways, a movement made for the internet. For all that the core texts of contemporary global jihadism strive to root themselves in authentic Islamic sources and interpretative traditions, and for all that they draw on a tradition of modern political Islam which is itself now more than a hundred years old, in many ways the global jihadism with which I have been primarily concerned was custom made for the internet age. Its most well-known and widely disseminated texts such as *39 Ways to Serve Jihad and the Mujahidin* and *Constants in the Path of Jihad* as well as the magazines *Sawt al-Jihad* and *Mu'askir al-Battar* were all produced circa 2004 by Al Qaeda in the Arabian Peninsula for the specific purpose of trying to produce a general uprising in one of the Arabic world's richest and most developed states. *The Global Islamic Resistance Call* was written with a similar purpose – the furtherance of the Al Qaeda struggle through the principle of 'organisation without *an* organisation' and, more recently, those publications associated with Anwar al-'Awlaqi have tried to renew the call.

Finally, jihadism is more firmly global and transnational than its alternatives. Of course, the various types of extreme right wing ideology with which I have just compared jihadism all have global or transnational dimensions to some degree. Of course jihadism is, in important strands of its overall vision, ideologically committed to a more geographically based vision than might sometimes be allowed. Of course jihadism, even specifically online jihadism, is in very important ways rooted in the very much localized and embodied practices of groups such as the various Al Qaeda affiliates, the Taliban, Al-Shabab Al-Mujahidin and so on. And of course it is obviously the case that what is apparently the same jihadist ideology is manifested and made use of very differently in different geographical and cultural contexts. Nonetheless, jihadi-salafism, in particular, is distinguished by being a fringe and subcultural phenomenon wherever it exists – in contrast to more amorphous movements such as anti-abortion, while existing across the world in both Muslim-minority and Muslim-majority contexts, in contrast (so far) to neo-Nazism or other forms of White Supremacism. Of course, jihadism is matched in its level of transnationalism by movements such as anti-capitalism and environmentalism, which also sometimes include offshoots that are somewhat violent. But these do not exist as nearly such well-developed 'violent radical' forms.

All in all then, the 'violent radical online milieu' examined in this book can be seen as rather a useful test case for the overall potential of such phenomena to produce actual violence. And, as I argued out the outset of this book, the results of this natural experiment seem to be quite clearly negative. That is not to say that jihadi violence has gone away. Far from it. But the new opportunities for the development of jihadi campaigns have come about primarily for old-fashioned reasons: the opening of new political opportunities, and the local availability or proximity of organizational and material resources for their exploitation. Hence the recent emergence of jihadi or somewhat jihadi groups in Libya, Syria, Sinai and Mali.

By contrast, constraining the resources and capabilities of 'Al Qaeda Central' and keeping a close watch on other organizations interested in 'going global' such as, notably, the second incarnation of Al Qaeda in the Arabian Peninsula has been largely effective at thwarting major acts of global terrorism. Constraining these groups has not been counterbalanced by an unstoppable wave of 'leaderless jihad' which has, in fact, amounted to no more than a handful of mostly rather limited incidents.

Of course the reason for the absence of *mass* participation in the kind of 'individual terrorism' called for by Abu Mus'ab al-Suri or for that matter Ayman al-Zawahiri[6] is undoubtedly the simple fact that only the minutest number of Muslims take this call for individual action seriously. But, as argued at the outset, it would seem that this cannot be the full story. For even if our concern is only with the subcultures of 'jihadis' who constituted, to repeat Adam Gadahn's memorable phrase, a 'fringe of a fringe', the paucity of actions from this grouping seems nonetheless to be remarkable on the naïve assumption that apparently sincere belief in a sufficiently uncompromising doctrine is sufficient to produce action.

What all this seems to hint at, at least, is that a shortfall in violence; and ostensibly surprising gap between speech and action may represent not just a puzzle for those trying to understand the relationship between the internet and actual *engagement* or *involvement* in terrorism, but actually one of the distinctive and possibly defining features of the online violent radical milieu as a class a phenomena. Indeed, once things are phrased in these terms, it seems that we might reasonably expect such a thing to be the case. The internet (as Johnny Ryan has previously observed),[7] whatever else it may do in terms of 'radicalising' people, is at least likely to make certain radical views which might once have been normal in certain very specific environments and contexts common knowledge to a wider world. But, more than this, it would also seem to be the case, as we saw in Chapter 4 for the case of jihadi forums, that it does more than this: creating polarized online environments characterized by the emergence of particularly extreme opinions. And yet, at the very same time as it does this, the internet would also seem to serve to isolate and constrain the actual practice of violent *practice*.

The first set of ways in which this would seem to work are negative. One can more or less have freedom of expression on the internet on condition of anonymity. Or one can use the internet to sustain more complex social interactions provided one is prepared to sacrifice anonymity. But one cannot have both, and jihadis (and likely other sorts of violent radical) well know it. Moreover, as suggested in Chapter 5, this knowledge itself can then go on to serve as another barrier, by offering a convenient explanation from those deeply involved in online activities as to why they are prevented from becoming engaged in a physical capacity.

However, as I have argued in this book, it would seem, paradoxically, that the online violent radical milieu may actually generate its own *positive* reasons for non-engagement. For once the barrier between online and offline has been securely established (and what better or more exciting way than the threat of intelligence listening in?), the online violent radical milieu is then able to develop a set of meaningful and, so it would seem, pleasurable practices of its own. Apparently supporting a particular cause, the violent radical group subtly subverts it by mining it for the affective benefits and subcultural capital resources it can yield, while contributing in return things which may, but quite possibly may not be of any serious value in terms of the movement's advancing towards its actual objectives.

This may seem to be rather a contentious statement. After all, the jihadis who carry out activities such as writing articles or producing graphic designs and so on, even as part of an 'art competition', are not, at least by their own estimation, simply playing around. Indeed, as I noted in the second chapter, what they are doing looks very much like alternative media of the sort produced by less contentious types of oppositional movement. And indeed, where we are talking quite specifically about the media apparatuses of groups like the Taliban or Al-Shabab Al-Mujahidin, approaching things from this angle might be more appropriate. And yet, as I also argued in that chapter, appearances can be deceptive. Indeed, it might be argued that jihadi media is actually furthest from being meaningfully comprehensible in terms of the repertoires of more familiar types of transnational contention precisely when it seems more closely to resemble them, as can be illustrated by the extract below.

> "I desire jihad, but the government has stopped the way to jihad." Are you constantly coming across this thinking? I believe that every respectable, decent person who won't stand for justice and shame thinks about jihad. And in any case: "who did not do jihad or decide in his heart to do jihad died with a portion of hypocrisy." The main point in the subject: do you want to be sure that you really desire jihad? And what stands in the path of your jihad? The government systems, not the desires of the soul. Put it another way: welcome to this field of jihad:
>
> 1 Stop smoking: mainly American cigarettes
>
> 2 Boycott products which support Zionism: "Starbucks" and so on
>
> 3 Boycott products which support American Zionism: Pepsi, Kentucky, McDonald's and so on . . .
>
> 4 Give a little time when you go shopping to read the sources of products and if they are American, discard them, and even if they are manufactured in an Arabic country under an American franchise, because the benefit will return to America and then to Israel to kill your brothers.
>
> 5 Did you disapprove of Israel's attacks on mosques? The least reply we can make is to develop our own safe, empty mosques, especially at the dawn prayer. (*How can you make war on the enemy, and you can't even make war on sleep and the blanket at dawn???*)
>
> 6 Du'a, du'a, du'a (and ask yourself before you sleep, did you do du'a for your people in Gaza today?)'[8]

Even in a relatively moderate text like this one (the tone of which would seem to be more in line with globalized Islamist politics generally than serious jihadi-salafism), jihad is presented as a moral duty in its own right, and the activities outlined are offered not as effective ways of putting pressure on a potentially pressurable opponent, but rather as acts of inherent moral worthiness. The boycotting of Israel and America, while intended to cause economic damage, is certainly not carried out in the expectation that it will cause either country to change its policies. The fact that it is listed alongside specifically ritual activities such as *du'a* further adds to the suggestion that its functional resemblance to conventional globalized activism is only superficial, or at any rate, that it taps more into notions of collective ritual that may be latent in consumer activist practices than into their explicit political purpose.

It was for this reason that, in the second chapter, I argued that those who have approached the jihadism, albeit in a rather limited way, through the lens of leisure, subcultures of consumption and, specifically, fandom may have more to contribute than has hitherto been acknowledged. To reprise, very briefly, the set of mechanisms I drew from that literature, it would seem that the major dynamics at work in fan communities are as follows:

- The emergence of a subcultural capital economy
- Subversive forms of reading
- Consumption practice versus textual content
- Synecdochic community

Based on the chapters that followed, I have tried to show that all of these mechanisms appear to be identifiable in jihadi contexts. With regard to the first, it is quite clear that it is possible to win prestige specifically through contributions to online jihadism, without any suggestion of engagement in actual violence. Indeed, with the development of a range of jihadi practices and forms of distinction, it increasingly seems to be the case that digital jihadi products, including ideological literature and art, are admired and appraised in their own right.

Jihadis do not subvert the core ideological texts which they read and virtually inhabit in any straightforward sense: on the contrary, they claim to revere them. It is true that jihadi content plays on and subverts a wide range of other media. For example, it has often been pointed out how the productions of official Islamic Media Foundations such as al-Sahab deliberately imitate the style and formats of mainstream news or with the production of so-called 'women's magazines' such as *Al-Shamikha*.[9] To some extent, this may be better understood as a process of substitution of the sort observed in rational choice perspectives on new religious movements, whereby these groups attempt to lower the costs of remaining within the group by trying to replicate some of the media forms available in the profane world outside. However, perhaps particularly with regard to English content such as *Inspire* magazine, it would seem that jihadi content clearly moves beyond this and into the domain of creative and subversive play.[10]

At a deeper level, however, the relationship jihadis have even with core ideological texts can be seen as subversive in a less obvious sense. Through the transgressive excess of the so-called fans identified by the passage quoted in Chapter 2, jihad is transferred from being a distant object which jihadis must soberly and incrementally attempt to serve, to being an immediate source of gratification, association with which can serve as the basis for a set of subcultural commitments. In this sense, the tactical, time-bound evasions of the internet jihadi can be seen as a form of 'resistant reading' by which the greater object of jihad is tacitly denuded of its binding force and liberated of its excitement and glamour.

As argued in Chapter 6, the seemingly obvious paradoxes of jihadi engagement are resolved in the practice of precisely those behaviours out of which these paradoxes arise. Like Janice Radway's romance-readers, who resisted traditional demands of husbands and domestic life in order to read books which apparently upheld precisely these traditionalist values, online jihadis involve themselves in demanding and self-affirming collective projects based on the dissemination of electronic content which calls for more or less immediate bodily action.

Finally, as explored in Chapters 5 and 6, jihadis seem to balance between their actual experience of online community and practice and their mediated experience of the mujahidin in order to produce a sense of mutual affect and meaningful action in which one fills out the other, infusing relatively fragmentary online interactions with significance, and at the same time helping to offer a taste of what the idealized companionship associated with the practice of jihad might mean.

Thus, so I have argued, fandom offers a useful analogy to jihadis' online behaviour in so far as both fans and internet jihadis make creative use of consumption practices in order to construct for themselves distinctive subcultures which serve as sources of collective identity which are related, but not explicitly reducible to what a 'dominant' reading of the texts engaged with might seem to imply.

And yet the complexity of the notion of fandom itself and the serious problems raised in comparing media fans to precisely the kind of 'fanaticism' which fan-studies scholars have struggled to move the term away from suggests that the need remains to think through the significance of this analogy more deeply.

In approaching this task, it is worth observing that recent developments in fan studies have increasingly opened up the notion to its application to a broader range of consumption behaviours and textual commitments. As once firm distinctions between cultural forms have become more plastic, and as fandom has become more culturally acceptable and mainstream, so the notion of 'fannish engagement' has come to be applied to a variety of consumption practices. For example, in a fairly recent collection of essays, engagement in high-cultural forms such as the plays of Chekhov[11] or the music of Bach[12] have been analysed as such. Still more striking, Jonathan Gray speculates in the same collection about whether one could speak of fandom in relation to the consumption of mediated news.[13]

However, attempts in this direction seem to remain conceptually limited and hesitant.

Gray's piece seeks to develop the idea by drawing on George Marcus' notion of sentimental citizenship – the claim that the division between emotion and reason is a false one, and that informed and engaged citizen decisions can only be founded on an ultimately emotional investment in politics.[14] But the problem with this line of thought seems to be that, however unwillingly and hesitantly, it reinstates the idea that fandom is to be located simply in the affective, emotional part of textual consumption, even while fan studies has often insisted on the rigour of analysis that fans bring to texts.

By contrast, Henry Jenkins' notion of a 'convergence culture' in which engagement with entertainment and activism are constantly and dynamically merging into one another is more nuanced. But its nuance seems to involve collapsing precisely the distinction which, albeit in idealized form, I am seeking to deploy. Moreover, it is unclear that, just because of a dizzying convergence of media forms and the possibilities of audience interactions with them, the salience of ideal-type categories of consumptive act is removed. The fact that one might one minute be collectively consuming Mitt Romney's address to the Republican National Convention *as comedy* and, in the next minute, making use of the cultural resonances of *Dr Who* to launch a devastating critique of new laws regulating political protest in the United Kingdom still implies the relevance of underlying frames of reference for such textual behaviours.

To develop an analysis further, then, it would seem to be necessary to move away from precisely such anti-essentialist thinking and to reassert, albeit only for conceptual purposes, some fundamental principle by which 'fannish' forms of engagement with texts can be distinguished from other types of engagement, without reducing fannish engagement to a mere pejorative, and without denying that fannish engagement with texts could in fact have 'serious' political or social potential.

A notion which seems to be helpful in this regard is that of fantasy. As multifarious as the forms of media fandom are, it would seem that all entail an engagement with fantasy in at least some, and sometimes multiple senses of the word. Thus, fans may fantasize about rock stars, sporting figures, actors or other celebrities, they may engage in fantasy worlds such as those of *Star Trek* or *The Lord of the Rings*, or they may even engage in fantasies regarding the inhabitants of fantasy worlds, such as the famous genre of 'slash' fiction involving imagined sexual relationships between figures such as Captain Kirk and Mr Spock.[15]

Now fantasy, where it is used to describe political phenomena, has characteristically pejorative connotations. To provide a topical example, here are the words of the anthropologist Nicola Khan drawing on the work of Freud, Klein and Zizek to argue that jihadist militants in Pakistan:

> . . . articulate their fantasies in ideological terms of desires to destroy the wholesale failures of Pakistani political democracy, neo-liberalism and US global capitalism, realise the ideal future of a truly Islamic Pakistan that can treat its citizens in accordance with its ideals, avenge the sufferings of the global community of Muslims, fulfil personal desires of becoming powerful and whole, and redeem the past through sacrifice. Yet practically, and in fantasy, in serving the state's methods of enforcing power and maintaining control, jihad structures protest conventionally rather than radically.[16]

An interesting point about Khan's use of 'fantasy' here is the way in which it seems to be specifically opposed to the notion of 'ideology'. By suggesting that 'ideological terms' are, in this case, mere clothing for underlying 'fantasies', the author necessarily suggests the idea that there is something mutually exclusive about the two, and that the integrity of one is violated by the other. Fantasy implies the intrusion of 'personal desires' and the irresponsible aspiration to impossible states of being premised on the unlimited fulfilment of these. By implication, authentic ideology is both altruistically motivated (premised on the vision of a better future for a whole collectivity, not just one in which individual desires are fulfilled) and at least to some degree realistic (premised on an attempt to analyse things as they actually are, and to propose possible, achievable futures based on this analysis).

What is interesting about this is that it seems to suggest the possibility not only of conceptualizing some kind of idealized distinction between the proper domains of 'fantasy' and 'ideology', but also of giving some unity to the apparently divergent senses of the word 'fantasy' itself. Generally speaking, the word 'fantasy' has at least two distinctive (albeit interconnected) sets of uses: psychologically, it refers broadly speaking to the imagination of an unlikely state of affairs which reflects the fulfilment of a 'conscious or unconscious wish'. Within literature, it refers to a genre characterized by unlikely or impossible things, particularly things which are or seem magical. Here, again, there is a further important distinction that has to be drawn. For theorists like Todorov, 'fantastic' literature is literature in which the everyday world is interrupted by extraordinary occurrences which seem to violate the laws of nature.[17] But this conception is at odds with fantasy as a popular genre today which is premised on the fact that the action takes place wholly or in part in an alternative world in which, generally speaking, magic and other aspects of what Todorov calls the 'marvellous' are part of ordinary existence.

And yet, if we consider the notion of fantasy as something essentially opposed to ideology, as suggested by the usage above, it would seem that both categories can be placed, in the whole diversity of senses in which we find them, along parallel spectrums of meaning. Taken in its broadest possible sense, fantasy would seem to relate to the imagining of alternative states of affairs such that the purpose and gratification is provided by the act of imagining itself. Thus, we say 'she fantasised about being a concert pianist' to mean that simply imagining being a concert pianist was a source of enjoyment and satisfaction to her. But if we say 'she aspired to be a concert pianist', then we immediately assume that the purpose of her present thoughts on the subject of being a concert pianist was instrumentally directed at actually becoming one.

Now, the relationship of the concept of 'ideology' to alternative states of being is not as obviously central to the term as for the case of fantasy. In Marxist understandings of the word such as that advanced by Althusser, ideology relates to 'the imaginary relationship of individuals to their real conditions of existence', a notion which gives a central role to imagination, but which deploys this imagination firmly in the attempt to give an account of the world as it is.[18] On the other hand, in social conservative discourse, ideology may be reserved solely for belief systems opposed to the status quo. For instance, some Islamophobic discourses from a 'cultural conservative' point of view attempt to claim that Islam is an 'ideology' as opposed to a religion because (so the argument claims) it aspires to alter the status quo.[19] And yet at some level, ideology, however it is understood, must, like fantasy, imply some possibility of envisaging alternative states of affairs, whether better or worse than the present one. In contrast to fantasy, however, ideological visions of alternative worlds are necessarily aspirational – and not just aspirational, but also conceived as collectivist and moral. Ideology, so it would seem, necessarily sets out an alternative state of affairs which *ought* to be achieved or avoided, which *can* be achieved or avoided by collective action, and the achievement or avoidance of which has collective implications.

In setting out what is required for a vision of an alternative world to be ideological, we have already touched on yet another possibility. While the idea of religion as a category fundamentally distinct from politics and ideology is – as Talal Asad, for example, has argued at length – premised on an arbitrary and itself ideological distinction,[20] it seems uncontroversial to assert that while many or even all religions may have political and ideological implications, there is something common to all religions which is not to be found in all political ideologies, namely, a professed belief in the reality of supernatural phenomena.[21]

Thus religion, too, seems to entail yet another possible relationship with an alternative world. Here, in contrast to ideology, the world concerned is one which cannot be brought into being through human action, collective or otherwise. And yet, in contrast to the alternative world envisaged by fantasy, the world we are concerned with is one that is taken actually to exist, and generally to be capable of being influenced in some way by human action whether in the form of ethical behaviour at an individual level, or ritual behaviour whether at an individual or collective level.

If we consider the implications of this approach, certain conclusions would seem to follow ineluctably.

First, the essential distinction between 'fantasy', 'ideology' and the religious perspective on the supernatural as visions of alternative realities lies not in the world being imagined, but rather in the propositional attitude of the one engaging with it. Thus, Anders Breivik, for example, had an elaborate vision of a future European Federation, for which he imagined a flag, a national anthem, a national holiday, a science budget, a guardian order of 'Justiciar Knights' complete with ranks and even an elaborate system of 'liberal zones' to be established for the benefit of those who did not wish to subscribe to cultural conservative values.[22] This world could, in principle, easily be the setting for a work of fiction, and indeed Breivik's character on 'World of Warcraft' was apparently a justiciar knight. For Breivik, however, this world was to be understood not as fiction, but as future aspiration.

Second, however, the fundamental nature of the way in which these different alternative realities are conceived would nonetheless seem to impose certain structural necessities on the parameters of the alternate reality envisaged. Ideological visions of alternate realities, because they must in principle be achievable by collective action, would seem to be heavily constrained in the ease with which they can incorporate elements of the supernatural – even if those subscribing to the vision believe in the supernatural themselves. By contrast, alternate realities encountered in specifically 'religious' terms, while they need not incorporate marvellous forms which violate the laws of the natural world, since they must be accessed by supernatural means, are very likely to do so. Again, fantasy, in order to be effective, generally requires a certain distance from quotidian reality.

Third, in each of these idealized relationships with alternate worlds, it seems possible to identify not only a particular propositional attitude but also an appropriate purpose to be served by the act of envisaging the alternative. Thus, in the ideological perspective, one envisages an alternative world with the object of either avoiding it or arriving at it through collective action. Where (as in Breivik's writing) an ideologically envisaged world is elaborated in excessive and frivolous detail or incorporates personal rather than collective ambitions, it would seem to violate the appropriate rules for ideological imagination. By contrast, in engagement with religious-supernatural visions of alternative worlds, the appropriate object would seem to be concern with salvation or damnation (or another supernatural equivalent). Here, it may be permissible to create highly elaborated descriptions of the supernatural world and its inhabitants, provided that all of this relates to the overarching moral purpose being served.

Finally, because of the latent tensions between adopted propositional attitude, the implied parameters of the alternative reality being envisaged and the purpose of the exercise of envisaging it, it seems to follow naturally that there will be situations in which one of these three relations to alternative worlds is 'misused' or, more accurately, in which one 'masquerades' as another. Thus, an alternate reality presented ostensibly as pure fantasy might, in fact, represent an allegory for an ideological aspiration. Or an ostensibly ideological vision of a possible future might be a thinly euhemerized vision of a supernatural world of personal salvation. Or, for that matter, an ostensibly ideological aspiration might, in reality, be engaged in as fantasy.

Thus, it is perfectly appropriate to say of, for example, *Star Trek* fans, that they may relate to the world of *Star Trek* as fantasy (i.e. as an imaginary alternative world enjoyed as such), while arguing that they may also produce ideological and politically engaged readings of the text as well (as a vision of a utopian future, or as an apologist allegory for American imperialism). But nor is it inappropriate to suggest that in ostensibly political or religious forms of engagement there may be elements of fantasy as well. According to this vision, then, media fandom (or, as Abercrombie and Longhurst would classify it, media *cult*)[23] can be tentatively defined as the formation of subcultural groupings based on consumption practices arising from a fantasy-based relationship with a media text.

This definition would not, as has just been pointed out, preclude the possibility that the collective consumption behaviours of fans would not move beyond fantasy. Indeed, the paradox implied in the notion of 'collective fantasy' seems automatically to imply the possibility of fan practices ultimately acquiring political or even quasi-religious content. Nor, again, need the notion of fantasy be seen as something pejorative or inappropriate. At the same time, however, this definition seems able to incorporate within the scope of 'fannish engagement' subcultural groupings based on other collective textual engagements which begin to develop collective consumption practices in which the sharing of a fantasy relationship *within* this alternative mode of consumption becomes important.

Having established fantasy and, with it, fannish engagement, as appropriate categories for applying to situations where political or religious forms of collective reading seem to apply, we may now move on to examine the significance of the category of fantasy itself in more detail. As we have seen, fantasy is a broad concept understood in many different senses, with notions of unreality and the exploration through unreality of personal desire as the only characteristics shared across all notions of the word. Even with regard to this latter characteristic, it is not immediately obvious how it applies to all senses of the word. Thus, in the type of 'fantastic' literature discussed by Tzvetan Todorov, it is not necessarily obvious how the intrusion of inexplicable events into ordinary reality reflects individual desires (although, in fact, Todorov believes it does, by offering a psychoanalytical interpretation in which the themes dealt with by 'the fantastic' represent otherwise suppressed wishes and appetites).[24] Similarly, there is no inherent reason for seeing the imaginary worlds of 'genre fantasy' as reflecting the exercise of any personal desire deeper than the desire to experience the pleasure of imagination itself. And yet for Tolkien, who perhaps remains not just the most influential author, but also the most influential theorist of this type of fantasy, the magical world of Faerie which is invoked by fantasy writing of this type is premised on the 'satisfaction of desires', as well as on 'return, or renewal', of 'regaining a clear view', of 'seeing things as they are'.[25]

The view of fantasy put forward by Tolkien here, as a space for personal exploration, for envisaging different possibilities and, ultimately, for coming to terms with the world as it is, is one which, it seems fair to say, can be made to fit fairly closely with other perspectives on fantasy. For example, this notion is very much the orthodoxy with regard to psychoanalytic readings of folklore. For Bettelheim, for example, the straightforward morality and difficult issues dealt with by fairy tales make them a hugely valuable resource for teaching children to deal with adult life.[26] Or for Joseph Campbell, the archetypal story of the hero's quest reflects the everyman's struggle to come to maturity.[27] More broadly, Winnicott proposed the idea of a transitional space between the self and the other which could help serve the developmental goal of coming to accept surrounding reality.[28]

And yet, later on in the same essay, Tolkien proposed something much more extraordinary.

> For my part, I cannot convince myself that the roof of Bletchley station is more "real" than the clouds. And as an artefact I find it less inspiring than the legendary dome of heaven. The bridge to platform 4 is to me less interesting than Bifröst guarded by Heimdall with the Gjallarhorn. From the wildness of my heart I cannot exclude the question whether railway-engineers, if they had been brought up on more fantasy, might not have done better with all their abundant means than they commonly do. Fairy-stories might be, I guess, better Masters of Arts than the academic person I have referred to.

> Much that he (I must suppose) and others (certainly) would call "serious" literature is no more than play under a glass roof by the side of a municipal swimming-bath. Fairy-stories may invent monsters that fly the air or dwell in the deep, but at least they do not try to escape from heaven or the sea.
>
> And if we leave aside for a moment "fantasy," I do not think that the reader or the maker of fairy-stories need even be ashamed of the "escape" of archaism: of preferring not dragons but horses, castles, sailing-ships, bows and arrows; not only elves, but knights and kings and priests. For it is after all possible for a rational man, after reflection (quite unconnected with fairy-story or romance), to arrive at the condemnation, implicit at least in the mere silence of "escapist" literature, of progressive things like factories, or the machine-guns and bombs that appear to be their most natural and inevitable, dare we say "inexorable," products.
>
> "The rawness and ugliness of modern European life"—that real life whose contact we should welcome —"is the sign of a biological inferiority, of an insufficient or false reaction to environment." The maddest castle that ever came out of a giant's bag in a wild Gaelic story is not only much less ugly than a robot-factory, it is also (to use a very modern phrase) "in a very real sense" a great deal more real.[29]

In contrast to the seeming universality and sophistication of psychoanalytical and structuralist analyses, Tolkien's refined horror at the intrusion of the ugliness of modern industrial life on a comfortable, privileged vision of the rural idyll may seem like the sort of reactionary conservatism that is most charitably passed over. And yet, regardless of whether we sympathize with Tolkien's views here, they are, from the point of view of the analysis of fantasy remarkable for at least two reasons.

First, at least since the brilliant work of Vladimir Propp on the morphology of folk tales, almost all attention on the subject has been focused firmly on issues of structure.[30] Even though Propp himself noted the interestingly specific nature of the world of fairy tales, and speculated about its origins, the elegance and analytical power he found in the tales was so compelling as to inform not only further work on fantasy (such as Todorov's), but also the study of narrative more generally.

What Tolkien's observation suggests, however, is that, notwithstanding its unique narrative structures, fantasy worlds cannot be constructed out of just any set of imaginative materials that happen to be to hand. Fantasy is distinguished not just by form, but also be specific sorts of *content*. Moreover, the types of setting and content which are suitable for constructing a 'faerie' world of the kind he envisages are much more limited than might be supposed.

Such a world must contain magic – or its effective equivalent, and it must be reached by magical means. 'Travellers' tales', so he insists, have no part in the genre, even where, as in *Gulliver's Travels*, the travels are wholly fictional and take place in imaginary lands. However, Tolkien recognizes that something akin to Faerie can be located in science fiction stories such as HG Wells' *The Time Machine* where the land reached is so remote, and the technology used to reach it so far beyond the imaginable capabilities of the present as to be effectively akin to magic.

One useful implication of this perspective for the case with which we are concerned is that it would seem to weaken to relevance of objections to the deployment of notions of fantasy even to texts which though perhaps 'fantastic' to an outsider's eye, are clearly, from a jihadi perspective, intended to be understood literally. A good example of this would be offered by an enduringly popular jihadi text, Abdullah Azzam's *Signs of the Merciful in the Afghan Jihad*.[31] This text, written in a dry, factual style in keeping with traditional Islamic epistemological norms, is concerned with accounts of miracles reported to have been experienced by those who considered themselves to be mujahidin fighting the Soviets in Afghanistan. In addition to more well-established motifs (corpses of martyrs exuding sweet smell, for example), a number of this anecdotes seem specifically to relate to the intersection of the miraculous power of God with the fearsome capabilities of modern military technology. Green birds outrun and obstruct modern fighter jets, for example; or angels arrive to provide artillery support. The fact that Azzam's text is obviously not written either stylistically or in terms of its intended manner of reading as 'fairy tale' or 'fantasy' need not – seen through Tolkien's eyes – get in the way of the fact that its *matter* (the superior 'reality' of natural – even if in fact supernatural – over technological phenomena) is the stuff of fantasy; nor of the likelihood that, for the jihadi consigned to consume this vision of the otherworldly nature of the lands of jihad, literature like this may nonetheless be *used* for fantastic as well as for more strictly religious purposes.

Moreover, widening our perspective somewhat, Tolkien's observations in this regard would seem to be closely (even presciently) borne out with regard to the state of genre fantasy in the present day. For example, as of February 2011,[32] the top ten most heavily subscribed massively multiplayer online role-playing games were estimated to be as follows:

With the exception of *Eve Online* (which is a space opera) and *City of Heroes* (which is based on a superheroes/supervillains theme), every single one of these games is set in an agrarian, pre-modern, quasi-medieval fantasy world populated by warriors, wizards and magical creatures. Nor would this seem to be an exclusively Western phenomenon, since it is also true of the world of the Korean game *Aion* and the Japanese game *Final Fantasy*.

World of Warcraft	12,000,000
Aion	3,400,000
Lineage/Lineage II	1,500,000
Runescape	1,300,000
Dofus	520,000
Final Fantasy XI	350,000
Eve Online	325,000
Lord of the Rings Online	210,000
City of Heroes/Villains	125,000
Age of Conan	125,000

FIGURE 9 *Top ten most popular massive multiplayer online role playing games.*

Still more profoundly, Tolkien's insistence on the superior 'reality' of premodern worlds of fantasy to the 'reality' of the industrial age would seem to utterly subvert the comfortable reading whereby fantasy represents a safely, reliably unreal alternative allowing a breathing space for contemplation away from the serious demands of the real world which we otherwise inhabit. For if we take Tolkien seriously, the neat, psychoanalytical idea that one can simply cross, for a time, into the transitional world of fantasy in order to slay one's inner demons before returning to the real world of mature adulthood would seem to fall apart. The fabricated nature of industrial civilization and the robot age means that there is simply no firmly grounded 'real world' left to return to.

What can fantasy mean in such a context? One clue would seem to be provided by an observation made by the Canadian critic and novelist Robertson Davies regarding the novel *Don Quixote*.[33] Robertson Davies notes that this novel is often taken as a satire on the outdated pretensions of Spain in the time of its author, Cervantes. The novel's protagonist is himself a fantasist, in both the psychological and generic senses of the term, whose obsession with romances about chivalric knights has created in him the insane delusion that he is himself a knight errant, who must travel the land, slaying giants and rescuing damsels in distress. And yet, what Davies insists is that the underlying power of the novel lies precisely in the fact that, despite the fact that Don Quixote is apparently the butt of the joke, for all the abuse and mockery he remains true to his high-minded ideals, however deluded. In the end, crazy or no, he is a better man than his persecutors.

Now, the fantasy of Don Quixote is not the potentially healthy fantasy of psychoanalysis. It is not a separate realm to be explored. Rather, it works by overlaying itself on the stuff of everyday reality, transforming an old nag into a charger, a farm-girl into a princess, an inn into an enchanter's castle. And yet, so Robertson Davies seems to be proposing, if Don Quixote's excessive love affair with a bygone age of chivalry is toxic at high doses, in a milder form it may be essential to the project of negotiating the complexities of life and especially the changes brought by an incipient modernity with which even Don Quixote had to contend.

What this notion of 'Quixotic' fantasy seems to suggest is a form of fantasy engagement in which the fantasy world is manifested not just as a self-contained 'virtual reality', detached from the everyday world and offering a source of escape, but rather a situation analogous to 'augmented reality', in which the fantasy functions in order to enrich the experience of everyday life. Moreover, following Tolkien's insight, part of the value of such fantasies might lie in their possession of a kind of 'reality' superior to the actual situation on which they are imaginatively overlaid. Thus, for instance, in watching a YouTube video of a horse, the horse itself is more easily grasped as a single, concrete reality than is the liquid crystal display, the thousands of minute transistors, the electrical currents, the radio waves and the vast server farms which are the actual reality underlying the superficial image.

Tolkien's misgivings, voiced in 1947, about the unreality of the industrial age therefore seem in some ways to anticipate the notion of 'hyper-reality' as later put forward by Jean Baudrillard and others. In *Simulacra and Simulation*,[34] Baudrillard insists that the industrial, media-saturated world has moved beyond representation, because the things which were once represented no longer exist. Instead, what we have is simulation: the production of signs which actually refer to nothing but themselves and exist to hide the ultimate absence of anything being represented.

But with all the dazzling virtuoso with which Baudrillard anatomizes the simulated unreality of the postmodern world, he says relatively little about the stuff which simulation is actually made of. One reason for this may be that the answer to this question – as Tolkien's lament suggests – may be rather banal: as 'real' reference points for representations recede so, paradoxically, the production of simulated reality must fall back ever more on a stylized emphasis on physicality and embodiment. As such the short shrift with Umberto Eco gives to the pulp-medievalism of the present day, on the grounds of historical illiteracy arguably misses the point.[35] The pseudo-medieval genre fantasy of the present day does not situate itself in a vaguely medieval world because it has any interest in the Middle Ages per se. Rather, the loosely medieval setting permits the deployment of a wide range of images (hand-to-hand combat, muscular physiques, forests, mountains, animals and even a highly essentialized conception of magic as the extension of a personal energy field) which are capable of brashly proclaiming a sense of reality from within the wholly simulated environment in which they are located.

I have previously argued in this book that the imaginative resources of internet jihadism seem to function in ways which are quite strikingly close to the model of 'Quixotic' fantasy which I have just proposed. That is to say that jihadism works, imaginatively, by trying to 'overlay' or better still 'integrate' its idealized, heroic and utopian visions of the mujahidin into the routine experiences of everyday life. Thus, it is perhaps no surprise to point out that, as we have seen – and as Tolkien's prescriptions would demand – it also seems to resemble it in the specific imaginative content out of which it is constructed. As was noted in Chapter 3, perhaps the single most important iconographic element by which 'global jihadism' can be distinguished from other, more localized forms, is the distinctive use it makes of specifically medieval (or 'pseudo-medieval') imagery such as horsemen, swords and banners.

Thus, to bring to a close this rather lengthy line of argument, I propose that we may speak of elements of 'fannish engagement' being present in a set of consumption practices where a relationship with the text of collectivized fantasy can be observed to be present. Fantasy, in turn, can be understood as an imagined relationship with a vision of a possible alternative reality in which the purpose of the alternative reality is served simply through the act of imagining it. Although fantasy can be invoked in relationship to any hypothetical reality, fantasy *worlds* are, in practice, far more structured and constrained than the supposed freedom of human imagination would seem to imply. Moreover, it would seem that the emergence of modernity has further strengthened this trend by paradoxically favouring a highly stylized set of icons of authentic reality, rooted in stereotypes of embodiment and the natural world. Finally, the deceptive complexities that underpin the representations produced by modern life are such as to give a new role to fantasy, as a way of overlaying a comprehensible 'reality' on the complex representation mechanisms of modern existence.

Now, in characterizing internet jihadism in these terms it may still seem that I am moving untenably far from the genuine violence and the genuine violent groups to which it continues to relate. For instance, it would seem to be important not to conflate the commitments of internet jihadis with what the literature on terrorism and the internet has sometimes called 'virtual terrorism'. As used by Dorothy Denning, this term refers to forms of 'terrorism' which occur in virtual worlds such as *Second Life*.[36] And yet it is not necessarily certain that the 'unreality' of such actions compares so unfavourably with phenomena such as that of the online violent radical milieu as might at first appear. Indeed, the case of 'virtual terrorism' and virtual forms of 'political' . . . 'violence' is in itself instructively complex. An interesting treatment of the phenomenon has been offered by a Master's dissertation produced by Tim Stevens of King's London, who has attempted to arrive at a conceptualization of this complex set of phenomena through studies of three cases which, so it seems, move incrementally closer to 'real' politics: 'The War of Jessie Wall', 'The Second Life Liberation Army' and 'Because I Hate Front National'.[37] The first of these cases concerns a dispute within the *Second Life* community concerning the anti-social (but technically permitted) use of computer game-type violence within the virtual world by visiting players of *Second World War Online*. The second concerns contentious attempts to wrest more input by the community from Linden Labs – the company which owns *Second Life* by means of techniques aimed at disrupting the underlying computational processes by which the virtual world is realized. The third relates to the response to the presence on *Second Life* of a real-world far-right political party.

Interestingly, however, Stevens' dissertation passes over the activities of a group within *Second Life* which may have been ignored on the grounds that its activities seem to be merely irritating, and of insufficient political relevance and which yet, looked at a certain way, might be construed as amounting to more 'genuinely' political action than any of the cases examined: this is the 'griefer group' Patriotic Nigras.[38] Patriotic Nigras were as group on *Second Life* which emerged as an offshoot of the 'something awful' online subculture (also, as it happens, loosely associated with the 'Anonymous' hacktivist phenomenon). Their actions on the virtual world consisted of being deliberately offensive (the members, who seem all to have been white in real life) presented themselves online as black, seemingly for reasons of pure provocation. Their actions amounted, at least superficially, to nothing more than rather crude 'cyberbullying', harassing and 'outing' the real-life identity, for example, of one member who was running a real-world business based on letting virtual land in *Second Life*. And yet, while Patriotic Nigras may not be the best example of their subculture's activities, it would seem that they did, nonetheless, have a deeper purpose. Specifically, members of 'something awful' are motivated in their seemingly unpleasant attempts to spoil online games precisely by the insistence that the internet and the types of environment it affords not be taken too seriously. The very nastiness of their actions therefore contain a clear subversive meaning, in that they are only as nasty as those committing their lives to online worlds ultimately controlled in every detail for by commercial operators construct them to be.[39]

Ultimately, the increasingly knotty complexities involved in disaggregating what is 'real' and what is merely 'virtual' in relation to seemingly political phenomena online would seem to provide an eloquent argument for taking up a rather deeper conceptualization of the meaning of these terms proposed by the theorist of cyberculture Pierre Levy. For Levy, the virtual must be understood as an antonym not to the 'real', but rather to the *actual*. That is to say that what is virtual *is real*, in the sense that it is a token of an indefinitely emergent future that is not here *yet*.[40] Owning ten cows is actual. Owning a contract which gives one the option to buy ten cows at some future date is virtual. Both are real. In this sense, 'virtual terrorism' would imply not terrorism that doesn't exist at all, but rather terrorism that *could* exist at some point, and some place, in the future.

Now, in this sense all terrorism is of course virtual in so far as it uses a relatively few incidents of high-profile violence in lieu of a comprehensive ground war involving the occupation of physical territory. And with the development of more thoroughly globalized forms of terrorism premised on creating the mediated impression of still fewer, but higher profile and more apparently extreme incidents the virtuality of the phenomenon is extended still further. As Ulrich Beck has influentially observed, even a very small amount of *actual* international suicide terrorism, by leveraging the *possibility* of future terrorism, is able to produce, via the institutionalization of counterterrorism measures, a universal, ambient terrorism threat everywhere.[41]

And yet, with the notion of a leaderless form of terrorism diffused through the internet, virtualization would seem to reach yet another level. We are no longer talking about even possessing the capacity to produce occasional violence, but rather about possessing *the capacity to possess the capacity*, in terms of raw human capital and stated intent.

And up to this point, jihadism, however remote it may grow from actual violence, is still underwritten by the promise of very extreme violence happening in principle. The 'training camp' section of *Shumukh al-Islam*, for example, continues to speculate about topics such as poison gas or mass poisoning. The figure of the mujahid 'knight' is still only a visual index of the kalaskhnikov or RPG wielding guerrilla in the field.

Thus, while internet jihadism has partially entered the world of simulation, it is accurate to say that its idiom remains tied in some ways to the principle of representation. In its relation to violence, internet jihadism can perhaps be said to have the character of a hall of mirrors all reflecting a single 'real' object placed before one of them, as opposed to a hall of screens in which no such object exists, and simulation is all there is.

Is it possible to imagine jihadism making this transition? The possibility is raised by a remarkable episode or, perhaps better, 'happening' which occurred in June 2009, when Jund Ansar Allah, a jihadi salafi group in Gaza, attempted to launch a horseback suicide bombing on an Israeli border-post. The raid itself was unsuccessful, in so far as five members of Jund Ansar Allah died without killing any Israelis. But it is difficult to disentangle the 'actual' operation from the video which the group produced, chronicling it, under the title of *The Raid of Al-Balagh*.[42] (Al-Balagh seems to be a place name, so we must presumably accept it as mere coincidence that the Arabic meaning of the word is 'reaching' or even 'eloquence'.)

In this film, virtually no mention is made of the purpose of the attack which the bulk of the footage sees members of the group preparing for. Indeed, sections of the video can be viewed almost more as a visual enactment of an Islamic sermon on the virtues of the horse than a piece of political communication. Large parts of the film are devoted to horsemen galloping around the Gaza landscape, either singly (usually in green areas) or in formation (in the desert). At one point, the camera is angled up to present a view of gently swaying branches and rolling clouds, as a voice-over narrates a prophetical hadith about the virtues of the horse. The camera then angles down to show us a horse grazing at the foot of the same tree. As well as the Qur'anic aya often quoted in jihadi materials from Surat al-Anfal (8) in which Muslims are enjoined to 'prepare for them whatever you are able to of force and of cavalry to terrify therewith the enemy of God and your enemy', a more unusual passage, the *Surat al-'Adiyat* is quoted three times, nearly in full.

> By the racers, panting
> And the producers of sparks striking
> And the chargers at dawn
> Stirring up thereby dust
> Arriving thereby in the centre collectively
> Indeed mankind to his Lord is ungrateful
> And indeed he is to that a witness

Other scenes describe how the group 'initiated a course of training in the arts of war and fighting, by means of an intensive training programme'. These show members of the group engaging in impressive-looking exercises with small arms. At the same time, elements of medieval (or even perhaps Eastern martial arts film) anachronism continue to intrude. A scene of troops advancing at night in single file shows a group in which one bears a large and conspicuous oblong banner. The language is confusing: are we supposed to read the modern warfilm language of stealth, or the medieval language of heroic display?

Either way, echoing Chase Knowles' confusion about 'Islamist neorealism' it is quite impossible to assign this extraordinary work any kind of generic status even as fiction or non-fiction. In a sense, it fulfils a prediction made by the theorist of global jihadism Faisal Devji, who, in analysing jihadist suicide attacks as 'ethical acts', asked the question as to whether one could envisage a suicide bombing in which only the perpetrator died.[43] Of course, this was not literally the case here in the sense that, unquestionably, the militants were hoping to kill Israeli soldiers. But at the same time, in the narrative of the video, it seems almost irrelevant whether they did or didn't. In terms of the intentions of the group, it would seem that the video here – in a sense somewhat similar, perhaps, to the *Juba* series – is more real than is the event itself. As much, perhaps more so than carrying out an attack, they were shooting a movie. This is 'propaganda of the deed' taken beyond its logical conclusion: in paradigmatic examples of 'made for television' acts of terrorism, the terrorists did the violence first and had to hope that something of the story they intended to tell with it would be conveyed via the television news media. Here, the terrorists have full control over every element of the story except the violence at the end (which, in a further irony, is blanked out on the video, as it claims, for security reasons).

Interestingly, the physical enactment of the medieval iconography of jihadism partially seen in *The Raid of al-Balagh* seems also to have been hinted at by Anwar al'Awlaqi in a section of a talk distributed online under the title 'Weapons of the End Times'.[44] Here, the cleric addresses what seems to have been an issue of wider current concern (the author also heard popular discussion along similar lines in Jordan), relating to the fact that hadiths speaking about the final battles at the end of time mention the use of medieval weaponry and equipment such as bows, swords and horses. The question that has arisen, therefore, is as to whether the last battle will occur in a post-apocalyptic, neo-medieval future in which Muslims will square off against their opponents using the technology of old. Al-'Awlaqi does not think so. Technological change is irreversible, so he argues, because of the incremental accumulation of knowledge by mankind. And yet he still advises his listeners to learn to follow Islamic injunctions by taking up archery and horse riding, as useful and constructive pastimes for a person interested in eventually taking up the duty of jihad.

These examples do not, of course, imply that we should imminently expect jihadism to abandon its guns, RPGs, IEDs and suicide belts in favour of the pursuits of medieval re-enactment and live action role-play. And yet they do, perhaps, hint at the future trajectory on which jihadism might find itself were it altogether starved of the more conventional representations of irregular combat which fighting groups in the 'lands of jihad' continue to supply.

What are the implications of all this? One crucial point would seem to be that governments, in responding to what are believed to be the threats presented by online radicalization or 'terrorism on the Internet' have, up to the present, tended to approach the phenomenon exclusively in terms of the presumption that it is only to be understood as a counterterrorism concern. In doing so, they have – as noted at the outset – essentially taken for granted a set of relationships between the two which are not proven, and certainly not proven to a level sufficient to reliably identify precisely what online content does and doesn't represent a concern in relation to political violence. Ironically, this point is demonstrated in a paper by Raphael Cohen Almagor which purports to prove the precise opposite: arguing that, because a particular college gun massacre was said to have been associated with the online actions of a particular person on the Goth forum *vampirefreaks*, that this provides a justification for the preventive monitoring of certain sections of the internet.[45] In reality, it should be clear that even if there turned out to be a causative link between the use of nihilistic language and violent fantasies online and the actual occurrence of incidents of this kind, the strength of this connection in relation to particular types of content would surely not be great enough to offer meaningful guidance to a panoptic authority as to precisely when to intervene in such cases.

Instead, it would seem that, if political or regulatory actions are indeed required in relation to online violent radical milieus, then these actions would be better conceived as a response to these phenomena in their own right – through frameworks similar to those which, in some jurisdictions for example, are used to regulate 'hate' content – material which, even if it does not have provable and direct links to specific real-world events – may be judged by a particular society to be undesirable for more general reasons, rooted in specific understandings of what that society holds to be good. Otherwise, we are all tilting at windmills.

Notes

Chapter 1

1 For a retrospective assessment of the impact of the Iraq War see Maura Conway, 'From Zarqawi to Al-Awlaki: The Emergence of the Internet as a New Form of Violent Radical Milieu', 2012, http://www.isodarco.it/courses/andalo12/doc/Zarqawi%20to%20Awlaki_V2.pdf.
2 See, for example, Eric Schmitt and Tom Shanker, 'U.S Adapts Cold War Idea to Fight Terrorists', *New York Times*, 18/3/2008.
3 See, for example, Scott Sanford, 'Faultlines in cyberspace', in Assaf Moghadam and Brian Fishman (eds), *Fault Lines in Global Jihad: Organizational, Strategic and Ideological Fissures*. London: Routledge, 2010.
4 Per Olof Wikström and Noémie Bouhana, 'Al Qa'ida Influenced Radicalisation: A Rapid Evidence Assessment Guided by Situational Action Theory', UK Home Office Report, 2011.
5 Terrorism has repeatedly been invoked as a justification for attempts by governments to extend control over the internet; a recent example would be the British government's suggestion of a law that would have allowed for unwarranted collection of real-time traffic data by government agencies. The reasons given (cybercrime, child pornography and terrorism) seem not to explain the need for such a measure, particularly given powers the government already possesses under its regulation of investigatory powers act.
6 For an effective critique of some of the difficulties with this term in contemporary counterterrorism contexts, see Anthony Richards, 'The Problem with "Radicalization, the Remit of "Prevent" and the Need to Refocus on Terrorism in the UK'. *International Affairs* 87(1), 143–252.
7 Michael Bonner, *Jihad in Islamic History: Doctrines and Practice*. Princeton, NJ: Princeton University Press, 2008; see also David Cook, *Understanding Jihad*. Berkeley: University of California Press, 2005.
8 Gabriele Marranci, *Jihad Beyond Islam*. New York: Berg, 2006.
9 John Esposito and Dalia Mogahed, *Who Speaks for Islam: What a Billion Muslims Really Think*. New York: Gallup Press, 2007.
10 For an up-to-date debate on this issue, see Paul Wilkinson and Dominic Bryan's chapters in Anthony Jackson and Samuel Justin Sinclair (eds), *Contemporary Debates on Terrorism*. London: Routledge, 2012, pp. 9–25.
11 Martin Kramer, 'Coming to terms: fundamentalists or Islamists?'. *Middle East Quarterly* 10(2), (2003), 65–77.
12 An important work in popularizing the notion of a 'global salafi-jihad' as an alternative to 'Al Qaeda' was Marc Sageman's, *Understanding Terrorist Networks*. Philadelphia: University of Pennsylvania Press, 2004.

13 For the evolution of Al Qaeda's plans over the decade before 2001, Lawrence Wright's, *The Looming Tower: Al Qaeda and the Road to 9/11*. New York: Knopf, 2006 remains an outstanding treatment.
14 Alan Stephens and Nicola Baker, *Making Sense of War: Strategy for the 21st Century*. Cambridge: Cambridge University Press, 2006, p. 190.
15 Michelle Zanini and Sean Edwards, 'The Networking of Terror in the Information Age', in Arquilla and Ronfeldt (eds), *Networks and Netwars: The Future of Terror, Crime and Militancy*. Santa Monica: RAND, 2001, p. 32.
16 Gabriel Weimann, *Terror on the Internet: The New Arena, The New Challenges*. Washington: United States Institute for Peace Press, p. 1.
17 Matthew Parker Voors, 'Encryption Regulation in the Wake of September 11, 2001: Must we Protect National Security at the Expense of the Economy?' *Federal Communications Law Journal* 55(2), (2003), 331–52.
18 National Commission on Terrorist Attacks Upon the United States, *The 9/11 Commission Report: Final Report of the National Commission on Terrorist Attacks on the United States*, Washington: 2004, p. 157.
19 Ibid., p. 169.
20 Evan Kohlmann, 'The Real Online Terrorist Threat', September/October, 2006.
21 Timothy Thomas, 'Al Qaida and the Internet, The Danger of Cyberplanning'. *Parameters* 33(2003), 112–24.
22 See Maura Conway, 'Hackers as Terrorists: Why it Doesn't Compute'. *Computer Fraud and Security* 12(2003), 10–13; Gabriel Weimann, 'Cyberterrorism: The Sum of all Fears?'. *Studies in Conflict and Terrorism* 28(2), (2005), 129–49.
23 Maura Conway, 'Terrorist "Use" of the Internet and Fighting Back'. *Information and Security: An International Journal* 19(2006), 9–30; Gabriel Weimann, Terror.net: Terror on the Internet, United States Institute for Peace report, 2004.
24 Laurel Sweet, 'Sudbury Terror Sympathizer Mehanna Sentenced to 17 Years', 14/4/2012, http://www.bostonherald.com/news/regional/view/20220412sudbury_terror_sympathizer_mehanna_its_because_of_america_that_i_am_who_i_am.
25 Gordon Corara, 'Al-Qaeda's 007: The Extraordinary Story of the Solitary Computer Geek in a Shepherds Bush Bedsit Who Became the World's Most Wanted Cyber Jihadist', *Times Online*, 1/16/2008.
26 See, for example, Joan Vennochi, 'Tarek Mehanna case puts first amendment on trial', *Boston Globe*, 19/4/2012.
27 *Terror on the Internet*, p. 5.
28 Ibid.
29 Gabriel Weimann, 'Al Qa'ida's Extensive Use of the Internet'. *CTC Sentinel* 1(2), (2008), 6–8.
30 This figure was given to the author by Richard Eaton of Hatewatch in 2008.
31 http://www.ai.arizona.edu/research/terror.
32 M. Dubowitz, 'Countering the Threat from Terrorist Media', *in Focus Quarterly*, Summer 2010, http//www.jewishpolicycenter.org/1746/terrorist-media-threat.
33 Yahya Ibrahim, 'Tips for our Brothers in the United States of America'. *Inspire* 2(2010), 55.
34 Gabriel Weimann and Yariv Tsfati, '*www.terrorism.com*: Terror on the Internet', 25(5), (2002), 317–32.

35 See Donald Holbrook, Gilbert Ramsay and Max Taylor, In Press. 'Terroristic Content: Towards a Grading Scale.' *Terrorism and Political Violence*.
36 Anne Braoche, 'Senators Voice Alarm over terrorist Net Presence', CNet news, 2007, http://www.news.cnet.com/Senators-voice-alarm-over-terrorist-Net-presence/2100-1028_3-6181269.html.
37 Lawrence Lessig, *Code 2.0*. New York: Basic Books, 2007.
38 Gabriel Weimann, 'www.terror.net How Modern Terrorism Uses the Internet', United States Institute of Peace report, 2004.
39 www.nussra.com, now defunct, from author's collection.
40 Michael Jacobson, 'Terrorist Financing and the Internet'. *Studies in Conflict and Terrorism* 33(4), (2010).
41 'The Threat of Money Laundering and Online Terrorist Financing through the Online Gambling Industry: A Report Prepared for the Remote Gambling Association by MHA Consulting', June 2009, http://www.rga.eu.com/data/files/final__mha_report_june_2009.pdf.
42 Ann. Stenersen, 'The Internet: A Virtual Training Camp?'. *Terrorism and Political Violence* 20(2), (2008), 215–33.
43 Michael Kenney, 'Beyond the Internet: Metis, Techne, and the Limitations of Online Artifacts for Islamist. Terrorists'. *Terrorism & Political Violence* 22(2), (2010)
44 Fernando Reinares, 'The Madrid Bombings and Global Jihadism'. *Survival* 52(2), April–May 2010.
45 See, for example, 'Coroner's Inquests into the London Bombings of 7th July, 2005', http://www.7julyinquests.independent.gov.uk/.
46 Perhaps the best presently available source on how Breivik prepared for his attacks is his own, see *2083: A European Declaration of Independence*, pp. 840 following.
47 Pantucci, 'Operation Praline: The Realisation of Al-Suri's *Nizam, La Tanzim?*' *Perspectives on Terrorism* 2(12), (2008).
48 Elaine Pressman, 'Risk Assessment Decisions for Violent Political Extremism, 2009–02', http://www.publicsafety.gc.ca/res/cor/rep/_fl/2009-02-rdv-eng.pdf.
49 Per Olof Wikström and Noémie Bouhana, Al Qa'ida Influenced Radicalisation, A Rapid Evidence Assessment Guided by Situational Action Theory, http://www.homeoffice.gov.uk/publications/science-research-statistics/research-statistics/counter-terrorism-statistics/occ97?view=Binary.
50 Mustafa Sittmariyam Nasar (Abu Mus'ab al-Suri), *The Global Islamic Resistance Call* (da'wat al-muqawamatial-islamiyya al-'alamiyya), pp. 1388 ff.
51 Abdul Aziz al-Muqrin, 'Targets inside Cities', *Al Battar Training Camp*, no. 7, March 2004.
52 www.al-sayf.com/vb (now defunct - author's collection).
53 http://www.jihadica.com/falluja-analytics/(accessed 8/08/2011).
54 http://www.xrdarabia.org/2007/11/29/saudi-terror-arrests-show-value-of-internet-monitoring/(accessed 12/5/2012).
55 For example, Muslm.net which, as we shall see, is home to a major online jihadi community is hosted in Mecca. This site's administrator, 'Al-Sarim Al-Maslul', himself a hardline jihadist sympathizer on the forum is said to be a faculty member of Abdul Aziz University.
56 This section is based on incident descriptions for attacks in Saudi Arabia available from the Global Terrorism Database.

57 For a succinct (re)-statement of the standard argument on terrorism and the media, see Paul Wilkinson, 'Terrorism and the Media: A Reassessment'. *Terrorism and Political Violence* 9(2), (1997), 51–64.
58 Victor Asal and Paul Harwood, 'Search Engines: Terrorism's Killer App'. *Studies in Conflict and Terrorism* 31(1), (2008), 641–54.
59 http://www.start.umd.edu/gtd/search/Results.aspx?start_yearonly=&end_yearonly=&start_year=&start_month=&start_day=&end_year=&end_month=&end_day=&asmSelect0=&asmSelect1=&criterion1=yes&criterion2=yes&criterion3=yes&dtp2=some&success=no&casualties_type=b&casualties_max=(accessed 28/08/2012).
60 Orla Lynch and Chris Ryder, 'Deadliness, Organisational Change and Suicide Attacks: Understanding the Assumptions Inherent in the Term 'New Terrorism'. *Critical Studies on Terrorism* 5(2), (2012), 257–75.
61 To date, US deaths in Afghanistan (between 2001 and 2011) total 2,104 (http://icasualties.org/oef/). The corresponding figure for Vietnam is 56,938 over a comparable period from the initiation of the American ground war (1963–73). http://www.archives.gov/research/military/vietnam-war/casualty-statistics.html.
62 The official civilian casualty figures for Afghanistan recorded by the United Nations Assistance Mission in Afghanistan (UNAMA) claim that a total of 6478 Afghani civilians were killed from 2007 to 2012. 'Conflict continues to take a devastating toll on civilians despite decrease in casualties during first six months', UNAMA press release, 2012. This total does not include a nearly equal number (5479) Afghan soldiers and police killed from 2007 to 2011 (Susan G. Chesser, 'Afghanistan casualties: military forces and civilians', Congressional research service, 12 July 2012). Proper records do not exist for earlier years, although a report by the *Guardian* newspaper suggested that as many as 8,000 may have been killed in the first year of the conflict, http://www.guardian.co.uk/world/2002/may/20/afghanistan.comment. Nor do the figures take into account Taliban casualties or indirect casualties. Compare this, however, with R. J. Rummel's estimate of 1,250,000 Vietnamese directly killed in the Vietnam war.
63 The Iraq body count project records a lower-end estimate of 108,428–118,482 documented civilian deaths in Iraq up to 2011, http://www.iraqbodycount.org/database/ (accessed 29/08/2012). Research by the company Opinion Research Business estimated on the basis of a survey of 2,414 adult Iraqis and data from Iraq's national census of 1997 concluded that between 946,000 and 1.12 million Iraqis had died as a result of the conflict by 2007.
64 Estimates of casualties in Iraq are based on one of two methods: survey research and attempts to amass comprehensive data on documented deaths. All attempts to arrive at a tally by the latter method have recorded in the region of 100,000 casualties, accepting that unrecorded deaths have occurred and will add to this total to some extent. The ORB survey, mentioned above, has been severely criticized on methodological grounds and seems no longer to be considered credible. This leaves two survey-based studies to consider: Gilbert Burnham, Riyadh Lafta, Shannon Doocy and Les Roberts, 'Mortality after the 2003 invasion of Iraq: a cross sectional cluster sample survey', 368(9545), 1421–8. This study estimated 654,965 'excess deaths' from violence by 2006, including 601,027 due to violence. The

other study, the Iraq Family Health Survey Study Group, 'Violence Related Mortality in Iraq from 2002–2006'. *New England Journal of Medicine* 48, 484–93, estimated 151,000 violent deaths – around double the contemporary estimates by projects such as the Iraq Body Count, but obviously far less than that estimated by *The Lancet*. Given that the latter is based on a larger-scale survey, and yields results closer to other estimates, it seems likely that the actual casualty figure is closer to the former estimate. A good overview of the various estimates and their plausibility is offered by Stephen Pinker in *The Better Angels of Our Nature: The Decline of Violence and its Causes*. London: Penguin, 2011, pp. 317–9.
65 http://www.globalsecurity.org/military/world/war/lebanon.htm (accessed 28/08/2012).

Chapter 2

1 See, for example, Muhammad Haniff Hassan and Redzuan Salleh, 'Jihadism studies in counter-ideology: time for initiation in universities', S. Rajaratnam School of International Studies, RSIS Commentaries series, 2010.
2 See, e.g Thomas Hegghammer, *Jihad in Saudi Arabia: Violence and Pan-Islamism since 1979*. Cambridge: Cambridge University Press, 2010.
3 Nelly Lahoud, *The Jihadis' Path to Self Destruction*. New York: Columbia University Press, 2010.
4 Jarret Brachman and William McCants, 'Stealing Al-Qaeda's Playbook'. *Studies in Conflict and Terrorism* 29(4), (2006)
5 For a measured discussion of this document, see Thomas Hegghammer and Brynjar Lia, 'Jihadi Strategic Studies: The Alleged Al Qaida policy study preceding the Madrid bombings'. *Studies in Conflict and Terrorism* 27(5), (2005).
6 See, again Reinares' groundbreaking study of these attacks, cited above.
7 Mustafa Sittmariyam Nasar (Abu Mus'ab al-Suri), *The Global Islamic Resistance Call*.
8 Abdul Aziz al-Muqrin, 'The Targets in the Cities'.
9 Osama bin Laden, 'Fight on, Champions of Somalia' (*ila nuzul ya abtal al-sumal*), 2009.
10 Jarret Brachman, *Global Jihadism: Theory and Practice*. London: Routledge, 2009.
11 See, for example, Jon Anderson, 'Internet Islam: New Media of the Islamic Reformation', in Donna Lee Bowen and Evelyn A. Early, *Everyday Life in the Muslim Middle East*; Jon Anderson and Dale Eickelman (eds), *New Media in the Muslim World: The Emerging Public Sphere*, 2nd Ed. Bloomington: Indiana University Press, 2003.
12 Kai Hafez, *Radicalism and Political Reform in the Islamic and Western Worlds*. Cambridge: Cambridge University Press, 2010.
13 Jocelyn Cesari, *Where Islam and Democracy Meet, Muslims in Europe and the United States*. New York: Palgrave Macmillan, 2004, pp. 115 ff.
14 Gary Bunt, *iMuslims: Rewiring the House of Islam*. London: Hurst, 2009, p. 1.
15 Ibid.

16 Gary Bunt, *Virtually Islamic: Computer Mediated Communication and Cyber-Islamic Environments*. Cardiff: Cardiff University of Wales Press, 2000, p. 1.
17 Howard Rheingold, *The Virtual Community: Homesteading on the Electronic Frontier*. Cambridge, MA: MIT Press, 2000, p. 30, originally published by Addison Wesley, 1993.
18 Marc MacWilliams, 'Techno-Ritualization: The Gohonzon Controversy on the Internet', Heidelberg Journal of Religions on the Internet, Vol. 2, Special Issue on Rituals on the Internet, ed. Kerstin Radde-Antweiler, 2006, http://www.archiv.ub.uni-heidelberg.de/volltextserver/volltexte/2006/6959/.
19 Karine Barzilai-Nahon and Gad Barzilai, 'Cultured Technology: Internet and Religious Fundamentalism'. *The Information Society* 21(1), (2004).
20 K. H. Karim, Book Review – *Islam in the Digital Age. The American Journal of Islamic Social Sciences* 21(4), (2004), 97–9.
21 *iMuslims*, p. 15.
22 Ibid., p. 179.
23 Frederic Volpi, *Political Islam Observed*. London: Hurst, 2010, p. 36.
24 For example of this discourse as expressed by an academic scholar, see Assaf Moghadam, 'Salafi-Jihad as a Religious Ideology'. *CTC Sentinel* 1(3), 14–16. This idea has been extended by Islamophobic extremists for whom Islam as such is an 'ideology' rather than a 'religion'.
25 Olga Guedes Bailey, Bart Cammaerts and Nico Carpentier, *Understanding Alternative Media*. Maidenhead: Open University Press, 2008.
26 Chase Knowles, 'Towards a New Web Genre: Islamist Neo-Realism'. *Journal of War and Culture Studies* 1(3), 357–80.
27 Hamid Mowlana, 'Foundation of Communication in Islamic Societies', in J. P Mitchell and S. Marriage (eds), *Mediating Religion: Conversations in Media, Religion and Culture*. New York: Continuum, 2003, pp. 305–17.
28 For an interesting example see L. M. Pitcher, 'The Divine Impatience: Ritual, Narrative and Symbolization in the Practice of Martyrdom in Palestine'. *Medical Anthropology Quarterly* 12(1), (1998), 8–30.
29 See, for example, Bill Rolston, 'Politics, Painting and Popular Culture: The Political Murals of Northern Ireland'. *Media, Culture and Society* 9(1), (1987); Jeffrey Sluka, 'The Politics of Painting: Political Murals in Northern Ireland', in Carolyn Nordstrom and JoAnn Martin (eds), *The Paths to Domination, Resistance and Terror*. Berkeley: University of California Press, 1992, pp. 190–218.
30 Paul Baines, Nicholas J. O'Shaghnessy, Kevin Moloney, Barry Richards, Sarah Butler and Mark Gill, 'Muslim Voices: The British Muslim Response to Islamic Video Polemic – an Exploratory Study', Cranfield University School of Management, Research Paper 3/06, 2006, www.som.cranfield.ac.uk/som/research/reserachpapers.asp; Marie Gillespie and Ben O'Loughlin, 'News Media, Threats and Insecurities: An Ethnographic Approach'. *Cambridge Review of International Affairs* 22(4), 667–85.
31 Dick Hebdige, *Subculture: The Meaning of Style*. London: Methuen, 1979. See also G. Mungham and G. Pearson, (eds), *Working Class Youth Culture*. London: Routledge, 1976.
32 Malcolm Muggleton, *Inside Subculture: The Postmodern Meaning of Style*. Oxford: Berg, 2000, pp. 14–15.
33 See, for example, Chris Atton, An Alternative Internet. Edinburgh: Edinburgh University Press, 2004.

34 John Downing, *Radical Media: Rebellious Communication and Social Movements*. Thousand Oaks: Sage, 2008, p. 8.
35 Saba Mahmood, *Politics of Piety: The Islamic Revival and the Feminist Subject*. Princeton, NJ: Princeton University Press, 2005.
36 Eugenia Siapera, 'Radical Democratic Politics and Online Islam', in *Radical Democracy and the Internet*. Basingstoke: Macmillan Palgrave, 2007, pp. 148–63.
37 A comprehensive essay on the nature of liberty is plainly impossible here. Rousseau conceives of liberty as attainable through an individual's participation in the general will, and Locke insists on the impossibility of freedom without laws. Even Marx's conception of liberty would seem to make more sense in terms of an ongoing dialectic than the final, utopian state in which the individual is at perfect liberty to perform a range of activities, the meaning of which, in the assumed utopian context in which they would take place, is of necessity unclear.
38 Lila Abu Lughod, 'The Romance of Resistance: Tracing Transformations of Power Through Bedouin Women'. *American Ethnologist* 17(1), (1990), 41–55.
39 Quoted by Henry Jenkins, 'Excerpts from Matt Hills Interviews Henry Jenkins', Henry Jenkins *Fans Bloggers and Gamers: Exploring Participatory Culture*. London: New York University Press, 2006, p. 11.
40 Anthony Giddens, *Modernity and Self-Identity: Self and Society in the Late Modern Age*. Cambridge: Polity, 1991, p. 46. See also Anthony Giddens, *The Consequences of Modernity*. Stanford: Stanford University Press, 1990.
41 Ibid., pp. 50–1
42 See e.g., William Montgomery Watt, *Muslim Intellectual: A Study of Al-Ghazali*. Edinburgh: Edinburgh University Press, 1963, pp. 128 ff.
43 http://www.gatewaystobabylon.com/myths/texts/classic/dialoguepessimism.htm.
44 *The Consequences of Modernity*, p. 36.
45 Ulrich Beck, 'What is Globalization?', Cambridge: Polity, 2000, p. 137.
46 Alasdair Macintyre, *After Virtue: A Study in Moral Theory*. Notre Dame: University of Notre Dame Press, 1984.
47 *The Consequences of Modernity*, p. 21.
48 Olivier Roy, *The Failure of Political Islam*. London: I. B. Tauris, 1994; see also Globalised Islam, The Search for a New Ummah. New York: Columbia University Press, 2004.
49 Patricia Gibbs, 'Alternative Things Considered: A Political Economic Analysis of Labour Processes and Relations at a Honolulu Newspaper'. *Media, Culture and Society* 25(5), (2003), 587–605.
50 Joseph Heath and Andrew Potter, *The Rebel Sell: Why The Culture Can't Be Jammed*. New York: Harper Collins, 2010.
51 Chris Atton, 'A Reassessment of the Alternative Press'. *Media, Culture and Society* 21(1), (1999), 51–76.
52 Jennifer Rauch, 'Activists as Interpretive Communities: Rituals of Consumption and Interaction in an Alternative Media Audience'. *Media, Culture and Society* 29(6), (2007), 994–1013.
53 Jarret Brachman, *Global Jihadism: Theory and Practice*. London: Routledge, 2009, p. 19.
54 Jarret Brachman, 'Ansarnet's Jihobby Orcs are at it again', *http://www.jarretbrachman.net/?p=170*, 22/11/2009.

55 'Meet a jihobbyist: week 1 analysis', http://jarretbrachman.net/?p=916.
56 Jarret Brachman and Alix Levine, 'The World of Holy Warcraft: How Al Qaeda is Using Online Game Theory to Recruit the Masses', *Foreign Policy*, 13 April 2011.
57 www.muslm.net (accessed 10/10/2009).
58 The emergence of splits in Iraq's jihadist groups is well described in, for example, Nir Rosen's *Aftermath: Following the Bloodshed of America's Wars in the Muslim World*. New York: Perseus, 2010.
59 Tom Hamilton, 'Scot freed after his terror sentence was quashed insists I'm not a terrorist, I'm more of a numpty', *Daily Record*, 10/02/2010, http://www.dailyrecord.co.uk/news/scottish-news/scot-freed-after-his-terror-sentence-1050167.
60 '"Lyrical terrorist" found guilty', BBC News 8/11/2007, http://news.bbc.co.uk/1/hi/7084801.stm.
61 Henry Jenkins, *Textual Poachers: Television Fans and Popular Culture*. London: Routledge, 1992, p. 10.
62 Joli Jensen, 'Fandom as Pathology: The Consequences of Characterisation', in L. Lewis (ed.), *The Adoring Audience: Fandom and Popular Media*. London: Routledge, 1992, pp. 9–29.
63 Camille Bacon Smith, *Enterprising Women: Television Fandom and the Creation of Popular Myth*. Philadelphia: University of Pennsylvania Press, p. 4.
64 Michel Maffesoli, *The Time of the Tribes: The Decline of Individualism in Mass Society*. London: Sage, 1996. Originally published 1988.
65 Emile Durkheim, *Elementary Forms of the Religious Life*, trans. Joseph Ward Swain. London: Allen and Unwin, 1976.
66 Lawrence Grossberg, 'Is There a Fan in the House? The Affective Sensibility of Fandom', in *The Adoring Audience*, pp. 50–68.
67 Matt Hills, *The Pleasures of Horror*. New York: Continuum, 2005.
68 Roland Barthes, *The Pleasure of the Text*, trans. Richard Miller. New York: Hill and Wang 1975.
69 Michel de Certeau, *The Practice of Everyday Life* (originally: *L'Invention du Quotidien*), trans. Steve Rendell. Berkeley: University of California Press, 1984.
70 Mikhail Bakhtin, *The Dialogic Imagination: Four Essays*, ed. Michael Holquist; trans. Caryl Emerson and Michael Holquist. Austin: University of Texas Press, 1981.
71 Janice Radway, *Reading the Romance: Women, Patriarchy and Popular Literature*. Chapel Hill: University of North Carolina Press.
72 Mikhail Bakhtin, 'Epic and the Novel: Towards a Methodology for the Study of the Novel', in *The Dialogic Imagination: Four Essays*.
73 Pierre Bourdieu, *The Field of Cultural Production*. New York: Columbia University Press, 1993, pp. 162–3; A useful discussion of the concept can be found in P. Thompson's, 'Field' in Michael Grenfall (ed.), *Pierre Bourdieu: Key Concepts*. Stocksfield: Acumen, 2008, p. 79.
74 Bourdieu's major empirical work on this subject is (trans. Richard Nice) *Distinction: A Social Critique of the Judgement of Taste*. London: Routledge, 1984; the concept is outlined earlier in Bourdieu's (trans. Richard Nice), *Outline of a Theory of* Practice. Cambridge: Cambridge University Press, 1977. A more concise statement is to be found in Bourdieu's 'The Forms of Capital', in J. Richardson (ed.), *Handbook of Theory and Research for the Sociology of Education*, Westport: Greenwood, pp. 241–58.

75 See John Fiske, 'The Cultural Economy of Fandom', in L. Lewis (ed.), *The Adoring Audience: Fandom and Popular Culture*, pp. 30–49. Also: Sarah Thornton, *Club Cultures: Music, Media and Subcultural Capital*. Hanover: University of New England, 1996.
76 *Textual Poachers*, p. 263.
77 Ibid. p. 46.
78 Howard Rheingold, *The Virtual Community: Homesteading on the Electronic Frontier*. Cambridge, MA: MIT Press, 2000, p. 30.
79 Robert Kozinets, *Netnography: Doing Ethnographic Research Online*. Thousand Oaks: Sage, 2010.
80 James J. Gibson, *The Ecological Approach to Visual Perception*. London: Houghton Mifflin, 1979.
81 Donald Norman, *The Design of Everyday Things*. London: MIT Press, 1998.
82 Ian Hutchby, 'Technologies, Texts and Affordances'. *Sociology* 35(1), (2001), 441–56.
83 Lev Manovich, *The Language of New Media*, Cambridge, MA: MIT Press, 2001.
84 See Henry Jenkins, *Convergence Culture: Where Old and New Media Collide*. New York: New York University Press, 2006.
85 Pierre Levy, *Collective Intelligence: Mankind's Evolving World in Cyberspace*. New York, and London: Plenum Press, 1997, p. 180.
86 Pierre Levy, *Becoming Virtual*, trans. R. Bononno. New York: Plenum, 1998.
87 Martin Heidegger, 'The Question Concerning Technology', 1954, available online from *http://www.wright.edu/cola/Dept/PHL/Class/P/Internet/PITexts/QCT.html*.

Chapter 3

1 Fawaz Gerges, *The Far Enemy: Why Jihad Went Global*. Cambridge: Cambridge University Press, 2005.
2 Popularized by Marc Sageman, *Understanding Terrorist Networks*. Philadelphia: University of Pennsylvania Press, 2004.
3 Bernard Haykel, 'On the Nature of Salafi Thought and Action', in Roel Meijer, (ed.), *Global Salafism: Islam's New Religious Movement*. London: Hurst, 2010, pp. 33–51.
4 For an excellent recent attempt to unpick this confusion, see H. Lauzière, 'The Construction of Salafiyya: Reconsidering Salafism from the Perspective of Conceptual History'. *International Journal of Middle East Studies* 42(3), (2010), 369–89.
5 Bernard Haykel, op. cit.
6 Quintan Wiktorowicz, 'Anatomy of the Salafi Movement'. *Studies in Conflict and Terrorism* 29, (2006), 207–39.
7 For a recent discussion which adds complexity and nuance to this typical characterization of the meaning of 'jihadi-salasim', see Joas Wagemakers, *A Quietist Jihadi: The Ideology and Influence of Abu Muhammad al-Maqdisi*. Cambridge: Cambridge University Press, 2012.

8 Thomas Hegghammer, 'Jihadi Salafis or Revolutionaries? On Religion and Politics in the Study of Militant Islamism', in Roel Meijer, (ed.), *Global Salafism: Islam's New Religious Movement*. London: Hurst, 2010, pp. 244–67.
9 Olivier Roy, *The Failure of Political Islam*. Cambridge, MA: Harvard University Press, 1996.
10 See, for example, Frédéric Volpi, 'Understanding the Rationale of the Islamic Fundamentalists' Political Strategies: A Pragmatic Reading of their Conceptual Schemes During the Modern Era'. *Totalitarian Movements and Political Religions* 1(2), (2000).
11 Abdullah Azzam, *Join the Caravan*. London: Azzam Publications, 2001.
12 op. cit. 'Jihadis or Revolutionaries?'
13 See Thomas Hegghammer, 'Global Jihadism After the Iraq War'. *The Middle East Journal* 60(1), (2006), 11–32.
14 Faisal Devji, *Landscapes of the Jihad: Militancy, Morality, Modernity*. Ithaca: Cornell University Press, 2005.
15 Johnny Ryan, 'The Internet, The Perpetual Beta and the State: A Long View of the New Medium'. *Studies in Conflict and Terrorism* 33(8), (2010), 673–81.
16 For example, according to Pew Global (2010), 60 per cent of the population in Jordan and 49 per cent in Egypt expressed support for Hamas, while 34 per cent and 20 per cent expressed support for Al Qaeda. Pew Global, 'Muslim Publics Divided on Hamas and Hezbollah', 2/12/2010, http://www.pewglobal.org/2010/12/02/muslims-around-the-world-divided-on-hamas-and-hezbollah/.
17 Lev Manovich, 'New Media from Borges to html', in Noah Wardrip-Fruin and Nick Montfort (eds), *The New Media Reader*. Cambridge, MA: MIT Press, 2003.
18 Jerome Bruner, 'Narrative and Paradigmatic Modes of Thought', in Elliot Eisner, (ed.), *Learning and Teaching the Ways of Knowing: Eighty Fourth Yearbook of the National Society for the Study of Education*. Chicago: University of Chicago Press, 1985, pp. 97–115.
19 Lev Manovich, *The Language of New Media*, pp. 45, 88, 35 ff.
20 Originally located at www.lokmaine.com, this content has recently moved to http://bg.omety.com/-a453764, (accessed 2/2/2013).
21 Jarret Brachman, Lianne Kennedy Boudali and Afshon Ostavar, 'The Islamic Imagery Project: Visual Motifs in Jihadi Internet Propaganda', Combating Terrorism Centre, Department of Social Sciences, 2006, available online from http://www.ctc.usma.edu/wp-content/uploads/2010/06/Islamic-Imagery-Project.pdf.
22 'Listen to the most beautiful and amazing jihadi nashids', http://www.syrianarmyfree.com/vb/showthread.php?t=19154 (accessed 14/01/2012).
23 http://uk.youtube.com/watch?v=LXhmCnpr6sw (accessed 12/01/2009).
24 Behnam Said, 'Hymns (Nasheeds): A Contribution to the Study of the Jihadist Culture'. *Studies in Conflict and Terrorism* 35(12), (2012), 863–79.
25 http://www.aw4h.net/showthread.php?t=33624 (accessed 25/6/2010).
26 "Abdur Rahman", "Anasheed: A Tool in Our Media's Warfare Arsenal", *Jihad Recollections*, No. 3, August 2009.
27 For an introduction to the position of various forms of music in Islamic law, see L. I. Al-Faruqi, 'Music, Musicians and Muslim Law'. *Asian Music* 17(1), (1985), 3–36.
28 See, e.g., Amnon Shiloah, *Islamic Music*. Detroit: Wayne State University Press, 1995, p. 156.

29 A useful description of the musical form of the contemporary nashid, albeit specifically applied to the case of Pashto material, is to be found in Alex Strick Van Linschoten and Felix Kuehn (ed.), *Poetry of the Taliban*. New York: Columbia University Press, 2012, p. 36.
30 This seems implicit, for instance, in Z. bin Abdul Ghani's paper for the Malaysian department of Islamic development, 'Entertainment in the Muslim Media: Unsettled Problem?'. *Jurnal Hadhari Bil* 2(2009), 53–63.
31 http://majdah.maktoob.com/vb/majdah65187/(accessed 5/1/2010). The majority of the nashid lyrics analysed here were located on one of two collections. The first was originally located at this URL (although the same collection appears elsewhere as well). The second was located on *http://wainuk2007.jeeran.com/anashed/*(accessed 6/6/2010).
32 Said, op. cit.
33 'Abu Ratib', *Khudhu Qalban*, available online from http://www.wainuk2007.arabblogs.com/anashed/archive/2008/2/465043.html, accessed 06/06/2010.
34 'It Pleased them that Blood Should Cover them', words to this nashid available from http://majdah.maktoob.com/vb/majdah66527/(accessed 5/1/2010).
35 The words to this nashid – *fajrī al-mal'ūn ya bint al-jihād* – can be found at *http://alhotah.net/vb/showthread.php?t=12606* (accessed 18/8/2010).
36 Mustafa al-Jaza'iri, *Labbayk, Islam al-Butula* (Here for you, Islam, heroism), http://wainuk2007.arabblogs.com/anashed/categories/بطولة_جهادية_إسلامية/.
37 op. cit. 'It Pleased them', http://majdah.maktoob.com/vb/majdah66527/ (accessed 5/1/2010).
38 Emile Durkheim, *The Elementary Forms of the Religious Life*. New York: Free Press, 1995, p. 226.
39 Muhammad al-Zuhayri, *On the path of the rightly guided Caliphs*, Zuhayri, known as 'Poet of Al Qaeda' was a well-known online activist who was sentenced to prison for a year and a half in Jordan in 2007. 'Prison for "Poet of Al-Qaeda" for a year and half after the publication of a poem impinging on the Jordanian monarch', *Al Arabiya*, 2007, http://www.alarabiya.net/articles/2007/10/01/39811.html.
40 'Where are our days, where?' http://majdah.maktoob.com/vb/majdah66527/, (accessed 5/1/2010).
41 'The Day the Whole Ummah Kneels', http://majdah.maktoob.com/vb/majdah66527/, (accessed 5/1/2010).
42 'Abu Abdullah al-Malik', 'O World, What Is This Silence?', http://www.3asq.com/showthread.php?t=211444 (accessed 3/02/2013).
43 'Blow them up', http://www.majdah.maktoob.com/vb/majdah66527/, (accessed 5/1/2010).
44 See, for example, Marwan Kreidy, 'Islamic Popular Culture', *Annenberg School of Communication, Departmental Papers*, University of Pennsylvania, 2006, http://repository.upenn.edu/cgi/viewcontent.cgi?article=1191&context=asc_papers&sei-redir=1&referer=http%3A%2F%2Fscholar.google.co.uk%2Fscholar%3Fhl%3Den%26q%3Dislamic%2Bmusic%2Bsami%2Byusuf%26btnG%3D%26as_sdt%3D1%252C5%26as_sdtp%3D#search=%22islamic%20music%20sami%20yusuf%22.
45 Ben Ando, 'The enigma that is the "lyrical terrorist"', BBC news, 2007, http://news.bbc.co.uk/1/hi/uk/7085889.stm.

46 See, for example, Hishaam Aidi, 'Don't Panic: Islam and Europe's "Hip Hop Wars"', http://www.aljazeera.com/indepth/opinion/2012/06/20126310151835171.html.
47 For further information on this group, see Shamim Miah and Virinder Kalra, 'Muslim Hip Hop – the Politicisation of Kool Islam'. *South Asian Cultural Studies* 2(1), (2010), 12–25.
48 'Muslim Belal', 'Like a Soldier', http://www.youtube.com/watch?v=nzW3GRbUd2w, (accessed 12/8/2012).
49 See, for example, BIAS (Brothers in a Struggle), 'Operation Revelotionary [sic] Liberation Jihad', http://www.youtube.com/watch?v=cQRzbbUpt44, (accessed 12/8/2012).
50 'Mother don't be sad – English jihad nasheed', http://www.youtube.com/watch?v=vIKQuZHw7qc, (accessed 12/08/2012).
51 It is interesting to note how this seems, on the one hand, to be a highly distinctive feature of new media (Manovich, for one, singles it out as such), while also perhaps representing the continuation of the high tradition of Islamic art.
52 http://www.muslm.net/vb/showthread.php?248922-روع-الفـلاشـات-الجـهاديـة**متـجددد, (accessed 20/06/2010).
53 *www.youtube.com/watch?v=co_RnlbBfkw&feature=related* (accessed 18/8/2010).
54 *www.archive.org/details/TheBaghdadSniper* (accessed 18/8/2010).
55 *www.youtube.com/watch?v=o7-f0_YhxJQ* (accessed 18/8/2010).
56 *Wassil sawt al-batal al-ghadib*, http://www.youtube.com/watch?v=cGKxUcZE4D8 (accessed 12/08/2012).
57 See Chapter 6 for a discussion of Jihadi nickname conventions.
58 Faisal Devji, *Landscapes of Jihad: Militancy, Morality, Modernity*. Ithaca: Cornell University Press, 2005.
59 This observation recalls Faisal Devji's notion of global jihadist violence as 'ethical' act, see *Landscapes of Jihad: Militancy, Morality, Modernity*. London: Hurst, 2005.
60 Search conducted 2/6/2010.
61 See, for example, Marc Lynch, 'Islam Divided between Salafi-Jihad and the Ikhwan'. *Studies in Conflict and Terrorism* 33(6), (2010), 467–87.
62 For a useful summary of key points of Salafist doctrine, see Bernard Haykel, 'On the Nature of Salafi Thought and Action', in Roel Meijer (ed.), *Global Salafism: Islam's New Religious Movement*. London: Hurst, 2010, pp. 33–57.

Chapter 4

1 Howard Rheingold, *The Virtual Community*, op. cit.
2 Pseudonymity here refers to the situation of being known by a single, stable pseudonym in which social capital is invested. By contrast, anonymity implies being totally unknown to those with whom one is interacting, even as an online persona.
3 See particularly Jürgen Habermas, *The Structural Transformation of the Public Sphere: An Enquiry into A Category of Bourgeois Society*, trans. Thomas Burger with Frederick Lawrence. Cambridge: MIT Press, 1989.

4 Mark Aakhus, 'The Design of Forums for Online Public Communication and the Consequences for Argumentation'. *Kentucky Journal of Communication* 21(2), Fall 2002.
5 Cass Sunstein, *Republic.com 2.0*. Princeton, NJ: Princeton University Press, 2007.
6 See Olivier Roy, *The Failure of Political Islam*, op. cit.
7 See Scott Sanford, 'Fault Lines in Cyberspace', op. cit.
8 See, for example, Henry Jenkins, *Convergence Culture*.
9 http://www.swalif.net/softs/swalif68/softs169433 (accessed 3/8/2009).
10 For this point (and much of the narrative of this paragraph) see Evan Kohlmann, 'Expert Report on the AQCORPO Website', 2006, available from http://nefafoundation.org/miscellaneous.FeatureDocs.ekirhaby0108.pdf.
11 Akil Awan and Mina al-Lami, 'Al Qa'ida's Virtual Crisis'. *The RUSI Journal* 154(1), (2009), 56–64.
12 Thomas Hegghammer, 'Spy Forums', *Jihadica.com* 2010, http://www.jihadica.com/spy-forums/.
13 This piece of information was provided to the author by a senior police officer heavily involved in the investigation.
14 Originally posted on the forum Madad al-Suyuf, this document remains accessible in its original from http://www.jihadica.com/wp-content/uploads/2009/03/01–04-09-madad-al-suyuf-the-jihadi-forums.pdf.
15 Anne Stenersen, 'The History of Jihadi Forums', *Jihadica*, 2009, http://www.jihadica.com/the-history-of-the-jihadi-forums/.
16 See comments to article above at same URL.
17 *http://www.alboraqforum.info/showthread.php?s=f181462ad503f0379100ef5020ac24&t=1677* (accessed 25/6/2010).
18 See, for example, Joas Wagemakers, 'Reclaiming Scholarly Authority: Abu Muhammad al-Maqdisi's Critique of *Jihadi* Practices'. *Studies in Conflict and Terrorism* 34(7), (2011)
19 For a good, brief summary of this dispute, see Brynjar Lia, 'More Fitna in Cyberspace: Mihdar vs Al-Maqdisi', *Jihadica*, 2009, http://www.jihadica.com/more-fitna-in-cyberspace-mihdar-vs-al-maqdisi/.
20 *http://www.qmagreb.org/pages/forums.html* (accessed 17/09/2007).
21 Hsinchun Chen, Arab Salem, Edna Reid, 'Sentiment and affect analysis of Dark Web forums: Measuring radicalization on the internet'. *ISI* (2008), 104–9.
22 Johnny Ryan, 'The Internet, The Perpetual Beta and the State: The Long View of the New Medium'. *Studies in Conflict and Terrorism* 33(8), (2010), 673–81.
23 Edna Erez, Gabriel Weimann and Aaron Weisburd, *Jihad, Crime and the Internet: Content Analysis of Jihadist Forum Discussions*, Report Submitted to the National Institute of Justice, 31 October 2011, available online from https://vubis.politieacademie.nl/pdf/82942.pdf.
24 Abbottabad letter SOCOM-2012-0000004, available online from http://www.ctc.usma.edu/posts/letters-from-abbottabad-bin-ladin-sidelined.
25 *http://al-hesbah.info/v/showthread.php?s=2c15369f2c489a89cbe010a218cc12f2&t=193033* (accessed 22/9/08).
26 'The jihadi forums!!!! Between the hammer of the members and the anvil of the Arabic and international intelligence', Sanam al-Islam network 18/-3/2012, http://snam-s.net/vb/.

27 Evgeny Morozov, *The Net Delusion: How Not to Liberate the World*. London: Allen Lane, 2010.
28 Gabriel Weimann, 'Virtual Disputes: The Use of the Internet for Terrorist Debates'. *Studies in Conflict and Terrorism* 29(7), (2006), 623–39.
29 This document, which at the time of writing remains available from http://archive.org/details/tagneed-Jhaaad0 (3/10/2012), seems to have first appeared online in late 2008, see Abdullah Warius and Brian Fishman, 'A Jihadist's Course in the Art of Recruitment', *CTC Sentinel* 2(2), February 2009.
30 *http://www.al-faloja.info/vb/showthread.php?t=29669* (accessed 12/8/2009).
31 'Jihadi Forums in the Balance', op. cit.
32 The information here is drawn from the author's archive of the site.

Chapter 5

1 See, for example, E. J. M. Kessells, (ed.), *Countering Violent Extremist Narratives*. The Hague: National Counterterrorism Coordinator, 2010.
2 Omar Ashour, 'Online Deradicalisation? Countering Violent Extremist Narratives: Message, Messenger and Media Strategy'. *Perspectives on Terrorism* 4(6), (2010).
3 For an example of the deployment of this term from a policy perspective, see https://www.mi5.gov.uk/home/the-threats/terrorism/international-terrorism/al-qaidas-history/al-qaidas-ideology.html (accessed 29/08/2012).
4 Michael Doran, 'The Pragmatic Fanaticism of Al Qaeda: An Anatomy of Extremism in Middle Eastern Politics'. Political Science Quarterly 117(2), 2002.
5 See, for example, Tim Stevens and Peter Neumann, 'Countering Online Radicalisation: A Strategy for Action'. London: ICSR, 2009.
6 For instance, see the uses of the term 'vulnerability' in the most recent version of the UK 'Prevent' strategy: http://www.homeoffice.gov.uk/publications/counter-terrorism/prevent/prevent-strategy/(accessed 29/08/2012).
7 Lina Khatib makes this point in 'Public Diplomacy 2.0: A Case Study of the Digital Outreach Team', CDDRL Working Paper Number 120, January 2011, http://iis-db.stanford.edu/pubs/23084/No.120-_Public_Diplomacy_2.0.pdf.
8 Ibid.
9 'Isa al-'Awshan, *39 Ways to Serve Jihad and he Mujahidin*, released online circa 2004.
10 For an introductory discussion, see Christopher Boucek, 'The Sakinah Campaign and Internet Counter-Radicalisation in Saudi Arabia'. *CTC Sentinel* 1(9), (2008).
11 A classical text much drawn on by jihadi writers which deals extensively with the matter of *qu'ud* is Ahmad bin Ibrahim al-Nuhas al-Dimashqi's *Water Holes for Those Who Yearn for the Places of Struggle, and Goading to those Who Love to Remain in the Abode of Peace* (mashari'al-'ushaq ila masari'al-jihad wa muthir al gharam ila dar al-salam), available online from http://www.tawhed.ws/dl?i=qvadc256.
12 'Conversation between a jihadi and a defeatist', http://joadalfajr.arabblogs.com/archive/2007/12/415477.html (accessed 14/8/2012).

13 See Joas Wagemakers, '"Seceders" and "Postponers?" An Analysis of the Khawarij and Murji'a Labels in Polemical Debates between Quietist and Jihadi Salafis', in Jeevan Deol and Zaheer Kazmi (eds), *Contextualising Jihadi Ideologies*. London: Hurst, Forthcoming. Presently available online from http://www.jihadica.com/wp-content/uploads/2012/04/Seceders-and-Postponers-An-Analysis-of-the-Khawarij-and-Murjia-Labels-in-Polemical-Debates-between-Quietist-and-Jihadi-Salafis.pdf.
14 Shaykh Hamid bin 'Abdullah al-'Ali "The danger of postponement and the reasons for the enmity of the murji'ites towards jihad"', http://www.tawhed.ws/r?i=fhmt0ia0 (accessed 14/08/2012).
15 Quoted in Y. Yehushoa, 'Re-Education of Extremists in Saudi Arabia', MEMRI, enquiry and analysis series report no. 260, 2006.
16 For a discussion of this debate see Joas Wagemakers, 'Defining the Enemy: Abu Muhammad al-Maqdisi's Radical Reading of Surat al-Mumtahana'. *Die Welt des Islams* 48(3–4), (2008), 348–71.
17 Frans van Eemeren and Robert Grootendorst, *A Systematic Theory of Argumentation: The Pragma-Dialectical Approach*. Cambridge: Cambridge University Press, 2003, p. 1.
18 Frans van Eemeren and Peter Houtlosser, 'Strategic Manoeuvering: A Synthetic Recapitulation'. *Humanities, Social Sciences and Law* 20(4), (2006), 381–92.
19 Frans van Eemeren, *Strategic Maneuvering in Argumentative Discourse*. Amsterdam: John Benjamins, 2010.
20 'Strategic Manoeuvering: A Synthetic Recapitulation'.
21 The basis for this statement is a detailed examination of thirty-six discussions on Muslm.net in which a critic of Al Qaeda attempted to advance argumentation against the group carried out by the author in 2010.
22 http://www.muslm.net/vb/showthread.php?376834-%D9%86%D8%AF%D8%A7%D8%A1-%D9%85%D9%86-%D8%A3%D9%85-%D9%85%D8%B3%D9%84%D9%85%D8%A9-%D8%A7%D9%84%D9%89-%D8%A7%D9%84%D9%82%D8%A7%D8%B9%D8%AF%D8%A9&p=2446036#post2446036, (accessed 20/08/2012).
23 *http://www.muslm.org/vb/showthread.php?t=381555*, (accessed 12/5/2010).
24 http://www.muslm.net/vb/showthread.php?384252-%D8%A7%D9%84%D8%B9%D9%88%D9%84%D9%82%D9%8A-%D9%8A%D8%AE%D9%84%D8%B7-%D8%A8%D9%8A%D9%86-%D8%A7%D9%84%D8%AC%D9%87%D8%A7%D8%AF-%D9%88%D8%A7%D9%84%D9%82%D8%AA%D8%A7%D9%84&p=2508300#post2508300 (accessed 20/08/2012).
25 The diagram below is taken from the Gilbert Ramsay, 'Online Arguments Against Al-Qaeda: An Exploratory Analysis'. *Perspectives on Terrorism* 6(1), (2012)
26 Abu Sa'ad al Bahili used flashing, coloured text for his post.
27 Hanzala is the famous creation of the Palestinian political cartoonist Naji al-Ali (1938–87). An emblem of the fate of the Palestinian people, he was always drawn with his back to the reader and his hands tied.
28 For a deeper discussion of this incident see Sandra Marie Phelps, 'The Limits of Admittance and Diversity in Iraqi Kurdistan: Femininity and the Body of Du'a Khalil'. *Gender and Political Religions* 11(3–4), (2010)

29 *http://www.muslm.net/vb/showthread.php?t=356855*, (accessed 10/5/2010).
30 http://www.muslm.net/vb/archive/index.php/t-380766.html, (accessed 24/11/2011).
31 *http://www.muslm.org/vb/showthread.php?t=381499*, (accessed 28/8/2012).

Chapter 6

1 https://www.as-ansar.org/vb/showthread.php?t=52265, (accessed 29/08/2012).
2 For further examples of this, see Thomas Hegghammer's 2009 *Jihadica* post 'Jihadists study jihadi studies', http://www.jihadica.com/jihadists-study-jihadi-studies/, (accessed 28/08/2012).
3 For a summary of some of the jihadi responses to Jenkins' report, see Nur Aziemah Binte Azman, 'Al Qaeda's Internet Strategy a Failure? Online Jihadists Disprove'. *Counter Terrorist Trends and Analysis*, International Centre for Political Violence and Terrorism Research, S. Rajaratnam School of International Studies, Nanyang Technological University 4(2), (2012), 1–4.
4 Omar Hammami, *The Story of an American Jihaadi: Part One*, published online, 2012, p. 116.
5 For a classic account of the thought of these two men, and its social and historical context, see Gilles Kepel, *Jihad: The Trail of Radical Islam*. Cambridge: Harvard University Press, 2002.
6 The idea that Muslims have a duty to fight as 'effectively' as possible is a mainstay of theological arguments justifying forms of violence normally forbidden in Islamic jurisprudence, advanced in, for example, Abu Muhammad al-Maqdisi's fatwa in defence of suicide bombing, Nasir al-Fahd's fatwa permitting the use of weapons of mass destruction, and Abu Yahiya al-Libi's vindication of the principle of tatarrus as a justification for attacks which it is known will cause Muslim casualties.
7 'Isa bin Sa'ad al-'Awshan's release of *39 Ways* should be understood originally as relating the specific dynamics of the doomed campaign of the first incarnation of Al Qaeda in the Arabian peninsula as chronicled by Thomas Hegghammer in *Jihad in Saudi Arabia*. Since then, however, it has become a widely circulated jihadist text well beyond this original context.
8 A useful overview of Al-'Awlaqi's publications is to be found in Alexander Meleagrou Hitchens and Jacob Amis, 'The Making of the Christmas Day Bomber'. *Current Trends in Islamist Ideology* 10(2010).
9 A slight ambiguity is presented here by the fact that Al-'Awshan's work suggests, early on in the document, participation in jihad 'bi nafs', which probably means 'in person'. There seems little doubt that Al-'Awlaqi's work, however (which does not include this), is intended to have something of the character of a pathway towards the ultimate end of physical engagement.
10 Indeed, this ambiguity carries over into the very title of the first of these works, which is given on the title page as *39 Ways to Serve Jihad and the Mujahidin* and on the first page of the actual text as *39 Ways to Serve* and Participate *in Jihad*.

NOTES

11 See: 'Al Asad: Prepared for War, and Israel Does not Understand other than the Language of Strength and the American Project Has Failed and the Arabs Have Abandoned Iraq', *Al Quds*, available online from http://www.alquds.com/node/245535, (accessed 10/8/2010).
12 Abu Muhammad al-Maqdisi, 'The Definition of Jihad in Islam' (*ta'rīf al-jihād fī islām*), available from www.tawhed.ws/dl?i=8zkfg6zh.
13 In the Qur'an (e.g. Al-Nisa' verse 95), the mujahidin 'with their wealth and their lives' are both explicitly contrasted to the 'qa'idun' who remain behind.
14 The context for this is Al-Awlaki's commentary on a medieval treatise by the 'embattled scholar' Ahmad bin Ibrahim al-Nuhas al-Dimashqi entitled, roughly, *Water Holes for Slaking the Longing of those who Yearn for Jihad* which is very popular in contemporary jihadi contexts.
15 Influentially, Jihad by the tongue is one of the four categories of jihad mentioned in Ibn Rushd's *Muqaddima*. The category of 'jihad with the tongue and proof' is also, significantly, retained in the work of Ibn al-Qiym al-Jawziya, a student of Ibn al-Taymiyya.
16 See Michael Cook's *Commanding Right and Forbidding Wrong in Islamic Thought*. Cambridge: Cambridge University Press, 2004 for a highly erudite discussion of the analogous division between acts with the sword, the tongue and the heart in traditional Islamic jurisprudence.
17 The classic story with regard to the virtue of incitement, or *tahrid* is that of Umm Ibrahim, who volunteered her son for the defence of Basra, paying the money that would have been his bride-price to equip him.
18 Abd al-Rahman Salum al-Rawashdi, *Media Jihad: Foundations and Practice (Readings in The Jihadi Media in Iraq)*, p. 22 ff.
19 Mustafa Sittmariyam Nasar (Abu Mus'ab al-Suri), *The Global Islamic Resistance Call*, p. 685.
20 For an overview of this movement see Stéphane Lacroix, *Awakening Islam: The Politics of Religious Dissent in Contemporary Saudi Arabia*, trans. George Holoch. Cambridge: Harvard University Press, 2011.
21 Al-Suri first introduces this term on p. 41.
22 ref 'enigma of al-takfir wa al-hijra'.
23 *The Global Islamic Resistance Call*, p. 1125.
24 Ibid., p. 1413.
25 Ibid., p. 1412.
26 Ibid.
27 i.e., member of RAND Corporation.
28 See Joby Warrick, *The Triple Agent: The Al Qaeda Mole Who Infiltrated the CIA*. New York: Doubleday, 2011.
29 http://www.muslm.net/vb/showthread.php?t=373832, (accessed 27/10/2010).
30 Jihadist writing oscillates between apocalyptic and revolutionary themes. Notwithstanding the significance of the Arab Spring in bringing the latter to the fore, the former remains important in online jihadi writing. For instance, a recent book by the popular Internet jihadi Asad al-Jihad 2, *Our War Has Not Started Yet*, seems to be fundamentally premised on the long term nature of the conflict between Islam and unbelief.
31 See, for instance Abdul Qadir ibn Abdul Aziz's (trans. And ed. Al Tibyan Publications), *Jihad and the Effects of Intention Upon It*.

32 This is true, for example, for *Al Sayf* – a forum downloaded in its entirety by the author at the end of 2007, the content of which deals extensively with military 'training' material.
33 These posts are all taken from the author's archive of Shumukh al-Islam's 'military camp', section, http://shamikh1.info/vb/showthread.php?t=120524.
34 http://www.alqimmah.net/showthread.php?t=7194, (accessed 30/07/2009).
35 Originally published by Shumukh al-Islam, presently available at http://www.airssforum.com/showthread.php?t=149667, (accessed 16/08/2012).
36 The low quality of the work in Irhabi007's Manual for Hacking Zionist and Crusader websites was confirmed by showing a translated copy to the data manager at the CSTPV.
37 http://www.alqimmah.net/showthread.php?t=7194, (accessed 30/07/2009).
38 *http://alflojaweb.com/vb/showthread.php?t=85273*, (accessed 1/02/2010).
39 Explanation of the word *nasr*, http://www.lesanarab.com/kalima/%D9%86%D8%B5%D8%B1, (accessed 7/06/2012).
40 Yusuf al-'Uyayri, *Thawabit 'ala Darb al-Jihad*, available from http://www.tawhed.ws/r?i=iftddsvn, (accessed 16/8/2012).
41 Presently available from http://www.youtube.com/watch?v=ajQWVMkQHTY, (accessed 14/8/2012).
42 Taken from the author's archive (2010) of the 'Questions and Answers' section of *Ansar al-Mujahidin* forum.
43 www.muslm.net (accessed 16/08/2010).
44 M. Maudoodi, 'The Mischief of Takfir', available online (in English) from *http://www.muslim.org/movement/maudoodi/art-takfir.htm*.
45 For an anatomization of Al-Maqdisi's argument here see again Joas Wagemakers, 'Defining the Enemy: Abu Muhammad al-Maqdisi's Radical Reading of Surat al-Mumtahana'. *Die Welt des Islams* 48(3-4), (2008), 348–71.
46 For the significance of irreducibly embodied moments to cyberculture see Live Gies, 'How Material are Cyberbodies: Broadband Internet and Embodied Subjectivity'. *Crime, Media, Culture* 4(3), (2008), 311–30.
47 www.al-sayf.com/vb (accessed January 2007, from author's archive of this site).
48 As an example of this, consider the video series by the Egyptian salafist preacher Muhammad Hisan *raqa'iq fi daqa'iq* (raqa'iq in minutes) – the notion that one can experience the 'subtlety' and emotional depth of this genre in minutes is, in itself, indicative of the postmodernist and consumerist dimensions of certain forms of contemporary Islam. http://www.youtube.com/watch?v=-O-rANpYN8s (accessed 21/08/2012).
49 See Juan Cole, 'The World as Text: Cosmologies of Ahmad al-Ahsa'i'.
50 *The Global Islamic Resistance Call*, p. 135 ff.
51 For example, it is interesting to note the motif of the tender-heartedness in eulogies of figures such as Usama bin Ladin, as, for example, in stories such as 'the story that made Shaykh Usama cry until he fainted'. Ayman al-Zawahiri's eulogy of bin Ladin 'Days Spent with the Imam' in which he praises bin Laden's 'subtle ethics' (*akhlaq al-raqiyya* and 'noble sentiments').

Chapter 7

1. QMI Agency, 'Sodomy: The New Jihadi Training Method?', *London Free Press*, 12/7/2012, http://www.lfpress.com/news/world/2012/07/12/19980551.html.
2. Benjamin Doherty, 'Sodomy for Jihad? Venerable LGBT Magazine the Advocate Spreads Vile Islamophobic Hoax', *The Electronic Intifada*, 07/13/2012, http://electronicintifada.net/blogs/benjamin-doherty/sodomy-jihad-venerable-lgbt-magazine-advocate-spreads-vile-islamophobic-hoax.
3. http://www.web.archive.org/web/20091002024147/http://www.montdiatna.com:8686/forum/showthread.php?t=105911, (accessed 21/8/2012).
4. 'The Muslim and the haircut', http://www.jihadidujour.blogspot.co.uk/, (accessed 21/8/2012).
5. Dr Babu Suseelan, "Jihadi Terrorism", http://www.faithfreedom.org/oped/BabuSuseelan40227.htm (accessed 21/8/2012).
6. Fernando Bravo Lopez, 'Towards a Definition of Islamophobia: Approximations of the Early 20th Century'. *Ethnic and Racial Studies* 1(4), (2011), 556–73.
7. See, for example, T. Marx, 'Islam and Media Discourses in India: Constructing Islamophobia'. *International Journal of South Asian Studies* 1(2), (2008), 284–95.
8. Lt. Col. Matthew Dooley, 'A Counter-Jihad Op Design Model'.
9. This is documented, along with the contents of Dooley's training course, in an outstanding series of articles by Spencer Ackerman and Noah Schachtman, *Wired* 2012, http://www.wired.com/dangerroom/2012/06/failure-oversight-war-islam/.
10. See Brian Jenkins, *Will Terrorists Go Nuclear?* New York: Prometheus Books, 2008.
11. Gabriele Marranci, 'Multiculturalism, Islam and the clash of civilisations theory: rethinking Islamophobia'. *Culture and Religion: An Interdisciplinary Journal* 5(1), (2004), 105–17.
12. Arun Kundnani, 'Blind Spot? Security Narratives and Far Right Violence in Europe', ICCT Research Paper, June 2012, http://www.icct.nl/download/file/ICCT-Kundnani-Blind-Spot-June-2012.pdf.
13. See, for example, Arun Kundnani, *Spooked: How Not to Prevent Violent Extremism*. Institute of Race Relations, 2009.
14. For example, Melanie Philips, *Londonistan: How Britain is Creating a Terror State Within*. New York: Encounter, 2006.
15. See, for example, Matthew Taylor, Guy Granjean and Teresa Smith, 'The English Defence League Uncovered', 28/05/2010, http://www.guardian.co.uk/uk/video/2010/may/28/english-defence-league-uncovered.
16. Robert Lambert and Jonathan Githens Mazer, *Islamophobia and Anti-Muslim Hate Crime: Case Studies 2010: An Introduction to a Ten-Year Europe-Wide Research Project*. University of Exeter and European Muslim Research Centre, 2010, p. 86.
17. Ibid., p. 33.
18. Matthew Goodwin, Vidhya Ramalingam and Rachel Briggs, 'The New Radical Right: Violent and Non-Violent Movements in Europe', Institute for Strategic Dialogue Briefing Paper, 2012, http://www.strategicdialogue.org/ISD%20Far%20Right%20Feb2012.pdf.

19 See, for example, http://ex-muslim.org.uk/.
20 'Blind Spot? Security Narratives and Far Right Violence in Europe'.
21 Fred Halliday, 'Anti-Muslimism and Contemporary Politics: One Ideology, or Many'. London: IB Tauris, 1996, pp. 160, 194.
22 Ibid., pp. 39–40.
23 Available online at the time of writing from: http://unitednations.ispnw.org/archives/breivik-manifesto-2011.pdf, (accessed 22/08/2012).
24 *Knights Templar 2083: A European Declaration of Independence*, p. 5.
25 This point has been widely observed, including by Kundani, above. *The Guardian*'s datablog produced an interesting map of sites referred to by Breivik based on services provided by the French analytics company Linkfluence which reinforces many of the complexities in defining the 'crusaderist' movement discussed in this chapter. http://www.guardian.co.uk/news/datablog/interactive/2011/sep/07/norway-breivik-manifesto-mapped.
26 *Knights Templar 2083: A European Declaration of Independence*, p. 5
27 Ibid., p. 6.
28 Ibid.
29 Ibid., p. 1352.
30 Ibid., p. 6.
31 Available online, http://www.youtube.com/watch?v=C35diYdLZ64, (accessed 22/08/12).
32 See, for example, Paul Rozen, Maureen Markwith and Clark McCauley, 'Sensitivity to indirect contacts with other persons: AIDS aversion as a composite of aversion to strangers, infection, moral taint and misfortune'. *Journal of Abnormal Psychology* 103(3), 495–505.
33 *Knights Templar 2083: A European Declaration of Independence*, p. 958.
34 Ibid., p. 492.
35 Ibid., p. 529.
36 Ibid., p. 58.
37 Max Abrahms, 'What Terrorists Really Want: Terrorist Motives and Counterterrorism Strategy'. *International Security* 32(4), (2008), 78–105.
38 *Knights Templar 2083: A European Declaration of Independence*, p. 858.
39 Ibid., p. 1208.
40 http://www.gatesofvienna.blogspot.co.uk/, (accessed 22/8/2012).
41 http://www.gatesofvienna.blogspot.co.uk/2007/11/danish-civil-war.html, (accessed 22/8/2012).
42 'El Ingles' *Our Muslim Troubles: Lessons from Northern Ireland*, (no date) available online from http://www.thebritishresistance.co.uk/downloadslink1/electronic-books/el-ingles-our-muslim-troubles-lessons-from-northern-ireland-pdf/detail, (accessed 22/8/2012).
43 http://www.gatesofvienna.blogspot.co.uk/2011/05/our-muslim-troubles-lessons-from_26.html.
44 *Our Muslim Troubles*, p. 9.
45 Ibid., pp. 11 ff.
46 Ibid., p. 20.
47 Ibid., p. 35.
48 Ibid., pp. 46 ff.
49 Ibid., p. 15.
50 Ibid., p. 37.

51 Ibid., p. 5.
52 'Abu Bakr Naji', *Idarat al-Tawahhush, Akhtar Marhala Satamurr biha Al-Umma*, first available online, 2004; available in English translation by Will McCants under the title *The Management of Savagery, The Most Critical Stage Through Which the Ummah Will Pass*. Harvard: John M. Olin Institute for Strategic Studies, 2006.
53 On page 75, Naji writes 'Thus, we need to massacre (others) and (to take) actions like those that were undertaken against Banu Qurayza and their like [a Jewish tribe reported to have been massacred by the prophet Muhammad for betrayal]. But if God should give us power and we take control and justice spreads, how tender the people of faith will be at that time, and they will say to the people: "Go, for you are free"'.
54 *The Management of Savagery*, pp. 54 ff.
55 Lars Bevanger, 'Breivik Trial: Psychiatric reports scrutinized', 14/06/2012, http://www.bbc.co.uk/news/world-europe-18440743.
56 Brynjar Lia, *Architect of Global Jihad: The Life of Al Qaeda Strategist Abu Mus'ab al-Suri*. London: Hurst, 2007.
57 http://www.jihadwatch.org/.
58 http://www.mypetjawa.mu.nu/.
59 http://littlegreenfootballs.com/
60 Qin et. al., 'The Dark Web Portal Project: Collecting and Analyzing the Presence of Terrorist Groups on the Web', *Intelligence and Security Informatics*, Lecture Notes in Computer Science, 3495, (2005), 359–78.
61 http://www.internet-haganah.com/haganah/.
62 For a rather fraught discussion of this issue, see the email debate between MEMRI's Yigal Carmon and *Guardian* Middle East editor Brian Whitaker.
63 Brian Whitaker, 'Selective MEMRI', http://www.guardian.co.uk/world/2003/jan/28/israel2.
64 The Wolf Pack's YouTube smackdown now seems to have moved to the following URL.
65 www.gotwarporn.com (now defunct).
66 T. J. O'Connor and David Shinberg, 'The Jester Dynamic: A Lesson in Asymmetric Unmanaged Cyber Warfare', SANS Institute Certificate Dissertation, 2011.
67 Weisburd reports that one member of the forum was future Al Qaeda in the Arabian Peninsula member and propagandist Samir Khan.
68 The following information is based on the author's interview with Hayden Hewitt.

Chapter 8

1 For a retrospective assessment of the impact of the Iraq War see Maura Conway, 'From Zarqawi to Al-Awlaki: The Emergence of the Internet as a New Form of Violent Radical Milieu', 2012.
2 Sophia Moskalenko and Clark McCauley, 'Measuring Political Mobilization: The Distinction Between Activism and Radicalism'. *Terrorism and Political Violence* 21(2), (2009), 239–60.

3 Anthony Richards, 'The Problem with "Radicalization, the Remit of "Prevent" and the Need to Refocus on Terrorism in the UK'. *International Affairs* 87(1), 143–252.
4 Mark Sedgwick, 'The Concept of Radicalization and a Source of Confusion'. *Terrorism and Political Violence* 22(4), 474–94.
5 Max Abrahms, 'What Terrorists Really Want: Terrorist Motives and Counterterrorism Strategy'. *International Security* 32(4), (2008), 78–105.
6 In *Knights Under the Banner of the Prophet* (both first and second editions), Al-Zawahiri famously wrote: 'Pursuing the Americans and Jews is not an impossible task, killing them is not impossible, whether by a bullet, a knife stab, a bomb or a strike with an iron bar'.
7 Johnny Ryan, 'The Internet, The Perpetual Beta and the State: The Long View of the New Medium'. *Studies in Conflict and Terrorism* 33(8), (2010), 673–81.
8 http://www.jihad1.com/vb/showthread.php?s=455c9fd9498294ca49cc41b946d13590&t=386, (accessed 16/7/2010), http://www.isodarco.it/courses/andalo12/doc/Zarqawi%20to%20Awlaki_V2.pdf, http://www.jihad1.com/vb/showthread.php?s=455c9fd9498294ca49cc41b946d13590&t=386 (accessed 16/7/2010).
9 http://www.muslm.net/vb/showthread.php?425786-ملل‌أرة-المسلمة-الفجر-يقدم- (-مجلة-الشماخة-(-العلاج-الدول-أل-إل-السمية-جهادية-نسوي, (accessed 16/06/2011).
10 See, for example, Al-'Awlaqi's mischievous (if that is the right word!) claim to have included a copy of *Great Expectations* in the parcel bomb which Al Qaeda in the Arabian Peninsula attempted to send to two synagogues in Chicago. *Inspire* no. 3, p. 8.
11 See John Tulloch, 'Fans of Chekhov: Re-Approaching "High Culture"', in Gray, Sandvoss and Harrington (eds), *Fandom: Identities and Communities in a Mediated World*. New York: New York University Press, 2007.
12 Robert Pearson, 'Bachies, Bardies, Trekkies and Sherlockians', in same vol.
13 Jonathan Gray, 'The News: You Gotta Love It', in same vol.
14 George Marcus, *The Sentimental Citizen: Emotion in Democratic Politics*. Philadelphia: Pennsylvania State University Press, 2002.
15 See, for example, Henry Jenkins, *Textual Poachers*, page 152 ff. Also Shoshanna Green, Cynthia Jenkins and Henry Jenkins, ' "Normal Female Interest in Men Bonking", Selections from the Terra Nostra Underground and Strange Bedfellows', in Cheryl Harris and Alison Alexander (eds), *Theorizing Fandom: Fans, Subculture and Identity*. Creskill, JJ: Hamptons Press.
16 Nicola Khan, 'Time and Fantasy in the Narratives of Jihad: The Case of Islami Jamiat-i-Tuleba in Pakistan'. *Human Affairs*, September 2010, 241–8.
17 Tzvetan Todorov, *The Fantastic: A Structural Approach to a Literary Genre*, trans. Richard Howard. Ithaca, NY: Cornell University Press, 1975, p. 25.
18 Louis Althusser, 'Ideology and Ideological State Apparatuses: Towards an Investigation', 1970 available online from http://www.marxists.org/reference/archive/althusser/1970/ideology.htm.
19 This point has been made by numerous people, a notable example being Robert Spengler's essay 'Islam: Religion or Political Ideology', in the *Asia Times*, 10 August 2004, http://www.atimes.com/atimes/Front_Page/FH10Aa01.html. A similarly binary distinction between 'religion' and 'ideology' has been drawn by Assaf Moghadam in 'The Salafi Jihad as a Religious Ideology'. *CTC Sentinel* 1(3), (2008).

20 Talal Asad, 'Formations of the Secular: Christianity, Islam, Modernity'. Stanford: Stanford University Press, 2003.
21 This point forms the minimal definition of religion proposed by Rodney Stark and William Sims Bainbridge in *A Theory of Religion*, New Brunswick: Rutgers University Press, 1996, p. 40.
22 *A European Declaration of Independence*, p. 1323 ff.
23 Nick Abercrombie and Brian Longhurst, *Audiences: A Sociological Theory of Performance*. London: SAGE, 1998, p. 138.
24 *The Fantastic*, pp. 91 ff.
25 J. R. R. Tolkien, 'On Fairy Stories', in *Tree and Leaf*, New York: HarperCollins, 2001.
26 Bruno Bettelheim, *The Uses of Enchantment: The Meaning and Importance of Fairy Tales*. New York: Vintage, 2010.
27 Joseph Campbell, *The Hero with a Thousand Faces*. Novato: New World Library, 2008.
28 Donald Winnicott, *Playing and Reality*. London: Routledge, 1991.
29 'On Fairy Stories'.
30 Vladimir Propp, *The Morphology of the Folk Tale*. Austin: University of Texas Press, 2010.
31 Abdul Azzam, *Signs of the Merciful in the Afghan Jihad*. Ayat al-Rahman fi Jihad al-Afghan, n.d.
32 This list is taken from http://www.alteredgamer.com/pc-gaming/35992-mmo-subscriber-populations/(accessed 30/08/2012). Figures for some of the games come from 2010 or 2009. In the original list, Lineage and Lineage II are listed in separate entries with 750,000 players each. Here these totals are combined.
33 Robertson Davies, *The Merry Heart: Reflections on Reading, Writing and the World of Books*. London: Penguin, 1996, p. 7.
34 Jean Baudrillard, *Simulacra and Simulation*, trans. Sheila Farrier Fraser. Ann Arbor: University of Michigan Press, 1995.
35 Umberto Eco, *Travels in Hyperreality*, trans. William Weaver. London: Pan Books, 1987, pp. 61 ff.
36 See, Dorothy Denning, 'The Jihadi Cyberterror Threat', presentation to SUMIT, 07, www.safecomputing.umich.edu/events/. . ./Cyber**terrorism**-UofM.ppt.
37 Tim Stevens, 'Second Life and Death: Political Violence and a Virtual World', MA dissertation, available online at www.acdemic.edu/1158396/Second_Life_and_Death_Political_Violence_and_a_Virtual_World.
38 See Julian Dibbell, 'Mutilated Furries, Flying Phalluses: Put the Blame on Griefers, the Sociopaths of the Virtual World'. *Wired Magazine*, No. 16.02, 2008.
39 Indeed, the complex layers of political meaning carried by this thicket of types of online engagement reached a recent climax in the tragic events that enveloped the US Consulate in Libya, where the last words in this world of a promising young American diplomat were a message of alarm sent to his long-standing friends among the 'something awful' inspired 'Goonswarm' of spoilers roaming the space opera world of *Eve Online*. See Robert Beckhausen, 'Diplomat Killed in Libya Told Fellow Gamers: Hope I "Don't Die Tonight"', *Wired Magazine*, 2012.

40 Pierre Levy, *Becoming Virtual*.
41 Ulrich Beck, World at Risk, p. 40.
42 http://www.youtube.com/watch?v=_zOquZlY6ks, (accessed 30/08/2012).
43 Faisal Devji, *The Terrorist in Search of Humanity*.
44 http://www.youtube.com/watch?v=6JByvsSE4gs, (accessed 30/08/2012).
45 Raphael Cohen-Almagor, 'Bloody Wednesday in Dawson College – The Story of Kimveer Gill, or Why Should We Monitor Certain Websites to Prevent Murder'. *Studies in Ethics, Law and Technology* 2(3), Article 1, December 2012.

Glossary of Arabic terms

The glossary here deals with terms which are used casually or inadequately defined in the text of the book (sometimes within quoted passages). It therefore excludes terms such as 'jihad', 'jihadi', 'murji'ite', the meaning of which is specifically discussed in the book itself.

Adab
'Culture, refinement; good breeding, good manners, social graces, decorum, decency, propriety, seemliness; humanity, humaneness; the humanities; belles-lettres' (Hans Wehr's dictionary of modern written Arabic). Improvement of the state of *adab* is identified as the primary goal of certain quiescent Salafist groups, according to jihadi writers.

Adhan
The call to obligatory prayer delivered five times daily by a mu'adhdhan, typically from the minaret of a mosque.

Al-Andalus
Present-day Andalucia, the medieval Islamic kingdom located in southern Spain.

Badr (battle of)
According to orthodox accounts of Islamic history, the battle of Badr occurred in 624 AD and was a decisive confrontation in the prophet Muhammad's war against his rivals from the Meccan tribe of Quraysh.

Caliph
Properly *Khalifa* (plural *Khulafa*) meaning, literally, 'successor', as in successor to the authority of the prophet Muhammad, the title given to rulers claiming to be the rightful political leader of all Muslims. The last person claiming to be a *Khalifa*, the deposed Ottoman Sultan Mehmed VI was deposed in 1922, with the last caliphate (to date) officially ending in 1924.

Da'wa
Da'wa (literally, 'calling') refers at least in the present day to attempts to convert non-Muslims to Islam or to encourage existing Muslims to return to observant practices. Da'wa to jihad or jihadi da'wa is specifically directed at calling Muslims to take up (militant) jihad.

Dhikr, literally, 'remembrance' is an Islamic spiritual practice which aims at spiritual development through the repetitive and formulaic invocation of the name of God. See, for example, *Dhikr*, in Cyril Glassé and Huston Smith, *The New Encyclopedia of Islam*. Singapore: Tien Wah Press, 2002, p. 116.

Du'a
Sometimes translated as 'supplication', the word *du'a* (from the same root as *da'wa*) refers to personal or collective 'calling' on God equivalent to what Western Christians would normally call 'prayer'. This is, however, a quite distinct activity from *sala*, the ritual prostration to God which Muslims are required to perform five times a day.

Fiqh
Literally 'understanding', *fiqh* is Islamic jurisprudence: the study of how the Islamic *shari'a* should be applied to everyday situations.

Hadith (plural Ahadith)
A saying attributed, by a chain of oral testimony of accepted reliability, to the prophet or one of his companions. *Ahadith* are the second source after the Qur'an for determining which practices are legitimate in Islam.

Hajj
The annual pilgrimage to Mecca established as one of the five 'pillars' of Islam.

'Ibada
'Ibada (literally 'obedience') means an act of worship in Islam, both in a ritual sense and also through any sincere attempt to follow a commandment of God.

'Id (often spelt Eid)
A religious festival (not necessarily Islamic). In Islam there are two main festivals, *'Id al-Adha*, held at the end of the month of *Hajj*, and *'Id al-Fitr* at the end of Ramadan.

Ikhwani
Pertaining to the school of thought associated with the *Ikhwan al-Muslimin* of 'Muslim Brothers', the most important mainstream Islamic political movement, presently the main ruling party in Egypt.

Islamiyyat
Collective noun referring to 'Islamic' publications or media items.

Istishhadi
Grammatically related to the word *shahid*, via the verb *istashhada* (to become a martyr), this is a modern term used by some groups to refer specifically to those who *deliberately* become martyrs, that is typically, suicide bombers.

'Izz al-Din al-Qassam Brigades
The armed wing of Hamas, founded in 1992. The original 'Izz al-Din al-Qassam, after whom the group is named led armed uprisings against the French in Syria and the British in Palestine during the 1920s and 1930s.

GLOSSARY OF ARABIC TERMS

Janna
Paradise. Like the word 'paradise' itself, the word 'janna' originally means 'garden'.

Jihad bi-l-Lisan
Literally, jihad waged with the tongue.

Jihad bi-l-Mal
Jihad waged with one's money or possessions.

Ka'ba
A cube-shaped shrine, located in Mecca, which Muslims circumambulate seven times as part of *Hajj* (or the lesser pilgrimage, *'Umra*). Muslims believe that the Ka'ba was built by the prophet Abraham.

Kafir (plural kuffar)
Typically rendered into English as 'unbeliever' or 'disbeliever', the question of who, exactly, is a *kafir* and what constitutes *kufr* (unbelief) is a long-running and contentious one in Islam. For jihadis most, if not all Christians and Jews would be considered to be *kuffar*, as well as political leaders ruling by elements of secular law.

Manhaj
Derived from the word *nahaja*, literally 'to approach', the word manhaj refers to a method, a way of life or a path. In contemporary Anglophone Islam, it is often translated as a 'methodology'. The concept seems to bridge the gap between belief (in Islam, *'aqida*) and actual behaviour.

Mujahid
'Active participle' of *jihad*, meaning literally, 'one who does jihad'.

Munshid
A singer of *anashid*.

Nafs
The 'self' or the 'soul'. A major theme of writing on jihad in Islam has always been the idea of a spiritual struggle against the whims and temptations of the *nafs* which the mujahid wages simultaneously with his material struggle against the enemies of Islam.

(Neo) Zarqawist/Al-Maqdisist
Supporter of the late leader of Al-Qa'ida in Mesopotamia with regard to his dispute with his former spiritual mentor, Abu Muhammad al-Maqdisi over his allegedly excessive and excessively sectarian killing in Iraq. Zarqawists have tended to take the view that al-Zarqawi, as a mujahid present in the field, was in a better position to judge what actions were appropriate (and potentially more likely to receive divine guidance on the matter) than was a scholar who was not present in the hostilities.

Qasida (plural Qasa'id)
Traditionally a particular form of classical Arabic poem. In contemporary online jihadi contexts it would seem that the term tends to be used to refer to jihadi poems in general.

Ramadan
The sacred month of fasting in the Islamic calendar.

Salafism
A term for several forms of contemporary Islamic thought and practice, having in common a rejection of *taqlid* – the automatic following of a particular Islamic tradition, especially the established schools of Islamic law, in favour of a return to the core Islamic sources. Early twentieth-century 'salafists' were mainly concerned with adapting Islamic societies to the challenges of modernity and Western domination. More recently, the term has become associated with fundamentalist forms of Islam premised on a literalistic approach to texts and a tendency to reject or severely limit the scope of analogical reasoning in interpreting them.

Shahid
A *shahid* is an Islamic martyr. Like the Greek word 'martyr' of which *shahid* may well be a gloss, the literal meaning of the word is 'witness', implying that, through sacrifice, the shahid 'bears witness' to the truth of the religion. The concept of martyrdom has long been associated in Islam with that of jihad and remains so to this day.

Shahada
Literally 'bearing witness', the *shahada* is the Muslim declaration of faith: 'there is no God but God, and Muhammad is the prophet of God'. In a distinct sense from this, the word shahada is also an abstract noun meaning 'martyrdom', analogous to the word *shahid*.

Shari'a
Islamic sacred law. For jihadi-salafis, failure by Muslim rulers to implement this law exclusively is tantamount to apostasy.

Shalwar Qamis
A flowing garment traditional to Pakistan and Afghanistan (*qamis*, in Arabic, means shirt). The garment has acquired iconic status for jihadis as part of the garb of the mujahidin.

Shaykh
In this book, the word *shaykh* specifically designates an authority on Islam.

Sufi
A follower of an Islamic mystical tradition. Jihadi-salafis, however, tend to refer to use the word 'Sufi' pejoratively (and inappropriately, not least because Sufis have historically been neither particularly quietist nor peaceful) to describe certain quietist Salafist groups.

Takfir
The act of declaring that a person is a *kafir*. Jihadis are often pejoratively labelled 'takfiris'.

Taqlid

Literally 'imitation', *taqlid* refers to the formal practice of following a particular Islamic authority – typically an established law school – rather than one's own specific interpretation of Islamic scripture.

Tawhid

Literally 'unification', the Islamic doctrine of the absolute oneness of God. The doctrine of tawhid is sometimes divided into two or more categories, including tawhid of names and attributes (recognition of the uniqueness of God's attributes), tawhid of Lordship (recognizing that only God has authority and power over the universe) and tawhid of worship (recognizing that only God is worthy of being worshipped and obeyed by man). Tawhid is a core principle – *the* core principle, for all Muslims. However, salafists tend to place a particular emphasis in the present day on its rigid interpretation.

Ummah

Literally 'nation', typically used to refer to the 'nation' of Muslims.

Wahhabism

A term – usually pejorative – associated with those who follow the teachings of the eighteenth-century Islamic reformer Muhammad ibn 'Abd al-Wahhab. Wahhabis have typically called themselves 'Muwahhidun' (Islamic monotheists). Wahhabi is often, though not strictly accurately, used as a synonym for 'Salafi'.

Yazidi

An esoteric religion, of obscure origin, practised by Kurdish people in parts of northern Iraq. Yazidis are reported to believe in a doctrine reminiscent of forms of Gnosticism whereby the creator of the world is removed from its day to day administration, which is instead handled by the 'Peacock Angel', formerly a rebel against God who may or may not be identifiable with Satan in the Abrahamic tradition. Whether this is so or not, Yazidis have been regarded as Satan worshippers by their neighbours and sporadically persecuted as such.

Bibliography

Aakhus, Mark, 'The Design of Forums for Online Public Communication and the Consequences for Argumentation'. *Kentucky Journal of Communication* 21(2), (Fall 2002), online: URL http://kycommunication.com/2002fall.htm (accessed 31/07/2013).

Abercrombie, Nick and Brian Longhurst, *Audiences: A Sociological Theory of Performance*. London: SAGE, 1998.

Abrahms, Max, 'What Terrorists Really Want: Terrorist Motives and Counterterrorism Strategy'. *International Security* 32(4), (2008), 78–105.

Abu Lughod, Lila, 'The Romance of Resistance: Tracing Transformations of Power Through Bedouin Women'. *American Ethnologist* 17(1), (1990), 41–55.

Ackerman, Spencer and Noah Schachtman, *Wired* 2012 ' "Institutional failures" led military to teach war on Islam', http://www.wired.com/dangerroom/2012/06/failure-oversight-war-islam/.

Aidi, Hishaam, 'Don't Panic: Islam and Europe's "Hip Hop Wars", http://www.aljazeera.com/indepth/opinion/2012/06/20126310151835171.html.

Al Arabiya, 'Prison for "Poet of Al-Qaeda" for a year and half after the publication of a poem impinging on the Jordanian monarch', 2007, http://www.alarabiya.net/articles/2007/10/01/39811.html.

Al-Faruqi, L. I., 'Music, Musicians and Muslim Law'. *Asian Music* 17(1), (1985), 3–36

Al Quds, 'Al Asad: Prepared for War, and Israel Does not Understand other than the Language of Strength and the American Project Has Failed and the Arabs Have Abandoned Iraq', available online from http://www.alquds.com/node/245535 (accessed 10/8/2010).

Althusser, Louis, 'Ideology and Ideological State Apparatuses: Towards an Investigation', 1970 available online from http://www.marxists.org/reference/archive/althusser/1970/ideology.htm.

Anderson, Jon and Dale Eickelman (eds), *New Media in the Muslim World: The Emerging Public Sphere*, 2nd Ed. Bloomington: Indiana University Press, 2003.

Ando, Ben, 'The enigma that is the "lyrical terrorist" ', BBC News, 2007.

Asad, Talal, 'Formations of the Secular: Christianity, Islam, Modernity'. Stanford: Stanford University Press, 2003.

Asal, Victor Paul Harwood, 'Search Engines: Terrorism's Killer App'. *Studies in Conflict and Terrorism* 31(1), (2008), 641–54.

Ashour, Omar, 'Online Deradicalisation? Countering Violent Extremist Narratives: Message, Messenger and Media Strategy'. *Perspectives on Terrorism* 4(6), (2010), online: URL http://www.terrorismanalysts.com/pt/index.php/pot/article/view/128/html (accessed 31/07/2013).

Atton, Chris, *An Alternative Internet*. Edinburgh: Edinburgh University Press, 2004.

—, 'A Reassessment of the Alternative Press'. *Media, Culture and Society* 21(1), (1999).

Awan, Akil and Mina al-Lami, 'Al Qa'ida's Virtual Crisis'. *The RUSI Journal* 154(1), (2009), 56–64.

Badawi, Elsaid. Michael Carter and Adrian Gully, *Modern Written Arabic: A Comprehensive Grammar*. London: Routledge, 2004.

Bacon Smith, Camille, *Enterprising Women: Television Fandom and the Creation of Popular Myth*. Philadelphia: University of Pennsylvania Press.

Baines, Paul, Nicholas J. O'Shaghnessy, Kevin Moloney, Barry Richards, Sarah Butler and Mark Gill, 'Muslim Voices: The British Muslim Response to Islamic Video Polemic – an Exploratory Study', Cranfield University School of Management, Research Paper 3/06, 2006. (online, URL Baines, Paul, Nicholas J. O'Shaghnessy, Kevin Moloney, Barry Richards, Sarah Butler and Mark Gill, 'Muslim Voices: The British Muslim Response to Islamic Video Polemic – an Exploratory Study', Cranfield University School of Management, Research Paper 3/06, 2006., accessed 31/07/2013).

Bakhtin, Mikhail, *The Dialogic Imagination: Four Essays*, ed. Michael Holquist; trans. Caryl Emerson and Michael Holquist. Austin: University of Texas Press, 1981.

Barthes, Roland, *The Pleasure of the Text*, trans. Richard Miller. New York: Hill and Wang 1975.

Barzilai-Nahon, Karine and Gad Barzilai, 'Cultured Technology: Internet and Religious Fundamentalism'. *The Information Society* 21(1), (2004), 25–40.

Baudrillard, Jean, *Simulacra and Simulation*, trans. Sheila Farrier Fraser. Ann Arbor: University of Michigan Press, 1995.

BBC News, '"Lyrical terrorist" found guilty', 8/11/2007, http://www.news.bbc.co.uk/1/hi/7084801.stm.

Beck, Ulrich, 'What is Globalization?'. Cambridge: Polity, 2000.

—, *World at Risk*. Cambridge: Polity, 2009.

Bettelheim, Bruno, *The Uses of Enchantment: The Meaning and Importance of Fairy Tales*. New York: Vintage, 2010.

Bevanger, Lars, 'Breivik Trial: Psychiatric reports scrutinized', 14/06/2012, http://www.bbc.co.uk/news/world-europe-18440743.

Bin Abdul Ghani, Z., 'Entertainment in the Muslim Media: Unsettled Problem?'. *Jurnal Hadhari Bil* 2(2009), 53–63.

Binte Azman, Nur Aziemah, 'Al Qaeda's Internet Strategy a Failure? Online Jihadists Disprove'. *Counter Terrorist Trends and Analysis*, International Centre for Political Violence and Terrorism Research, S. Rajaratnam School of International Studies, Nanyang Technological University 4(2), (2012), 1–4.

Bonner, Michael, *Jihad in Islamic History: Doctrines and Practice*. Princeton, NJ: Princeton University Press, 2008.

Boucek, Christopher, 'The Sakinah Campaign and Internet Counter-Radicalisation in Saudi Arabia'. *CTC Sentinel* 1(9), (2008).

Bourdieu, Pierre, *Outline of a Theory of Practice*. Cambridge: Cambridge University Press, 1977.

—, *Distinction: A Social Critique of the Judgement of Taste*, trans. Richard Nice. London: Routledge, 1984.

—, *The Field of Cultural Production*. New York: Columbia University Press, 1993.
Bowen, Donna Lee and Evelyn A. Early, *Everyday Life in the Muslim Middle East*. Bloomington: Indiana University Press, 2002.
Brachman, Jarret, *Global Jihadism: Theory and Practice*. London: Routledge, 2009.
Brachman, Jarret and Alix Levine, 'The World of Holy Warcraft: How Al-Qaeda is Using Online Game Theory to Recruit the Masses'. *Foreign Policy*, 13 April 2011, http://www.foreignpolicy.com/articles/2011/04/13/the_world_of_holy_warcraft (accessed 31/07/2013).
Brachman, Jarret and William McCants, 'Stealing Al Qaeda's Playbook'. *Studies in Conflict and Terrorism* 29(4), (2006), 309–21.
Braoche, Anne, 'Senators Voice Alarm over terrorist Net Presence', CNet news, 2007, http://www.news.cnet.com/Senators-voice-alarm-over-terrorist-Net-presence/2100-1028_3-6181269.html.
Bunt, Gary, *iMuslims: Rewiring the House of Islam*. London: Hurst, 2009.
—, *Virtually Islamic: Computer Mediated Communication and Cyber-Islamic Environments*. Cardiff: University of Wales Press, 2000.
Burnham, Gilbert, Riyadh Lafta, Shannon Doocy and Les Roberts, 'Mortality after the 2003 invasion of Iraq: a cross sectional cluster sample survey'. *The Lancet* 368(9545), (2006), 1421–8.
Campbell, Joseph, *The Hero with a Thousand Faces*. Novato: New World Library, 2008.
Cesari, Jocelyn, *Where Islam and Democracy Meet, Muslims in Europe and the United States*. New York: Palgrave Macmillan, 2004, pp. 115 ff.
Chen, Hsinchun, Arab Salem, Edna Reid, 'Sentiment and affect analysis of Dark Web forums: Measuring radicalization on the internet'. *ISI* (2008), 104–9.
Chesser, Susan G., 'Afghanistan casualties: military forces and civilians', Congressional research service, 12 July 2012.
Cole, Juan, 'The World as Text: Cosmologies of Shaykh Ahmad al-Ahsa'i'. *Studia Islamica* 80(1994), 1–24.
Cook, David, *Understanding Jihad*. Berkeley: University of California Press, 2005.
Cook, Michael, *Commanding Right and Forbidding Wrong in Islamic Thought*. Cambridge: Cambridge University Press, 2004.
Conway, Maura, 'Hackers as Terrorists: Why it Doesn't Compute'. *Computer Fraud and Security* 12(2003), 10–13.
—, 'Terrorist "Use" of the Internet and Fighting Back'. *Information and Security: An International Journal* 19(2006), 9–30.
—, 'From Zarqawi to Al-Awlaki: The Emergence of the Internet as a New Form of Violent Radical Milieu', 2012, http://www.isodarco.it/courses/andalo12/doc/Zarqawi%20to%20Awlaki_V2.pdf.
Corera, Gordon, 'Al-Qaeda's 007: The Extraordinary Story of the Solitary Computer Geek in a Shepherds Bush Bedsit Who Became the World's Most Wanted Cyber Jihadist', *Times Online*, 1/16/2008.
Davies, Robertson, *The Merry Heart: Reflections on Reading, Writing and the World of Books*. London: Penguin, 1996.
De Certeau, Michel, *The Practice of Everyday Life* (originally: *L'Invention du Quotidien*), trans. Steve Rendell. Berkeley: University of California Press, 1984.
Deol, Jeevan and Zaheer Kazmi (eds), *Contextualising Jihadi Ideologies*. London: Hurst, Forthcoming.

De Saussure, Ferdinand *Course in General Linguistics*, trans. Wade Buskin, ed. Charles Bally and Albert Sechehaye. London: McGraw-Hill, 1966.

Devji, Faisal, *Landscapes of Jihad: Militancy, Morality, Modernity*. Ithaca: Cornell University Press, 2005.

—, *The Terrorist in Search of Humanity*. New York: Cornell University Press, 2008.

Doherty, Benjamin, 'Sodomy for Jihad? Venerable LGBT Magazine the Advocate Spreads Vile Islamophobic Hoax', *The Electronic Intifada*, 07/13/2012.

Doran, Michael, 'The Pragmatic Fanaticism of Al Qaeda: An Anatomy of Extremism in Middle Eastern Politics'. *Political Science Quarterly* 117(2), (2002), 177–90.

Downing, John, *Radical Media: Rebellious Communication and Social Movements*. Thousand Oaks: Sage, 2008.

Dubowitz, M., 'Countering the Threat from Terrorist Media', *in Focus Quarterly*, Summer 2010, http//www.jewishpolicycenter.org/1746/terrorist-media-threat.

Durkheim, Emile, *Elementary Forms of the Religious Life*, trans. Joseph Ward Swain. London: Allen and Unwin, 1976.

Eco, Umberto, *Travels in Hyperreality*, trans. William Weaver. London: Pan Books, 1987.

Elias, Elias A., *Elias' Modern Dictionary, Arabic-English*. Cairo: Modern Press, 1929.

Erez, Edna Gabriel Weimann and Aaron Weisburd, *Jihad, Crime and the Internet: Content Analysis of Jihadist Forum Discussions*, Report Submitted to the National Institute of Justice.

Esposito, John and Dalia Mogahed, *Who Speaks for Islam: What a Billion Muslims Really Think*. New York: Gallup Press, 2007.

Fanon, Frantz, *The Wretched of the Earth*, trans. Constance Farrington, preface Jean Paul Sartre. Harmondsworth: Penguin, 1967.

Gibbs, Patricia, 'Alternative Things Considered: A Political Economic Analysis of Labour Processes and Relations at a Honolulu Newspaper'. *Media, Culture and Society* 25(5), (2003), 587–605.

Gibson, James J., *The Ecological Approach to Visual Perception*. London: Houghton Mifflin, 1979.

Giddens, Anthony, *The Consequences of Modernity*. Stanford: Stanford University Press, 1990.

—, *Modernity and Self-Identity: Self and Society in the Late Modern Age*. Cambridge: Polity, 1991.

Gies, Lieve, 'How Material are Cyberbodies: Broadband Internet and Embodied Subjectivity'. *Crime, Media, Culture* 4(3), (2008), 311–30.

Gillespie, Marie and Ben O'Loughlin, 'News Media, Threats and Insecurities: An Ethnographic Approach'. *Cambridge Review of International Affairs* 22(4), (2009), 667–85.

Goodwin, Matthew, Vidhya Ramalingam and Rachel Briggs, 'The New Radical Right: Violent and Non-Violent Movements in Europe'. London: Institute for Strategic Dialogue Briefing Paper, 2012.

Gray, Jonathan, Cornel Sandvoss and C. Lee Harrington (eds), *Fandom: Identities and Communities in a Mediated World*. New York: New York University Press, 2007.

Grenfall, Michael (ed.), *Pierre Bourdieu: Key Concepts*. Stocksfield, Acumen, 2008.

Guedes Bailey, Olga Bart Cammaerts and Nico Carpentier, *Understanding Alternative Media*. Maidenhead: Open University Press, 2008.

Habermas, Jürgen, *The Structural Transformation of the Public Sphere: An Enquiry into A Category of Bourgeois Society*, trans. Thomas Burger with Frederick Lawrence. Cambridge: MIT Press, 1989.

Hafez, Kai, *Radicalism and Political Reform in the Islamic and Western Worlds*. Cambridge: Cambridge University Press, 2010.

Halliday, Fred, 'Anti-Muslimism and Contemporary Politics: One Ideology, or Many'. London: IB Tauris, 1996, pp. 160, 194.

Hamilton, Tom, 'Scot freed after his terror sentence was quashed insists "I'm not a terrorist, I'm more of a numpty', *Daily Record*, 10/02/2010, http://www.dailyrecord.co.uk/news/scottish-news/scot-freed-after-his-terror-sentence-1050167.

Haniff Hassan, Muhammad and Redzuan Salleh, 'Jihadism studies in counter-ideology: time for initiation in universities', S. Rajaratnam School of International Studies, RSIS Commentaries series, 2010.

Harris, Cheryl and Alison Alexander (eds), *Theorizing Fandom: Fans, Subculture and Identity*. Creskill, JJ: Hamptons Press.

Heath, Joseph and Andrew Potter, *The Rebel Sell: Why The Culture Can't Be Jammed*. New York: Harper Collins, 2010.

Hebdige, Dick, *Subculture: The Meaning of Style*. London: Methuen, 1979. See also G. Mungham and G. Pearson, (eds), *Working Class Youth Culture*. London: Routledge, 1976.

Hegghammer, Thomas, *Jihad in Saudi Arabia: Violence and Pan-Islamism since 1979*. Cambridge: Cambridge University Press, 2010.

Hegghammer, Thomas and Brynjar Lia, 'Jihadi Strategic Studies: The Alleged Al Qaida policy study preceding the Madrid bombings'. *Studies in Conflict and Terrorism* 27(5), (2005).

Heidegger, Martin, 'The Question Concerning Technology', 1954, available online from http://www.wright.edu/cola/Dept/PHL/Class/P/Internet/PITexts/QCT.html.

Hills, Matt, *The Pleasures of Horror*. New York: Continuum, 2005.

HM Coroner, 'Coroner's Inquests into the London Bombings of 7th July, 2005', http://www.7julyinquests.independent.gov.uk/.

Holbrook, Donald, Gilbert Ramsay and Max Taylor, In Press. 'Terroristic Content: Towards a Grading Scale.' *Terrorism and Political Violence*. 202–23.

Hutchby, Ian, 'Technologies, Texts and Affordances'. *Sociology* 35(1), (2001).

Ibrahim, Yahya, 'Tips for our Brothers in the United States of America'. *Inspire* 2(2010).

Iraq Family Health Survey Study Group, 'Violence Related Mortality in Iraq from 2002–2006'. *New England Journal of Medicine* 48(2008), 484–93.

Jackson, Anthony and Samuel Justin Sinclair (eds), *Contemporary Debates on Terrorism*. London: Routledge, 2012.

Jacobson, Michael, 'Terrorist Financing and the Internet'. *Studies in Conflict and Terrorism* 33(4), (2010), 353–63.

Jenkins, Brian, *Will Terrorists Go Nuclear?* New York: Prometheus Books, 2008.
Jenkins, Henry, 'Strangers No More, We Sing: Filking and the Social Construction of the Science Fiction Fan Community,' in Lisa Lewis (ed.), *The Adoring audience fan culture and popular media.* London: Routledge, 1992, pp. 208–32.
Jenkins, Henry, *Textual Poachers: Television Fans and Popular Culture.* London: Routledge, 1992.
—, *Fans Bloggers and Gamers: Exploring Participatory Culture.* London: New York University Press, 2006.
—, *Convergence Culture: Where Old and New Media Collide.* New York: New York University Press, 2006.
Karim, K. H., Book Review – *Islam in the Digital Age. The American Journal of Islamic Social Sciences* 21(4), (2004).
Kenney, Michael, 'Beyond the Internet: Metis, Techne, and the Limitations of Online Artifacts for Islamist. Terrorists'. *Terrorism & Political Violence* 22(2), (2010) 177–97.
Kepel, Gilles, *Jihad: The Trail of Radical Islam,* Cambridge: Harvard University Press, 2002.
Kessells, E. J. M. (ed.). *Countering Violent Extremist Narratives.* The Hague: National Counterterrorism Coordinator, 2010.
Khan, Nicola, 'Time and Fantasy in the Narratives of Jihad: The Case of Islami Jamiat-i-Tuleba in Pakistan'. *Human Affairs* 20(3), (September 2010), 241–8.
Khatib, Lina, 'Public Diplomacy 2.0: A Case Study of the Digital Outreach Team', CDDRL Working Paper Number 120, January 2011, http://iis-db.stanford.edu/pubs/23084/No.120-_Public_Diplomacy_2.0.pdf.
Knowles, Chase, 'Towards a New Web Genre: Islamist Neo-Realism'. *Journal of War and Culture Studies* 1(3), (2008), 357–80.
Kohlmann, Evan, 'The Real Online Terrorist Threat', September/October, 2006.
Kozinets, Robert, *Netnography: Doing Ethnographic Research Online.* Thousand Oaks: Sage, 2010.
Kramer, Martin, 'Coming to terms: fundamentalists or Islamists?'. *Middle East Quarterly* 10(2), (2003), 65–77.
Kreidy, Marwan, 'Islamic Popular Culture', *Annenberg School of Communication, Departmental Papers,* University of Pennsylvania, 2006.
Kundnani, Arun, 'Spooked: How Not to Prevent Violent Extremism'. London: Institute of Race Relations, 2009.
—, 'Blind Spot? Security Narratives and Far Right Violence in Europe', ICCT Research Paper, June 2012, http://www.icct.nl/download/file/ICCT-Kundnani-Blind-Spot-June-2012.pdf.
Lacroix, Stéphane, *Awakening Islam: The Politics of Religious Dissent in Contemporary Saudi Arabia,* trans. George Holoch. Cambridge: Harvard University Press, 2011.
Lahoud, Nelly, *The Jihadis' Path to Self Destruction.* New York: Columbia University Press, 2010.
Lambert, Robert and Jonathan Githens Mazer, *Islamophobia and Anti-Muslim Hate Crime: Case Studies 2010: An Introduction to a Ten-Year Europe-Wide Research Project,* University of Exeter and European Muslim Research Centre, 2010, p. 86.
Lessig, Lawrence, *Code 2.0.* New York: Basic Books, 2007.
Levy, Pierre, *Becoming Virtual,* trans. R. Bononno. New York: Plenum, 1998.

—, *Collective Intelligence: Mankind's Evolving World in Cyberspace*. New York and London: Plenum Press, 1999.

Lewis, Lisa (ed.), *The Adoring Audience: Fandom and Popular Media*. London: Routledge, 1992.

Lia, Brynjar, *Architect of Global Jihad: The Life of Al Qaeda Strategist Abu Mus'ab al-Suri*. London: Hurst, 2007.

Lopez, Fernando Bravo, 'Towards a Definition of Islamophobia: Approximations of the Early 20th Century'. *Ethnic and Racial Studies* 1(4), (2011), 556–73.

Lynch, Marc, 'Islam Divided between Salafi-Jihad and the Ikhwan'. *Studies in Conflict and Terrorism* 33(6), (2010), 467–87.

Lynch, Orla and Chris Ryder, 'Deadliness, Organisational Change and Suicide Attacks: Understanding the Assumptions Inherent in the Term "New Terrorism"'. *Critical Studies on Terrorism* 5(2), (2012), 257–75.

Macintyre, Alasdair, *After Virtue: A Study in Moral Theory*. Notre Dame: University of Notre Dame Press, 1984.

MacWilliams, Marc, 'Techno-Ritualization: The Gohonzon Controversy on the Internet', Heidelberg Journal of Religions on the Internet, Vol. 2, Special Issue on Rituals on the Internet, ed. Kerstin Radde-Antweiler, 2006' http://archiv.ub.uni-heidelberg.de/ojs/index.php/religions/article/view/371 (accessed 31/7/2013).

Maffesoli, Michel, *The Time of the Tribes: The Decline of Individualism in Mass Society*. London: Sage, 1996. Originally published 1988.

Mahmood, Saba, *Politics of Piety: The Islamic Revival and the Feminist Subject*. Princeton, NJ: Princeton University Press, 2005.

Manovich, Lev, *The Language of New Media*. Cambridge, MA: MIT Press, 2001.

Marcus, George, *The Sentimental Citizen: Emotion in Democratic Politics*. Philadelphia: Pennsylvania State University Press, 2002.

Marranci, Gabriele, 'Multiculturalism, Islam and the clash of civilisations theory: rethinking Islamophobia'. *Culture and Religion: An Interdisciplinary Journal* 5(1), (2004), 105–17.

—, *Jihad Beyond Islam*. New York: Berg, 2006.

Marx, T., 'Islam and Media Discourses in India: Constructing *Islamophobia*'. *International Journal of South Asian Studies* 1(2), (2008), 284–95.

Meijer, Roel (ed.), *Global Salafism: Islam's New Religious Movement*. London: Hurst, 2010.

Meleagrou Hitchens, Alexander and Jacob Amis, 'The Making of the Christmas Day Bomber'. *Current Trends in Islamist Ideology* 10(2010), 116–42.

MHA Consulting, 'The Threat of Money Laundering and Online Terrorist Financing through the Online Gambling Industry: A Report Prepared for the Remote Gambling Association by MHA Consulting', June 2009, http://www.rga.eu.com/data/files/final__mha_report_june_2009.pdf.

Miah, Shamim and Virinder Kalra, 'Muslim Hip Hop – the Politicisation of Kool Islam'. *South Asian Cultural Studies* 2(1), (2010), 12–25.

Moghadam, Assaf, 'Salafi-Jihad as a Religious Ideology'. *CTC Sentinel* 1(3), (2008), 14–16.

Morozov, Evgeny, *The Net Delusion: How Not to Liberate the World*. London: Allen Lane, 2010.

Mowlana, Hamid, 'Foundation of Communication in Islamic Societies', in J. P Mitchell and S. Marriage (eds), *Mediating Religion: Conversations in Media, Religion and Culture*. New York: Continuum, 2003.

Muggleton, Malcolm, *Inside Subculture: The Postmodern Meaning of Style*. Oxford: Berg, 2000.

Musawi, Muhammed Ali, *Cheering for Osama: How Jihadists Use Internet Forums*. London: Quilliam Foundation, 2010.

Nasar, Mustafa Sittmariyam (Abu Mus'ab al-Suri), *The Global Islamic Resistance Call* (da'wat al-muqawamat al-islamiyya al-'alamiyya).

National Commission on Terrorist Attacks Upon the United States, *The 9/11 Commission Report: Final Report of the National Commission on Terrorist Attacks on the United States*, Washington: 2004.

Nordstrom, Carolyn and JoAnn Martin (eds), *The Paths to Domination, Resistance and Terror*. Berkeley: University of California Press, 1992.

Norman, Donald, *The Design of Everyday Things*. London: MIT Press, 1998.

O'Connor, T. J. and David Shinberg, 'The Jester Dynamic: A Lesson in Asymmetric Unmanaged Cyber Warfare'. SANS Institute Certificate Dissertation, 2011.

Ostovar, Afshon, Jarret Brachman and Lianne Boudali, *The Islamic Imagery Project: Visual Motifs in Jihadi Internet Propaganda*, United States Military Academy Combating Terrorism Centre, Department of Social Sciences, 2006.

Pantucci, Rafaello, 'Operation Praline: The Realisation of Al-Suri's *Nizam, La Tanzim?*' *Perspectives on Terrorism* 2(12), (2008), http://www.terrorismanalysts.com/pt/index.php/pot/article/view/59/html (31/7/2013).

Parker Voors, Matthew, "Encryption Regulation in the Wake of September 11, 2001: Must we Protect National Security at the Expense of the Economy?" *Federal Communications Law Journal* 55(2), (2003), http://www.repository.law.indiana.edu/fclj/vol55/iss2/7/ (31/7/2013).

Phelps, Sandra Marie, 'The Limits of Admittance and Diversity in Iraqi Kurdistan: Femininity and the Body of Du'a Khalil'. *Gender and Political Religions* 11(3-4), (2010)

Philips, Melanie, *Londonistan: How Britain is Creating a Terror State Within*. New York: Encounter, 2006.

Pinker, Stephen, *The Better Angels of Our Nature: The Decline of Violence and its Causes*. London: Penguin, 2011, 317–9, http://www.globalsecurity.org/military/world/war/lebanon.htm (last accessed 28/08/2012).

Pitcher, L. M., 'The Divine Impatience: Ritual, Narrative and Symbolization in the Practice of Martyrdom in Palestine'. *Medical Anthropology Quarterly* 12(1), (1998).

Pressman, Elaine, 'Risk Assessment Decisions for Violent Political Extremism, 2009–02', http://www.publicsafety.gc.ca/res/cor/rep/_fl/2009–02-rdv-eng.pdf.

Propp, Vladimir, *The Morphology of the Folk Tale*. Austin: University of Texas Press, 2010.

Qin, Jialun, Zhou, Yilu, Lai, Guanpi, Reid, Edna, Sageman, Marc, Chen, Hsinchun, 'The Dark Web Portal Project: Collecting and Analyzing the Presence of Terrorist Groups on the Web'. *Intelligence and Security Informatics*, Lecture Notes in Computer Science 3495(2005), 359–78.

QMI Agency, 'Sodomy: The New Jihadi Training Method?', *London Free Press*, 12/7/2012, http://www.lfpress.com/news/world/2012/07/12/19980551.html.

Radway, Janice, *Reading the Romance: Women, Patriarchy and Popular Literature*. Chapel Hill: University of North Carolina Press, 1991.
Ramsay, Gilbert, 'Online Arguments Against Al-Qaeda: An Exploratory Analysis'. *Perspectives on Terrorism* 6(1), (2012), http://www.terrorismanalysts.com/pt/index.php/pot/article/view/ramsay-online-arguments.
Rauch, Jennifer, 'Activists as Interpretive Communities: Rituals of Consumption and Interaction in an Alternative Media Audience'. *Media, Culture and Society* 29(6), (2007), 994–1013.
Reinares, Fernando, 'The Madrid Bombings and Global Jihadism'. *Survival* 52(2), April–May 2010, 83–104.
Rheingold, Howard, *The Virtual Community: Homesteading on the Electronic Frontier*. Cambridge, MA: MIT Press, 2000.
Richards, Anthony, 'The Problem with "Radicalization, the Remit of "Prevent" and the Need to Refocus on Terrorism in the UK'. *International Affairs* 87(1), 143–252.
Richardson, John, (ed.), *Handbook of Theory and Research for the Sociology of Education*. Westport: Greenwood, 1986.
Rolston, Bill, 'Politics, Painting and Popular Culture: The Political Murals of Northern Ireland'. *Media, Culture and Society* 9(1), (1987), 5–28
Rosen, Nir, *Aftermath: Following the Bloodshed of America's Wars in the Muslim World*. New York: Perseus, 2010.
Roy, Olivier, *The Failure of Political Islam*. London: I. B Tauris, 1994.
—, *Globalised Islam: The Search for a New Ummah*. New York: Columbia University Press, 2004.
Rozen, Paul, Maureen Markwith and Clark McCauley, 'Sensitivity to indirect contacts with other persons: AIDS aversion as a composite of aversion to strangers, infection, moral taint and misfortune'. *Journal of Abnormal Psychology* 103(3), (1994), 495–505.
Ryan, Johnny, 'The Internet, The Perpetual Beta and the State: The Long View of the New Medium'. *Studies in Conflict and Terrorism* 33(8), (2010), 673–81.
Sageman, Marc, *Understanding Terrorist Networks*. Philadelphia: University of Pennsylvania Press, 2004.
Sanford, Scott, 'Faultlines in cyberspace', in Assaf Moghadam and Brian Fishman (eds), *Fault Lines in Global Jihad: Organizational, Strategic and Ideological Fissures*. London: Routledge, 2010.
Schmitt, Eric and Tom Shanker, 'U.S Adapts Cold War Idea to Fight Terrorists', *New York Times*, 18/3/2008.
Shiloah, Amnon, *Islamic Music*. Detroit: Wayne State University Press, 1995.
Siapera, Eugenia, 'Radical Democratic Politics and Online Islam', in Lincoln Dahlberg and Eugenia Siapera (eds), *Radical Democracy and the Internet*. Basingstoke: Macmillain Palgrave, 2007.
Spengler, Robert, 'Islam: Religion or Political Ideology', in the *Asia Times*, 10 August 2004, http://www.atimes.com/atimes/Front_Page/FH10Aa01.html.
Stark, Rodney and William Sims Bainbridge, *A Theory of Religion*. New Brunswick: Rutgers University Press, 1996, p. 40.
Stenersen, Anne, 'The Internet: A Virtual Training Camp?'. *Terrorism and Political Violence* 20(2), (2008), 215–33.

Stephens, Alan and Nicola Baker, *Making Sense of War: Strategy for the 21st Century*. Cambridge: Cambridge University Press, 2006.

Stevens, Tim, '*Second Life* and Death: Political Violence in a Virtual World', http://www.kcl.academia.edu/TimStevens/Papers/1221463/Second_Life_and_Death_Political_Violence_and_a_Virtual_World.

Stevens, Tim and Peter Neumann, 'Countering Online Radicalisation: A Strategy for Action'. London: ICSR, 2009.

Strick, Alex Van Linschoten and Felix Kuehn (ed.), *Poetry of the Taliban*. New York: Columbia University Press, 2012.

Sunstein, Cass, *Republic.com 2.0*. Princeton, NJ: Princeton University Press, 2007.

Sutton, Philip and Stephen Vertigans, 'Islamic New Social Movements: Radical Islam, Al Qaeda and Social Movement Theory'. *Mobilization* 11(1), (2006), http://www.mobilization.sdsu.edu/volumes/Volume11.html.

Sweet, Laurel, 'Sudbury Terror Sympathizer Mehanna Sentenced to 17 Years', 14/4/2012.

Taylor, Matthew Guy Granjean and Teresa Smith, 'The English Defence League Uncovered', 28/05/2010, http://www.guardian.co.uk/uk/video/2010/may/28/english-defence-league-uncovered.

Thomas, Timothy, 'Al Qaida and the Internet, The Danger of Cyberplanning'. *Parameters* 33(2003), 112–23.

Thornton, Sarah, *Club Cultures: Music, Media and Subcultural Capital*. Hanover: University of New England, 1996.

Todorov, Tzvetan, *The Fantastic: A Structural Approach to a Literary Genre*, trans. Richard Howard. Ithaca, NY: Cornell University Press, 1975.

Tolkien, J. R. R, *Tree and Leaf*. New York: HarperCollins, 2001.

UNAMA, 'Conflict continues to take a devastating toll on civilians despite decrease in casualties during first six months', press release, 2012. This total does not include a nearly equal number (5479) Afghan soldiers and police killed 2007–2011.

Van Eemeren, Frans, *Strategic Maneuvering in Argumentative Discourse*. Amsterdam: John Benjamins, 2010.

Van Eemeren, Frans and Robert Grootendorst, *A Systematic Theory of Argumentation: The Pragma-Dialectical Approach*. Cambridge: Cambridge University Press, 2003.

Van Eemeren, Frans and Peter Houtlosser, 'Strategic Manoeuvering: A Synthetic Recapitulation'. *Humanities, Social Sciences and Law* 20(4), (2006), 381–92.

Van Linschoten, Alex Strick and Felix Kuehn (eds), translated by Mirwais Rahmany and Hamid Stanikzai, *Poetry of the Taliban*. London: Hurst, 2012.

Vennochi, Joan, 'Tarek Mehanna case puts first amendment on trial', *Boston Globe*, 19/4/2012.

Volpi, Frederic, *Political Islam Observed*. London: Hurst, 2010.

Wagemakers, Joas, 'Defining the Enemy: Abu Muhammad al-Maqdisi's Radical Reading of Surat al-Mumtahana'. *Die Welt des Islams* 48(3–4), (2008), 348–71.

—, 'Reclaiming Scholarly Authority: Abu Muhammad al-Maqdisi's Critique of Jihadi Practices'. *Studies in Conflict and Terrorism* 34(7), (2011), 523–39.

Warius, Abdullah and Brian Fishman, 'A Jihadist's Course in the Art of Recruitment'. *CTC Sentinel* 2(2), February 2009, http://www.ctc.usma.edu/wp-content/uploads/2010/06/Vol2Iss2-Art5.pdf (accessed 31/7/2013)

Warrick, Joby, *The Triple Agent: The Al Qaeda Mole Who Infiltrated the CIA*. New York: Doubleday, 2011.

Watt, Montgomery William, *Muslim Intellectual: A Study of Al-Ghazali*. Edinburgh: Edinburgh University Press, 1963.

Weimann, Gabriel, 'www.terror.net How Modern Terrorism Uses the Internet', United States Institute of Peace report, 2004.

—, 'Cyberterrorism: The Sum of all Fears?'. *Studies in Conflict and Terrorism* 28(2), (2005), 129–49.

—, *Terror on the Internet: The New Arena, The New Challenges*. Washington: United States Institute for Peace Press, 2006.

Weimann, Gabriel, 'Virtual Disputes: The Use of the Internet for Terrorist Debates'. *Studies in Conflict and Terrorism* 29(7), 2006, 623–39.

—, 'Al Qa'ida's Extensive Use of the Internet'. *CTC Sentinel* 1(2), (2008)

Weimann, Gabriel and Yariv Tsfati, '*www.terrorism.com*: Terror on the Internet', 25(5), (2002), 317–32.

Whitaker, Brian, 'Selective MEMRI', http://www.guardian.co.uk/world/2003/jan/28/israel2.

Wikström, Per Olof and Noémie Bouhana, 'Al Qa'ida Influenced Radicalisation: A Rapid Evidence Assessment Guided by Situational Action Theory', UK Home Office Report, 2011.

Wilkinson, Paul, 'Terrorism and the Media: A Reassessment'. *Terrorism and Political Violence* 9(2), (1997), 51–64.

Winnicott, Donald, *Playing and Reality*. London: Routledge, 1991.

Wright, Lawrence, *The Looming Tower: Al Qaeda and the Road to 9/11*. New York: Knopf, 2006.

Yehushoa, Y., 'Re-Education of Extremists in Saudi Arabia', MEMRI, enquiry and analysis series report no. 260, 2006.

Zanini, Michelle and Sean Edwards, 'The Networking of Terror in the Information Age', in Arquilla and Ronfeldt (eds), *Networks and Netwars: The Future of Terror, Crime and Militancy*. Santa Monica: RAND, 2001.

Index

9/11 attacks 1, 20, 83, 145, 162
9/11 Commission Report 7
39 Ways to Serve Jihad and the Mujahidin 136, 139
44 Ways to Serve Jihad and the Mujahidin 63, 136, 144

Aakhus, Mark 80
Abbottabad (documents released) 90, 110
Abduh, Muhammad 52–3
Abercrombie, Nick and Brian Longhurst 194
Abrahms, Max 182, 167
Abu 'Amru al-Qa'idi 94–5
Abu Harith al-Mihdar 85–92
'Abu Jihad' (nickname of Omar Hammami/Abu Mansur al-Amriki) 133, 143, 151
Abu Lughod, Lila 35
Abu Maysara al-Iraqi 83
Abu Mus'ab al-Suri 18, 26–7, 53, 115, 138–9, 155, 171–2, 185
Abu Mus'ab al-Zarqawi 83, 86, 147, 177
A Course in the Art of Recruitment 139
Adab 139
Adbusters 38
affordance 47–8
Afghanistan 1, 6, 20–1, 95, 110, 124, 146, 174–6, 197
Al-Afghani, Jamal al-Din 52–3
Al-Albani, Nasir al-Din 52
Al-'Ali, Hamid 106
Al-Anbar Awakening 41
Al-Aqsa 130
Al-Aqsa Gate (forum) 81

Al Arabiya 85
Al-Asad, Bashar 136
Al-'Awlaqi Anwar 16, 63, 136, 151, 184, 204
Al-'Awshan, 'Isa 136
Al-Baghdadi, Abu Umar 147
Al-Balawi, Humam Khalil (Abu Dujana al-Khurasani) 141, 147–8, 152–3
Al-Banna, Hassan 76
Al-Buraq (forum) 81, 83, 86, 91–2, 99
Al-Daour, Tareq 15
Al-Fajr media network 83
Al-Falluja (forum) 56, 84, 95
Al-Fida' (forum) 99
Al-Firdaws (forum) 56, 83, 89, 91–2, 99
Al-Ghazali 36
Al-Hisba (forum) 83–4, 87, 89, 91–3, 95, 99
Al-Ikhlas (forum) 83, 91, 99, 148
Al-Jihad al-'Alami (forum) 82, 99
Al-Khallaf, Abdullah 159
Al-Maqdisi, Abu Muhammad 2, 53, 58–60, 76, 86, 94, 97, 137, 154
Al-Mis'ari, Muhammad 93
Al-Qaeda 6, 39–40, 117, 121
 in the Arabian Peninsula 16, 19, 25, 68, 83, 113, 184–5
 'Central' 185
 in the Islamic Maghreb 87, 125–6, 151
 in the Land of the Two Rivers 73, 120
Al-Qaradawi, Yusuf 77
Al-Rawashdi, Abd al-Rahman Salum 138
Al-Sahab 84–5, 188

Al-Shabab Al-Mujahidin   120, 133, 184, 186
Al-Shamikha (magazine)   188
Al-Sharkawi, Ahmed   86
Al-Siba'i, Hani   86
Al-Tartusi, Abu Basir   53, 58
alternative media   31, 34–5, 37–8, 100, 186
alternative public sphere   38
Althusser, Louis   192
Al-Tubayhi, Muhammad (Abu 'Ayna' al-Muhajir)   142
Al-'Uyayri, Yusuf   67, 122, 144
Al Watan   110
Al-Wuhayshi, Nasir 'Abd al-Karim   147
Al-Zawahiri, Ayman   185
Amish   30
Anderson, Jon   28
Ansar al-Mujahidin (forum)   82, 99, 102, 133, 140
anti-globalization   105
argumentative activity types   115
Arrow of Yesterday Continues, The   69
Arson   17, 163
art world   102
Asad, Talal   192
Asal, Victor and Paul Harwood   19
Aswad, Du'a Khalil   128
Atif Siddique, Mohammed   41
aviation terrorism   5
Azzam, Abdullah   53, 76, 197
Azzam.com   83

Bach 'fans' of   189
Bacon Smith, Camille   42, 46
Badawi, Elsaid, Mike G. Carter and Adrian Gully   54
Badr, battle of   125
Bailey, Olga, Bart Cammaerts and Nico Carpentier   31
Bakhtin, Mikhail   44–5, 147
Bandana (motif)   62
Banner (motif)   47, 60, 62, 70, 105–6, 118, 123
Barthes, Roland   44
Beck, Ulrich   36, 202
Birmingham School   34

Blow Them Up (nashid)   67
Blow up the cursed one O daughter of jihad   63, 65
Bourdieu, Pierre   45
Brachman, Jarret   26, 39–40, 42
Breivik, Anders Behring   16, 162, 164–8, 171–3, 179, 193
'Building' communities   101
Bunt, Gary   29–31, 33

Campbell, Joseph   195
"cards"   59, 61–2, 68, 70–1
Carderplanet   15
Cesari, Jocelyn   29
Cook, David   26
Chechclear   176
Chechnya   67, 83, 177
Cheering for Osama   86
Chekhov (fans of)   189
Choudhry, Roshonara   16
civilians   125
Cold War against Islam   162
conflict in Northern Ireland, study of cultural products of   33, 168
Constants in the Path of Jihad   151, 184
convergence (media)   82, 190
Convey the Voice of the Wrathful Hero (nashid)   72
Conway, Maura   8–9, 11, 182–3
"counter-jihad"   173
Counternarrative   105–6, 110, 129
'Crusaderism'   163, 183–4
cultural, subcultural capital   15, 45, 130, 156–7, 186, 188
'cultural conservatism'   167–8
'cultural Marxism'   166
cultural studies   34, 44
cyber-attack   5, 84
cyberculture   5, 7, 13, 47–9, 157, 201
cyberjihad   29
"cyberplanning"   8
cyberspace   1, 8, 13, 29, 97, 157

'Danish Civil War, The', (Article)   168
Dark Web Portal   11, 89
Da'wa   97, 100, 107, 144–5, 151

INDEX

Deadheads 46
De Certeau, Michel 44, 49, 157
Defensive jihad 52, 77, 134, 154
De Graaf, Janny 17
Deleuze and Guattari 31
'demographic jihad' 167
Devji, Faisal 53–4, 75, 203
Dialogue of Pessimism 36
Digital Outreach Team 106–7
Dirty Kuffar (song) 68
Don Quixote 45, 198–9
Downing, John 34–5
dread 36, 166
Dunblane Massacre 17
Durkheim, Emile 66, 43

Eickelman, Dale 28
electronic bulletin board 46, 48, 79–80, 100
Electronic Colonialism Theory 30
'El Ingles' (blogger) 168–71
English Defence League 162–3
Erez, Edna 90, 94
ethnographic market research 47, 101
European Declaration of Independence, A, 164

Fans 41–3, 46–8, 73, 102, 188, 190, 194
Fantastic, The (book) 195
fantasy 190–200
Faraj, 'Abd al-Salam 59, 134
Fiqh al-Jihad (book) 77
Fiske, John 45
flash animation 68, 81
Fort Hood shooting 16
Fortuyn, Pim 162
Frankfurt School 32
full face veil ban 162
fund-raising 9, 14, 136

Gadahn, Adam Yahiya 90–1, 93, 185
gamification 40
Gates of Vienna (website) 168
Gaza 33, 73, 81, 187, 202–3
'geeking' communities 101
Gibson, James J. 47
Giddens, Anthony 36, 132, 166

Githens-Mazer, Jonathan and Lambert, Robert 163
Glischomorphic tendency 43
Globalised Islam 139, 155, 184
Global Islamic Resistance Call, The (book) 15, 18, 27, 113, 126, 138, 171
Global Jihadism: Theory and Practice 39
Global Terrorism Database 19–20
Global terrorism trends 19–20
Gohonzon 30
Google trends 55–6
Gray, Jonathan 190
Grossberg, Lawrence 36, 43
group polarization 80

Habermas, Jürgen 35, 80
Hafez, Kai 28
Hajj 63, 72, 75–6
Hamas 6, 14, 53, 57, 63, 72, 75–6
Hammami, Omar 133, 143, 151
Hassan, Nidal Malik 16
hate crime 163
Hatib ibn Abi al-Balta'a 112–13
Heath, Joseph and Andrew Potter 38
Hebdige, Dick 34, 154
Hegghammer, Thomas 25, 52–3, 173
Heidegger, Martin 49
heteroglossia 45, 157
Hewitt, Hayden 176–8
Hijra 91
Hills, Matt 43
Holocaust 28
Holy Land Foundation 14
'home grown terrorism' 17
Honolulu weekly 38
Horseman (motif) 70–1, 81, 151
hostages 124–7

iMuslims (book) 30
'Individual terrorism' 139, 185
Information war 95, 105, 138
'Infospiritualism' 32
Infovlad (forum) 174–5, 178–9
Inhizami 108
Inspire (magazine) 11, 68, 188
Internet Wolf Pack 173

INDEX

Iraq (casualties) 20–1
Iraq (insurgency) 20, 41, 67, 72, 128, 138–9, 177
Iraq (invasion and occupation of) 1, 83, 138, 146
Irredentist, revolutionary, classical, global jihad 51
Islamic Army of Iraq 2, 14, 72–5, 81, 138
Islamic Awakening (in Al-Suri's thought) 138–9
Islamic Awakening (forum) 95
'Islamic media foundations' 73, 81–2, 188
Islamic State of Iraq 10, 21, 40, 63, 72–3, 92, 94, 120, 128
Islam in the Digital Age (book) 30
Islamist neorealism 32, 203
Islam Online (forum) 85
Islamophobia 160–4, 172
Islam, Yusuf 67
Istilahi (technical) vocabulary 138

Jawa Report, The (Website) 173
Jenkins, Brian 133, 143
Jenkins, Henry 42, 49, 82, 190
Jensen, Joli 42
Jerusalem 65
Jihad (meaning of) 3–4
Jihad al-Akbar 3
Jihad bi-l-Lisan 137
Jihadica 25, 173
Jihadi current 51, 138–9
'Jihadi Forums: What they Have, What they Need' (article) 85
Jihadi (grammatical meaning of) 51
'Jihadi Iraq: Hopes and Dangers' 26
'Jihadiness' 57–8, 74–6
"Jihadism studies" 25
jihadi strategic studies 28, 170
Jihadwatch (Website) 173
Jihobbyist 39–40
Juba, Baghdad Sniper 73–4, 204
Judgement Day 73, 109, 143
Justiciar Knights 165–6, 193

Kafir 68
Kalashnikov 71–2, 81

Kenney, Michael 15
Khan, Nicola 191
Kharijite 26, 109
Khatib, Lina 106
Kierkegaard 36
Knights of Martyrdom 74
Knowles, Chase 32–3, 203
Kozinets, Robert 47, 101
Kundnani, Arun 162

Lahoud, Nelly 25–6, 173
Late modernity 36
Layuth al-Islam (forum) 82
Lebanese civil war, casualties 21
leisure 40, 188
Lennon, John 42
Lessig, Lawrence 13
Levine, Alix 40
Levy, Pierre 49, 201
Lewinski, Marcin 115
Lia, Brynjar 25, 171–2
liberation (meaning of) 34–5
Libya (jihadist violence in) 18, 185
Lieberman, Joseph 13
'Like a Soldier' (song) 68
Lisan al-'Arab 150
London bombings 16, 53
Lord of the Rings, The 190
Lux Aeterna 168
Lynch, Orla and Christopher Ryder 20

Macintyre, Alasdair 36
Madad al-Suyuf (forum) 85–6, 88–9
Madrid bombings 16, 26, 162
Maffesoli, Michel 43
Mahmood, Saba 35
Mali (jihadist violence in) 185
Malik, Samina 42, 67
Manual on Hacking Zionist and Crusader Websites 148
Maqdisists 2
Management of Savagery, The (book) 170
Manovich, Lev 48–9, 58–9, 157, 164–5
Martyrdom 26, 33, 58, 64–5, 72–4, 94, 108, 121, 142, 145, 153, 156, 212, 234

Mawdudi, Abu al 'Ala   153
McCants, Will   25, 173
Mecca   27, 54, 71, 85, 91, 107, 162
media contagion   17
Mehanna, Tarek   10
MEMRI   11, 110, 173
meta discussion/meta argument   114–16, 118, 122, 124, 126, 136
metis and techne   15
Mexican drug cartel beheading videos   177
Millat Ibrahim   154
Millenarianism   105, 184
Minaret Ban   162
montage   48, 69, 72–3, 165–6, 168
Morozov, Evgeny   93
Mowlana, Hamid   32
Mu'askir al-Battar   27, 144, 184
Murji'ite   94, 109–10, 148, 153
MUDs and MOOs   13
Muggleton, Malcolm   34
Muhibb al-Shaykhayn al-Tunisi   83, 148
music in Islamic tradition   64
Muslim Brothers   35, 53, 72, 76
Muslim minority populations   18, 169, 185
Muslm.net (forum)   41–2, 86, 107, 128, 141

Naji, Abu Bakr   138, 170–1
Nashid   39, 55–6, 63–70, 72–3, 76, 82, 102, 146, 157, 145
NATO   1, 20
Neda.com   83
neofundamentalism   37, 53
neo-Zarqawists   2, 86, 97
Network (versus hierarchy)   9
Nisba construction   54
Nusra (I'dad, and Da'wa)   144, 147, 150–1

Obama administration   161
Ofex   176
ontological security   36–7
Open Fire (Flash animation)   69
Orientalism (book)   129
Orthodox Jews   30

Osama bin Laden   1, 6, 27–8, 83, 90, 110, 112–13, 124, 147, 156
'Our Muslim Troubles' (online article)   168, 170
O World What is this Silence? (nashid)   67
'oxygen of publicity'   19

Pakistan (terrorism in)   20, 85, 163, 191
Palestinian Islamic Jihad   4, 6, 63
Palestinian resistance   31, 33
PalTalk   82, 84
Pantucci, Raphael   16
pathological stereotype of fandom   42
Plaisir/Jouissance   44
Pleasure of the Text, The (book)   44
poet of Al-Qaida   66
Politics of Piety (book)   35
Port Arthur Massacre   17
Pragma-Dialectics   114
Prison is a Paradise or an Inferno   69
prosumption   47
pseudonymity   79, 115
Purist, Political and Jihadi Salafism   52

Qasida   64
Qoqaz.net   86
Quilliam Foundation   74
Qur'an   30, 51, 71, 73–4, 81, 137–8, 161, 203, 223, 232
Qutb, Sayyid   56, 73, 134
Qu'ud   108

Radway, Janice   44–5, 189
RAND Corporation   6, 40–1, 107, 131–2, 140
Rap   68
Raqa'iq   61, 155
Rauch, Jennifer   38
Reading the Romance (book)   44, 189
Rebel Sell, The (book)   38
recruitment   14, 79
reflexivity   53, 132
Rheingold, Howard   46–8, 80

rhetoric   28, 32, 44, 46, 93, 106, 108, 113–16, 119, 152, 170–1
rhizomatic media   31–2
Roy, Olivier   37, 39, 53
Ryan, Johnny   90, 186

sacred space (online)   29–30
safe haven (Internet as)   1, 92
Sakinah project   107, 110–14, 116–17, 126
Salafism   4, 22, 51–3, 56, 58, 80–1, 153, 183, 185, 187
Sami Yusuf   67
Sanam al-Islam (forum)   82, 99
Saudi Arabia   7, 18, 27, 107, 110–11, 113, 116
Sawt al-Jihad (magazine)   184
science fiction fans   42
Second Life   201
Shadowcrew   15
Shalwar Qamis   71
Shari'a   52, 59, 74, 96–7, 119–23, 125, 135, 154
Shumukh Al-Islam (forum)   81–2, 84, 93, 99, 133, 144, 146, 202
signatures (on Web forums)   2, 59, 151–2
Sinai (jihadist violence in)   185
single narrative (Al Qaeda)   105
SITE Institute   173
social media   79
Soldiers of Allah   68
Somalia   27–8, 120, 133
Song of Terror   91
Soul Salah Crew   68
Star Trek   190, 194
Stenersen, Anne   15
Stevens, Alan and Nicola Baker   5–6
'Strategic Theory for the Second Generation of Jihadis: Foundations and Practice, The', (online article)   146
subcultures   3, 18, 33–4, 37–8, 185, 188–9
suicide bombing   20, 73, 75, 95, 110, 202–3
Sunstein, Cass   80
'Surrender, Genocide or What?'   168
Swalifsoft   82
sword (motif)   70–1, 200, 204
synecdoche   46
Syria (jihadist violence in)   18, 63, 185
Schmid, Alex   17

Tahrid   136–8
Tajdid (forum)   85, 93
Takfir   83, 107, 109, 138, 153
Talbiya   64
Taliban   21, 110, 120, 142, 184, 186
Taqiyya (in Breivik's manifesto)   167
Taqlid   52–3, 77
Targets Within Cities, The (article)   18
Tea Party (social movement)   161
technological determinism   47
television fans   42, 46
'The mischief of takfir' (article)   153
Th3J35t3r   174
Todorov, Tzvetan   191, 195
training manuals   9, 15, 39
transformations (in argument analysis)   126
Tsouli, Younes (irhabi007), 10, 14–15, 83–4, 110, 147–8

Ummah   27, 63, 67, 72–4, 81, 120, 122, 151, 170
Umar, Mullah   121, 124, 147
'Umra   64
US Department of State (list of foreign terrorist organisations)   11
'Ushaq al-Hur (forum)   82
Usud al-Sunna (forum)   159
Utøya Island Massacre   162

Van Eemeren, Frans and Rob Grootendorst   115
Van Gogh, Theo   162
Vietnam war (casualties in)   20–1
violent extremism   33, 105
violent radicalization   2, 16
virtual community   45–6, 79
virtuality   29, 49, 73, 202
Virtually Islamic (book)   29
Volpi, Frederic   31

War on Terror, (online supporters of) 179
War Porn 174–5, 178–9
Web forums (properties of) 79–80, 115
Weimann, Gabriel 7–11, 16, 90, 93, 95
Weisburd, Aaron 85, 90, 94, 99, 173–4
Westpoint Military Academy 39, 61
Wikileaks 174
Wikström, Per Olof and Noémie Bouhana 17

Wiktorowicz, Quintan 52
World of Warcraft 13, 193, 198

Yazidi 128
Youssef, Ramzi 5
Youth Movement (Al Qaeda in the West as) 37
YouTube smackdown 173

Zaid, Sayyid 85
Zuhd 155

Lightning Source UK Ltd.
Milton Keynes UK
UKHW02f0035020318
318744UK00005B/222/P